$ ECONOMICS,
$ ENTREPRENEURSHIP,
$ ETHICS

The "E"s of Business

The basic economic problem is scarcity.
Human wants are unlimited.
Resources are limited.

$$$

Daniel R. Hogan, Jr., Ph.D.

authorHOUSE®

AuthorHouse™
1663 Liberty Drive
Bloomington, IN 47403
www.authorhouse.com
Phone: 1-800-839-8640

Published by AuthorHouse 06/17/2013

ISBN: 978-1-4817-6699-9 (sc)
ISBN: 978-1-4817-6698-2 (e)

Library of Congress Control Number: 2013911082

Any people depicted in stock imagery provided by Thinkstock are models, and such images are being used for illustrative purposes only. Certain stock imagery © Thinkstock.

This book is printed on acid-free paper.

Because of the dynamic nature of the Internet, any web addresses or links contained in this book may have changed since publication and may no longer be valid. The views expressed in this work are solely those of the author and do not necessarily reflect the views of the publisher, and the publisher hereby disclaims any responsibility for them.

DEDICATION

To the Grand Children:

Zachary Hogan Guzzo

Hannah Elizabeth Guzzo

Grace Elizabeth Guzzo

Daniel Richard Hogan, IV

David Alexander Hogan

Dean Vincent Hogan

Grateful that there appears to be no limit to this resource

TABLE OF CONTENTS

PART THREE
Ethics

APPENDIX

PREFACE

Economics, Entrepreneurship, Ethics, three subjects one does not often see addressed in one book. Yet upon reading and studying the different treatments, an overlap can be perceived and the interrelation of the three becomes evident for a successful business.

The entrepreneur cannot live in isolation. To be successful and start, grow, and manage a profitable business with sustainability, he/she must be cognizant of all the factors that may impact (favorable and unfavorable) the business. In this regard a true internal locus-of-control, a firm belief that "if it is to be it is up to me" must exist. It is not enough to be expert in a particular line of business or trade. One must know the business-of-the-business. In so doing a working knowledge of the environment in which the business is to survive is essential. Besides the technical knowledge which may be necessary for operations, and besides the sales and marketing acumen possessed, the financial language of the business must be understood and constantly analyzed and monitored. As does the economic conditions of the market, industry, country, and the world; for all will have an effect on the future and success of the venture. Constant attention must be paid to government regulations and legislation. Ethical considerations and behavior must always be in the forefront of decision-making.

In the final analysis the true entrepreneur is all alone. No matter how many key employees are hired, business partners and investors are acquired, advisors and consultants are made available, the founder and perhaps the CEO and COO for an extended period of time, can never delegate ultimate responsibility. It is therefore necessary to always be working on the business and not simply working in the business.

A business person, founder, owner, manager, entrepreneur certainly does not deal with economics, entrepreneurship, and ethics in isolation. They are interwoven and necessary for every productive decision made.

This book, *$Economics, $Entrepreneurship, $Ethics*, accompanying the others in the series, *$The Entrepreneur's Edge—Finding the Money, $The Entrepreneur's Manager—The Business Man's Business Plan*, and *$The Entrepreneur's Guide—To Start, Grow, and Manage a Profitable Business*, helps to fill the tool box necessary for every entrepreneur and business manager.

> *"Entrepreneurship is based upon the same principles, whether the entrepreneur is an existing large institution or an individual starting his or her new venture singlehanded. The rules are pretty much the same, the things that work and those that don't are pretty much the same, and so are the kinds of innovation and where to look for them. In every case, there is a discipline we might call Entrepreneurial Management."*
> Peter Drucker

Our current entrepreneurial revolution is just beginning. The 21st century will belong to the entrepreneurs, enterprisers, and leaders of the world. Essential will be the transition from founding entrepreneur with the vision to see what is possible to the entrepreneur manager with the skills to bring that vision to fruition. An awareness of the ever-changing economic systems of the world and the impact it holds for a successful, self-sustaining business will be crucial. Ignorance to ethical consideration will be costly. A basic understanding of ethics where business owners face the dilemma of balancing their own moral standards with those of the business will always be present. Customers, employees, stockholders, and the environment are all considerations that business managers ignore at their peril. The business as a separate corporate entity is not an artificial arena where the rules business managers may choose to live their lives are different from the values of the work-place.

Bureaucracy, governments, and large corporations have not sufficiently fueled economic growth for business to compete in the world marketplace. As a result, these large organizations are restructuring, reengineering, downsizing, and trimming their staffs. We are experiencing an age in which the large corporations are becoming inefficient, while resilient, flexible, and innovative entrepreneurial companies are emerging. Increasingly this demand requires entrepreneurs not only equipped with visionary skills but also with leadership and managerial skills. The most powerful ten two letter expression of "If it is to be it is up to me," is not enough for the entrepreneur who must soon realize that a truly successful, growing enterprise cannot be realized alone but with require qualified and talented others to join the organization who will share the vision and be motivated to achieve objectives and the goal as communicated. To build and maintain a needed competitive advantage in the market place an inspired team applying continuous innovation and new ideas are required.

Business leaders and scholars from various disciplines have attempted to define the term "organization". A formal organization is defined by Louis (Allen Louis *Management and Organization,* McGraw-Hill) "the process of identifying and delegating responsibility and authority, and establishing relationships for the purpose of enabling people to work most effectively in accomplishing objectives." And Barnard (Chester Barnard *The Function of the Executive,* Harvard Press) defines a formal organization as a "system of consciously coordinated activities of two or more people."

Accordingly the three essential elements of an organization are:

- Common Purpose
- Willingness to serve and
- Communication

Most of the definitions of organizations appear to stress the following factors:

- Organization symbolizes a group effort
- The group effort is directed toward a goal
- The group effort can be achieved by coordination
- Authority and responsibility help to achieve coordination

Most of the firms of the early 1900s were small retailing and manufacturing enterprisers operating in a vacuum with little knowledge of social economic changes. Management was essentially informal, mainly because products or services were unsophisticated, as were the firm's production process and operations. Also contributing was the lack of intervening levels of management between the top manager (the owner) and workers. Insofar as subordinates were concerned, the supervisor or foreman was the ultimate authority, whose power was absolute.

Most entrepreneurs (owners) possess an inner locus-of-control which hinders the very growth and development of their firms. The very traits which sparked the enterprises often prove to be a serious problem. This need for control and distrust of delegation impacts the interrelationships which are vital to the success and growth of the business.

Entrepreneurs obsessed with being in control for fear of others controlling them, taking advantage, or making costly mistakes have little patience with employees who act with initiative and think for themselves. This micro-management may have serve well as a start-up business, but now will stifle the development and restrict attracting the very assistance from others, be they employees, advisers, or vendors, required to grow a profitable business.

It is overcoming this difficulty that enables a business to mature and become a thriving, growing, profitable business rather than remain a life-style, small business, or a failed business. The expression that leaders and entrepreneurs do the right thing while managers simply do things right is not enough. Entrepreneurs who by necessity are also managers-owners must do it the right way to start, grow, and manage a profitable business that continues to build value. The transition of the visionary start-up entrepreneur to a pragmatic thinking leader aware of the economic climate and behaving in an ethical manner to all concern as an entrepreneur-manager willing to invest in learning the necessary management skills without fear of delegation to others is the mission of this book.

It was Will Rogers who commented that *"Common sense ain't necessarily common practice."* It is relatively easy to enumerate the best management practice, but another altogether to implement them.

PART ONE

ECONOMICS

INTRODUCTION

*"An economist is a man (or woman) who states
the obvious in terms of the incomprehensible."*
Alfred A. Knopf

Few, if any, are qualified to write about the economy as an economist; yet, I do. For I, like you, are part of the economy, strive to live in it, endure it, and understand it every day. I teach basic economics. I have read many texts by eminent economist, and follow the economy. As a lifelong student of human behavior, I am perhaps as qualified as any to expound upon the economy which is a result of that behavior.

Very few economists agree on any one theory or practice in resolving the essential economic problem of scarcity in satisfying unlimited human desires with limited resources. I have concluded that the multitude of economic theories, beliefs, and practices, although well-intended, do not work. Whether applied in solidarity or, as is so often attempted, in aggregate simply does not accomplish the goals of stabilizing price levels, reducing unemployment, stemming inflation, avoiding recession, and providing for economic growth.

Why not?

Primarily because for the most part they have abandoned the premises set forth in 1776 by Adam Smith in his *The Wealth of Nations* and the philosophy of "the invisible hand."

What is Economics?

*"Economics has never been a science—and it
is even less now that a few years ago."*
Paul Samuelson

Economics is the study of our market system; it is the study of how people make choices about what they buy, what they produce, and how our

3

market system works (refer to the Ten Principles of Economics to follow). It is the study of how limited resources are used to try to satisfy unlimited wants

People want many things in life; in fact, the more they have, the more they want. When a desire is fulfilled, another desire replaces it. Our desires are infinite, but the resources to fulfill these desires are limited. There aren't enough resources to give everyone what they want.

The concept of scarcity is one of the most important concepts in economics. If we had the resources to fulfill every desire we had, everybody would have everything they wanted. But life is not like that; we have limited resources, and we must make decisions on how to use these resources. Economics is the study of those decisions.

Scarcity cannot be resolved. It will always persist and be with us. As we continue to strive for higher and higher standard of living, scarcity will remain. Therefore the goal of dealing with scarcity is **not** to satisfy all of our wants. That is impossible. It is to produce as much satisfaction as possible with those limited resources available.

Opportunity Costs

Since we have more desires than resources to fulfill them, we must choose one desire to fulfill over another. The opportunity cost of the decision is what you had to give up to get what you wanted. You may want a new stereo system, but you also want a television set, but you don't have the money to buy both. If you choose to buy the stereo, the television set was the opportunity cost of that decision. You might decide to go to dinner instead of going to a movie. You might choose to stay up late studying, at the cost of some sleep. In each example, a choice was made; something was sacrificed; there was a cost, not necessarily a monetary cost but an opportunity cost.

The Four Questions

There are four basic questions that every economy must answer.

What should be produced?

This is determined in a market economy by consumer demand.

How many should be produced and for whom?

> This is determined by the distribution of income and consumer demand, and markets for resources. If a person owns resources that are highly valued in the market place, that person can receive a large share of the income.

What methods should be used?

> This is determined by the least cost method of production which will satisfy the consumer's wants and desire for quality and value.

How should goods and services be distributed?

> As determined to be the least costly and most efficient method possible to assure consumer satisfaction while securing a profit.

There are two kinds of economies: A Command Economy and a Market Economy.

In a Command Economy, the government would answer all these questions. In a Market Economy, the marketplace decides how to answer the four basic questions. A Market Economy would answer these questions by saying that each producer can answer these questions themselves. A producer can make their own decisions, but these decisions would be determined by the marketplace. In other words, a producer makes decisions that will make his product sell, and make him money. So the buying public really makes these decisions, by choosing to buy, or not to buy, a product.

Here in the United States, we live in a Market Economy.

In a market economy, resources are owned by individuals, for example each person owns his own labor and personal investment capital. These individuals are making most of their production decisions and most of their consumption decisions. How do they make these decisions? By pursuing their own self-interest in respond to incentives (the invisible hand and the rational person assumption as you will find in the Ten Principles of Economics to follow in Chapter One).

Adam Smith introduced this concept in *The Wealth of Nations* published in 1776. *"It is not from the benevolence of the butcher, the brewer, or the baker that we expect our dinner, but from their regard to their own interest."*

CHAPTER ONE

THE BASIS ECONOMIC PROBLEM

Scarcity and Choices

"The first lesson of economics is scarcity. There is never enough of anything to satisfy all those who want it. The first lesson of politics is to disregard the first lesson of economics."
Thomas Sowell

The basic economic problem is **scarcity.** Human wants are unlimited. Resources are limited. Scarcity is the problem that human wants exceed the production possible with the limited resources available. Economics is the study of how individuals and societies use their limited resources to try to satisfy their unlimited wants.

Macroeconomics is the branch of economics that focuses on overall economic behavior such as inflation, unemployment, economic growth, and deficits.

Microeconomics is the branch of economics that focuses on components of the economy. Households, firms, specific markets and industries are examples.

The basic goal in dealing with the problem of scarcity is to produce as much consumer satisfaction as possible with the limited resources available.

Resources are the inputs that make production possible. The four categories of resources are **labor, land, capital, and entrepreneurship.** Most resources are owned by private persons. In economics, people are assumed to behave rationally, which means that they will respond to incentives in the pursuit of their own self-interest. As resource owners pursue self-interest in the use of their resources, the best interest of society will also generally be served (the invisible hand).

Opportunity cost is the value of the best alternative surrendered when a choice is made. Scarcity creates the necessity to ration the limited resources to production and to ration the limited goods to consumers. The primary rationing device is the dollar price.

The four categories of resources:

> Labor—the physical and mental efforts that people contribute to production. Human capital which is the developed ability that increases individual productivity; it is developed through education, training, and experience.

> Land—the naturally occurring resources, such as unimproved land, water, minerals, fossil fuels, forest, and weather.

> Capital—money, equipment, and produced goods that are used in the production of other goods

> Entrepreneurship—the special skill involved in organizing labor, land, and capital for production. Entrepreneurs organize labor, land, and capital for production. Entrepreneurs start new businesses, grow existing businesses, develop new production techniques, introduce new products, and employ people. They are generally motivated by the goal of profit-maximization. They bear the risk of loss. Profits (and loss) direct entrepreneurs and the resources that they control into (and out of) different types of production. They strive to use their resources as efficiently as possible.

TEN PRINCIPLES OF ECONOMICS

How people make decisions:

1. **People face tradeoffs**—There is no such thing as a free lunch. To get one thing we like, we usually have to give up another thing we like. Making decisions require trading off one goal against another.

2. **The cost of something is what you give up to get it**—Because people face tradeoffs, making decisions requires comparing the costs and benefits of alternative courses of action.

3. **Rational people think at the margin**—Economist use the term "marginal changes" to describe small incremental adjustments to an existing plan of action. "Margin" means edge, so marginal changes are adjustments around the edge of what you are doing. At dinnertime the decision is not between fasting or eating, but whether to take that extra serving. In a market economy people are assumed to behave rationally in their own best interest. Economic decisions are made by comparing the marginal (extra) benefits of a choice with the marginal (extra) costs. Any activity should be continued as long as the marginal benefit of the activity exceeds the marginal cost.

4. **People respond to incentives**—Because people make decisions by comparing costs and benefits, their behavior change when the costs or benefits change. When the price of apples rises, people decide to eat more pears and fewer apples. An incentive changes the benefit or cost associated with an action.

How people interact:

5. **Trade can make everyone better off**—Trade allows each person to specialize in the activities he or she does best. By trading with others, people can buy a greater variety of goods at lower cost. Most resource owners choose to engage in trade rather than the low-yields of self-sufficiency. They will use

their resources to produce what they do best and trade for everything else. A person has a comparative advantage when he can produce a good or service at a lower opportunity cost than other producers. Producing as such leads to a more productive use of resources and a higher standard of living. If a person values what is received in trade more than what is giving, the trade is beneficial.

Countries as well as families benefit from the ability to trade with one another.

6. **Markets are usually a good way to organize economic activity**—Communist and Socialist countries work on the premise that central planners in the government are in the best position to guide economic activity. They decide what is to be produced, at what cost, and who would produce and consume these goods. The theory behind central planning is that only the government can organize economic activity to promote economic well-being for the country as a whole. Most of these countries have abandoned central planning and are trying to develop a market economy. In a market economy, the decisions of central planners are replaced by the decisions of millions of firms and households. Firms decide whom to hire and what to make. Households decide what firms to work for and what to buy from what firms with their income.

In Adam Smith's 1776 book, *The Wealth of Nations,* he made the observation that markets are guided by an "invisible hand" that leads to desirable market outcomes. Prices are the instrument with which the invisible hand directs economic activity. Prices reflect both the value of a good to society and the cost to society of making the good. Because people look at prices when deciding what to buy and sell, they unknowingly take into account the social benefits and costs of their actions. As a result prices guide these decisions to reach outcomes that maximize the welfare of society as a whole.

When the government prevents prices from adjusting naturally to supply and demand, it impeded the invisible hand's ability to coordinate the decisions that make up the economy. This explains why taxes adversely affect the allocation of resources. Taxes distort price and thus the decisions of households and firms.

7. **Governments can sometimes improve market outcomes**—If the invisible hand of the market is so great, why do we need government? The invisible hand does need government to protect it. Markets work only if property rights are enforced. A farmer won't grow food if he expects his crops to be stolen, and a restaurant won't serve meals if it feels the customer will leave without paying.

How the economy as a whole works:

8. **A country's standard of living depends on its ability to produce goods and services**—The difference in living standards around the world are staggering. In 2000 the average American had an income of about $35,000. In the same year, the average Mexican earned $8,500, and the average Nigerian earned $800. This large variation in income is reflected in the quality of life within those countries. High-income countries have more TV sets, cars, better nutrition, better health care, and longer life expectancy. The explanation for these better living standards is attributed to a country's productivity.

9. **Prices rise when the government prints too much money**—"Inflation"—What causes inflation?—Growth in the quantity of money, too much money chasing too few goods. When a government creates large quantities of a nation's money, the value of the money falls. The economic history of the United States reveals this: the high inflation of the 1970s was associated with rapid growth in the quantity of money, and the low inflation of the 1990s was associated with slow growth in the quantity of money. It is feared by many that the growth of money in the 2000s will also produce high inflation.

10. **Society faces a short-run tradeoff between inflation and unemployment**—When the amount of money increases, one result is inflation. Another result, in the short run, is a lower level of unemployment.

CHAPTER TWO

ECONOMIC GROWTH

The basic economic problem is scarcity.
Human wants are unlimited.
Resources are limited.

Economic growth is one of the three macroeconomic goals (the three are price level stability, full employment, and economic growth). A society's success in dealing with the basic problem of scarcity depends on its success in achieving economic growth. Growth will not allow a country to satisfy all human wants. But economic growth will help to produce as much consumer satisfaction as possible with the limited resources available.

A Brief History U. S. Economic Growth

From humble beginnings in Jamestown, the U.S. economy has achieved remarkable growth. Economic growth is an increase in the productive capacity of an economy. Today, the U.S. economy is the largest national economy in the world and produces the highest standard of living in the world.

From Jamestown to the Present

In 1607, the Jamestown colony was established. Jamestown was the first permanent English settlement in what would become the United States of America. The colonists were drawn to the new world not seeking religious freedom but largely by economic motivation. They and their financial backers hoped to strike it rich by discovering gold, silver, and cooper. The initial 105 colonists included a number of goldsmiths and jewelers, but no farmers.

The original colonists did not strike it rich. Instead, they confronted the basic economic problem of scarcity. They had only limited resources to satisfy their unlimited wants and needs.

Of the 105 original colonists, only 38 were still alive when a second group of colonist arrived in 1608. There were 214 colonists in 1609. By 1610 only 60 were still alive. The Jamestown colony was on the verge of failure.

By 1612 there were more colonists with ships bringing more supplies. In 1612, Jamestown began growing and exporting tobacco earning a very high return. Nonetheless, the colony continued to struggle with the majority of colonists either dying or returning to England.

Condition began to improve when more people arrived and other colonies were established. As the population grew, the labor force became more specialized providing for the opportunity of profitable trade. During this colonial era the economy and population grew rapidly.

By 1790, after the Revolutionary War, there were nearly 4 million Americans. They had established a Constitution that balanced a strong central government with individual freedom. They had achieved a much higher standard of living than most in the world at this time; yet, their standard of living was extremely low by our modern standards.

The primary economic activity in pre-Civil War America was agriculture. Economic growth was disrupted by the Civil War (1861-1865). The Civil War was fought at incredible cost to the nation. Over 600,000 Union and Confederate soldiers died. Another 500,000 were wounded. The total population of both the North and the South was only about 30 million at the time. Therefore about 4% of the population was either dead or incapacitated. The total financial cost at that time was estimated to have been $6.7 billion, about double the national income of 1860.

After the Civil War, agriculture again began to increase and the nation really begins to recover with the Industrial Revolution. There were major technological breakthroughs and Americans were assured a very high standard of living. Workers were much more productive able to produce a considerable amount of good than previously.

However in 1929, the Great Depression began. The unemployment rate would average 18% for nearly 10 years.

In spite of the depression with advances in technology, in the 20th century per capital output in the U.S. increased by about eight-fold. This rapid growth caused remarkable improvements in the quality of life for the average American. In many ways, even a wealthy American in 1900 would have been at an economic disadvantage compared to the average American in 2000. In 1900, there were no airplanes, no radio, no television, no cell phones, no penicillin, no open-heart surgery, no organ transplants, no computers, and no air conditioning.

Measures of Economic Growth

Economic growth is defined as an increase in Gross Domestic Product (GDP).

The factors that determine a country's ability to increase its productive capacity are:

1. **Natural Resources.** The United States has been blessed with an abundance of natural resources; fertile farmlands, temperate weather, fossil fuels, minerals, navigable waterways, etc.

2. **Labor.** Labor, physical and mental, contributes in two ways:

   A. An increase in the quantity of labor will increase GDP. Simply, a larger labor force, properly executed, can produce more than a smaller labor force particularly when supplemented with an increase in capital and technology.

   B. An increase in labor productivity (output per unit of labor) will increase GDP.

3. **Capital.** Increases in capital lead to increases in labor productivity and in GDP.

4. **Technology.** Technological advances are the ability to produce more output per resources.

Governmental Policies

"The point to remember is that what the government gives it must first take away."
John Coleman

Governmental policies are conducive or constraining to economic growth. Governments that have utilized the following policies have been more successful in achieving economic growth:

1. **Private property rights.** The strength of private property rights determines the incentive that resource owners will have in using their resources.

2. **Free and competitive markets** lead to economic efficiency in the allocation of resources. Governments may discourage free markets by regulating entry via licensing, by restricting international trade with tariffs and quotas, and by imposing price controls with ceilings and floors. Governments can encourage free markets by permitting free entry, free international trade, free market prices, and by prohibiting anticompetitive behavior.

3. **Free International trade** is a type of technological advance, in that it allows for more production from the same amount of resources. Governments should resist the pressure to restrict international trade from special interest groups and by maintaining favorable exchange rates.

4. **A stable price level** depends upon proper monetary policies. A government must avoid excessive money supply growth in order to avoid excessive inflation. Excessive money supply contraction must also be avoided to avert deflation; either can have a negative effect on investment. Lack of investment will hinder economic growth.

5. **A small government.** The private sector tends to use resources more efficiently than the public sector. As the government grows larger, more resources are transferred from the private sector to the less efficient public sector. A larger government also means higher tax rates to support it. High tax rates weaken private property rights.

The Invisible Hand

Adam Smith

In 1776, Adam Smith wrote *The Wealth of Nations,* and capitalism was born. The word *capital* comes from the Latin word *capitalis,* meaning head. Under capitalism, you could use your head to get ahead.

The Invisible hand is the concept that producers will be guided, as if by an "invisible hand", to produce what the public wants. The reason for this, ironically, is greed; a producer will produce what the public wants simply because that is what will create profit for him. Likewise, a producer also will not produce something harmful to the public, since it would cause him to lose profits.

According to Adam Smith, the owner of the resource, be it labor, land, capital, or the entrepreneur's skills, pursuit of self-interest will generally serve the best interest of the community as a whole: *[The resource owner]* *"intends only his own gain, and he is in this…led by an invisible hand to promote an end which is no part of his intention…By pursuing his own intention he frequently promotes that of society more effectually than when he really intends to promote it."*

The Law of Demand

The law of demand states that when the price of an item goes down, the demand for it goes up. When the price drops, people who could not afford the item can now buy it, and people who weren't willing to buy it before will now buy it at the lower price. Also, if the price of an item drops enough, people will buy more of the product, and even find alternate uses for the product; for example, if the price of a sweaters drops enough, people would start buying to put on their pets.

The Law of Supply

The law of supply states that when the selling price of an item rises, more people will produce the item. Since a higher price means more profit for the producer, as the price rises, more people will be willing to produce the item when they see that there's money to be made.

Equilibrium Price

If a sample "demand graph" was drawn with price on the X-axis and quantity of a product demanded on the Y-axis, the graph would look like a downward-sloping curve; as price increases, demand goes down. If a "supply graph" was drawn, it would be an upward-sloping curve; as price increase, supply increases. If both curves are drawn on the same graph, the point at which they meet is the "Equilibrium Price".

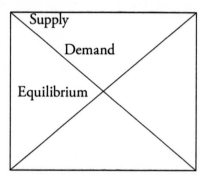

This is the price at which the amount of product demanded is equal to the amount of product supplied; in other words, if the price of a product is set at its equilibrium price, then for each individual product produced, there is a buyer for it. If the price of the products is set too high, then there will be more products produced than brought; a surplus of goods would occur. If the price is set too low, there would be demand for a higher quantity of product than is being produced; a shortage would occur.

When we say that "demand goes up", we are talking about moving along the demand curve; i.e. at a lower price, more people are willing and able to buy it. When we say that "total demand goes up", we mean that the amount of demand at all prices goes up; i.e. the entire curve shifts up. If the price of an item drops and more people buy it, the demand for it goes up; if something has made the product more popular and more people are willing to buy at any price, the total demand has gone up.

How Pilgrims Embraced the Market

The next time you sit down for Thanksgiving dinner, perhaps you should give thanks not only for the turkey on your plate but also for the economic system in which you live.

Most Americans think of Thanksgiving as a time to gather with friends and family and celebrate with a huge feast. Children are educated to know that the Pilgrims were grateful for a good harvest in their new land and set aside this day to give thanks.

What they don't know is that things weren't always so good for the Pilgrims, who came to the new world from England to escape religious persecution. Their first winters after they landed at Plymouth Rock in 1620 and established the Plymouth Bay colony were harsh. The weather was lousy and crop yields were poor. Half of the Pilgrims died or returned to England.

Those who remained went hungry. Despite their deep religious convictions, they took to stealing from one another. In the spring of 1623, following three grueling winters and widespread famine, Governor Bradford and the others began to think how they might raise as much as they could, and obtain a better crop then they had done.

One of the traditions the Pilgrims brought with them from England was something called "farming in common." The colonists pooled the fruits of their labor and the harvest was rationed among them.

This idea of not having personal property to work, but to bring all into the common community was found to breed too much confusion and discontent. Young and able men resented working hard for other men and their wives, without compensation or a larger share of the harvest for themselves and their families.

So after these three winters of hardship and starvation due to poor crops, Bradford instituted a new policy when it came time to plant the following spring. He set aside a plot of land for each family, allowing each to plant for his own needs and wants, and in that regard trust each to themselves for the winter.

For the pilgrims the results were miraculous. Even the women went willingly into the field to help their husband and family. Those who had previously claimed to be too ill or weak to work were now eager to till their own soil.

Yet it was no miracle. Without knowing it, Governor Bradford and the Pilgrims had discovered that **socialism does not work.** Deprived of property rights and lacking economic incentives to work, produce and save, human beings behave in a predictable manner.

Pretty soon, the colonist had more than enough food for their own needs and started to trade their excess corn for other commodities, such as furs and tobacco.

After three winters of famine, the Pilgrims viewed their time of plenty as a stroke of good fortune when they were merely responding to market signals. Even before there was an official market, the "invisible hand" was at work.

Thanksgiving is a time to give thanks for our system of government, which allows the "invisible hand" to guide, provide for, and protect us.

CHAPTER THREE

MARKETS

Characteristics of a Market Economy

"An economist is an expert who will know tomorrow why the things he predicted yesterday didn't happen today."
Lawrence J. Peter

There are five characteristics of a pure market economy:

1. Economic Freedom

2. Economic Incentives

3. Competition

4. Private Ownership

5. Limited Government

Economic Freedom: In a market economy, people have the freedom to make their own economic decisions. People have the right to decide what job they work in, and their salary. A producer has the freedom to produce whatever product or products they want, and what price to sell them at. Everyone has the freedom to choose what is in their best interests as long as they don't interfere with the rights of others. (Principle #6, Markets is usually a good way to organize economic activity.)

Economic Incentives: While everyone has economic freedom, in practice it doesn't necessarily mean that people can simply do what they want. A producer has the freedom to charge an unreasonably high price for an item, but chances are people won't buy it. This is an example of an economic incentive. Economic incentives are the consequences, positive or negative, of making an economic decision. A positive incentive, such as making a profit on an item, encourages a producer to produce what the consumer wants. A negative incentive, such as a drop in profits or a boycott, would discourage producers from acting against the public interest. (Principle #4, People respond to incentives.)

Competition: There is competition in a pure market economy. This means that there isn't just one producer producing an item for the public. There are usually many producers of any given item. This gives consumers a choice in buying something. If they don't like the price or quality of a product made by one company, they can buy the product from another company. This encourages the producer to produce a quality product, and charge a reasonable price for it. If they don't, they will lose business to the other company.

Private Ownership: In a market economy, the individual, people or company, own the factors of production that they use to make their product, as opposed to the factors of production being owned by the government.

Limited Government: A pure market economy requires a "limited" government, that is, a government that does not have absolute power over its people, and plays no role in the economic decisions of the people. If the government was not limited, it would have control over the economy, and there would be no economic freedom, and the economy would, by definition, be a Command economy, rather than a market economy. (Principles #6, Markets are usually a good way to organize economic activity.)

The Factors of Production

To produce goods and services, resources must be used. These resources are the Factors of Production. These factors are:

- Land
- Labor
- Capital
- Entrepreneurship

Land: The natural resources that people use: Forest, pasture land, minerals, and water.

Labor: The human ability to produce a good or service: Talents, skills, and physical labor.

Capital: Goods made by people to be used specifically to produce goods and services: Tools, equipment, roads, factories, and the money to purchase and provide for these goods as well as labor and land.

Entrepreneurship: An entrepreneur is someone who accepts the personal risk of loss to put together all the factors of production together to make a good or service for the probability of gain; without entrepreneurship no good or service would be produced.

Circular Flow

In a market economy, there are two markets: The "Factor Market", and the "Product Market".

In the factor market, the people, who own the factors of production, sell their services to the companies that produce products. In exchange, the companies give the workers' wages, and pay rent and interest to factor owners. In the factor market, the people are the sellers, and the companies are the buyers. The people are selling their services to the production firms.

In the product market, companies sell the products they have produced to the people who pay money to the companies for them. The money is flowing in the opposite direction this time; people are buying products from the producing firms.

In this way, money flows through the economy in a circle. The money goes from the producers to the workers in the form of wages, and the money then flows back to the producers in the form of payment for products.

Rent, Interest, and Profit

One of the factors of production, labor, is paid with wages, salary, and perhaps other benefits. The other three, land, capital, and entrepreneurship, are paid with rent, interest, and profit.

Economic rent is the price paid for the use of land and other natural resources. The difference in land rent usually results from the difference in demand often stemming from differences in the fertility of the land, locations, climate, or natural reachable supply. The payment of land rents is useful to the land owners because it puts an opportunity cost on the use of land so that the owners are motivated to put the land to its best possible use.

Interest is the price paid for the use of money. Money is not itself an economic resource, people do not value money for its own sake; they value it for its purchasing power and what it can produce. The market interest rate on money loans determine the interest income earned by the lender for providing the funds. Interest will vary in size due to difference in loan risk, maturity, amount, and taxability.

Entrepreneurs receive profits (revenue minus cost) in exchange for assuming risk associated with running a business. The corporate form of business organization has allowed many by owning stock in the corporation to share in the financial risk and profits of entrepreneurship. Profits are the key incentive of business firms within our capitalist economy system. In order to obtain profits, the entrepreneur must allocate resources above cost in accordance with consumers' preference.

Market Structures

Market power—the ability of a seller or a buyer to affect market price

The market structure that a firm operates in will affect the firm's market power. The market power will affect the output and pricing decisions that the firm makes as it attempts to maximize profits.

For any given product that is produced, its production market falls into one of four categories:

Pure Competition,

Monopolistic Competition,

Oligopoly,

Monopoly

These categories are called the "Market Structures". The category that a product falls into depends on how many people are producing it.

In a **purely competitive market**, there are many buyers and sellers. It is easy for a new person to enter the market, and the products are all pretty much identical. For example, an egg market that has 5,000 firms, each making 10,000 eggs per year. 50,000 eggs are being produced each year, and each egg is the same as every other egg.

In a market with **monopolistic competition**, there are a large number of firms producing a product. Each firm has a small amount of control over the price, and it is fairly easy for a new producer to enter the market. Each firm utilizes nonprice competition, that is, they compete with the other firms, not by competing in price, but by trying to make their product unique; different from the product made by other companies in the market. This is called product differentiation. Examples of monopolistic competition are barber shops, restaurants, and book stores. There are many firms in these markets. Each one is different, and they compete with each other by emphasizing how their product or service is different from the others.

In an **oligopoly,** there are just a few firms producing the product. There is limited entry into an oligopoly (in other words it is difficult for a new firm to enter into the market and be widely recognized and accepted), and oligopolies utilize nonprice competition and product differentiation. An example of an oligopoly is the automobile industry; just a few large firms producing the products.

In a **pure monopoly,** there is no competition at all, just one large firm making a given product. A monopoly can charge any price it wants for a product, since there is no other producer with a lower price that consumers can go to. Since monopolies hurt consumers by not providing people with any choice of where to go, the government often breaks up monopolies, e.g. the telephone company.

Market	Number of firms	Control over price	Type of product	Entry	Competition
Pure competition	Very large	None	Standardized	Very easy	Price-based
Monopolistic	Large	Small	Differentiated	Easy	Non-price
Oligopoly	Few dominant	Fair amount	Standardized or differentiate	Difficult	Non-price
Monopoly	One	Large	One	Blocked	Non-existent

Major Economic Theories

"There can be no real individual freedom in the presence of economic insecurity."
Chester Bowles

Scarcity forces every society to answer economic questions by choosing an economic system to address those questions. The two primary economic systems are capitalism and socialism. These two are the product of two very different economic visions; the capitalist vision and the socialist vision as they relate to private property, personal incentives, market prices, and government.

CAPITALISM, Laissez-Faire, Supply and Demand—ADAM SMITH

Adam Smith (1723-1790), a philosopher and Scotsman is considered the founder of modern economic theory. Smith had infinite faith in humanity; he believed that people would act in their own self-interest and produce the goods required by society as a whole. He contended that an **invisible hand** was the mechanism behind self-regulation. His book outlining this theory *The Wealth of Nations* was published in the year of our independence, 1776. Smith expressed that a **free market economy** could run on its own. This supported a *laissez-faire (French for "leave it be")* attitude. He felt that the markets would take care of themselves. He was an outspoken opponent of government intervention, product regulation, trade restrictions, and labor laws. He perceived the invisible hand as the self-regulating nature of the marketplace. The invisible hand was the simultaneous occurrence of the forces of self-interest, competition, and supply and demand which he felt would be inherently capable of allocating resources in society.

The capitalist vision contends that private property is economically and politically desirable. It leads to the efficient use of resources. Self-interest (profit-maximization) will lead resource owners to use their resources in ways that benefit society (the invisible hand). The more consumer satisfaction that a resource gives, the more income the resource owner receives.

Private property is politically desirable because it contributes to individual freedom. Resource owners use their private property as they see fit for their own best use. Collective ownership would require collective decision-making instead of individual decision-making, and sharing of proceeds with little regard toward individual effort. Collective ownership would reduce individual freedom and incentive.

KEYNESIAN, John Maynard Keynes

John Keynes (1883-1946), felt quite differently than Adam Smith. In 1936, Keynes published *"The General Theory of Employment, Interest, and Money"*. He advocated interventionist economic policy encouraging governments to leverage fiscal and monetary policies to allay the adverse consequences of downturns in business cycles, economic recessions, and depressions. He argued that individuals in the private sector can, at times, produce negative economic results which can be mitigated by monetary measures and policy actions by governments in the public sector. He felt that a collective demand for goods might be deficient in times of economic crises fueling high unemployment and damaging output (production). He asserted that government policies should be applied to enhance the aggregate demand thereby stimulating growth and in turn decreasing unemployment. His strategy for recovering from a great recession or a depression involves the government stimulating the economy by reducing interest rates and government investment. DADDY TO THE RESCUE!

CLASSICAL, The Law of Market, Say's Law

Jean-Baptiste Say (1767-1832), stated that "products are paid for with products" and a glut can take place only when there are too many means of production applied to one kind of product and not enough to another. In Say's view a rational businessman will never hoard money; he will promptly spend it for the value of money is also perishable. The validity of Say's Law was that "supply creates its own demand," as a market mechanism to avoid that general glut. There will always be sufficient demand to purchase as much total output as is supplied.

Classical economic theory was introduced by Adam Smith and adopted and supplemented by Jean-Baptiste Say, John Stuart Mill, and other economist. Classical economic theory was the predominant theory in industrialized nations from the 18th century until the Great Depression of the 1930s.

SOCIALISM, Communism, Marxism, Karl Marx

Karl Marx (1818-1883), the founder of modern communism and socialism, has a completely different perspective. Marx merges politics and economics. He contended that the history of all existing society is the history of class struggles. He argued that capitalism would produce internal tensions which would lead to the destruction of society. Just as capitalism replaced feudalism, Marx believed that socialism would replace capitalism and lead to a stateless, classless society which he referred to as pure communism. He theorized that first there must be a **dictatorship of the proletariat** from which would emerge this stateless classless society the "worker's democracy." He asserted that workers should own the production since they were the means of production. He expounded that workers, in a market economy, would be exploited. Capitalists would pay the workers less than the value of the worker's output. The exploitation of labor would mean that income would be distributed very unequally in a free market economy. This unequal distribution of income would mean that workers would not have enough income to consume all that they produced. Inadequate demand would result leading to increasingly downturn in the business cycle. Eventually the economy would collapse.

There is no place for incentives, individual differences, or investment entitlements. Private property is considered as economically and politically harmful. Socialism holds that some people will be more successful in accumulating private property than others. Consequently, Private property will come to be concentrated in the hands of a few. Better that it is owned by the government for the benefit of all. In this way the government protects the masses from exploitation by the rich and big business.

The government should be large and strong in order to protect the weak from the powerful.

Capitalism holds the opposite to be true, whereas a government that controls economic activities has tremendous power over its citizens. Socialism can punish dissenters by depriving them of employment (since the government is the only employer). It can silence dissenters by withholding the resources necessary for communicating their dissent (television, newspapers, radio, internet, etc.)

MONETARISM, Milton Friedman

Milton Friedman (1912-2006), a Nobel Prize winning economist, specialized in consumption theory, monetary policy, and stabilization policy. He has been called the first counterrevolutionary against Keynesianism. He endorsed an economic policy which became known as **monetarism.** He believed in a natural rate of unemployment which governments could modulate at the risk of creating inflation. He objected to a good deal of government regulation, and favored free market economies. His views are outlined in his book *Capitalism and Freedom.* According to Friedman (Nobel Prize winner in Economics, 1976), capitalism is a necessary condition for individual freedom.

Monetarism is a tendency in economic thought that emphasizes the limited role of government in controlling the amount of money in circulation. Too much creates inflation, too little could result in recession. It is the view that variations in the money supply has a major influence on national production in the short run and the price level over longer periods and that objectives of monetary policy are best met with a controlled targeted growth rate of the money supply. As such the Federal Reserve should be striving at keeping the supply and demand for money at equilibrium, as measured by growth in productivity and demand.

Milton Friedman asserts that the proper limited role of a government in a capitalist system is to establish and enforce property rights and contract rights. The government should also function in areas which cannot be performed well by the free market system such as: to provide and control the money supply, correct for market failure by promoting competition, and to supplement private efforts to care for those who cannot care for themselves.

CHAPTER FOUR

DEMAND, SUPPLY, AND EQUILIBRIUM

The basic economic problem is scarcity.
Human wants are unlimited.
Resources are limited.

Because resources are limited, only a limited amount of products can be produced. In our free market system, the problem of scarcity is handled through markets.

A product market has two sides. The buying side is called DEMAND. The selling side is called SUPPLY.

DEMAND—the willingness and ability of **buyers** to buy different quantities of a good at different prices.

LAW of DEMAND—the price and the quantity demanded of a good are inversely related.

The Law of Demand indicates that as the price of a good increase, the quantity demanded decreases. And as the price of the good decreases, the quantity demanded increases.

There are two reasons for this inverse effect:

The primary reason is the **substitution effect.** The substitution effect is caused by the basic economic problem of scarcity. Because of scarcity, a consumer will have only limited income from which to try to obtain as much satisfaction as possible. Therefore a consumer will substitute lower-priced goods for higher-priced goods.

The secondary reason for the inverse relationship between price and quantity demanded is the **income effect.** The income effect is also caused by scarcity. Because of scarcity, a consumer will have only limited income.

SUPPLY—the willingness and ability of **sellers** to sell different quantities of a good at different prices

LAW of SUPPLY—the price and the quantity of a good are directly related. (as one variable {price} increases, the other variable {quantity} increases, and vice-versa.

The reason for the direct relationship between price and quantity supplied is the seller's goal of profit-maximization.

EQUILIBRIUM—Putting Demand and Supply together; what will the actual price of a good be and what quantity of the good will be produced and consumed is determined in a free market by the interaction of demand (buyers) and supply (sellers).

In a free market system the price is free to adjust up or down in response to demand and supply. In a free market, the market price will be the equilibrium price.

The **equilibrium price** is the price where quantity demanded equals quantity supplied.

Elasticity

Elasticity—a measure of the responsiveness of one variable to changes in another variable

If the Demand for a product is not affected by a change in price, the product is said to have "inelastic demand". Products that people need to survive, such as food, are inelastic. People will buy them no matter what the price is, because they need the product.

If the Supply for a product is not affected by a change in price, it is said to have "inelastic supply". If a product is difficult (or impossible) to produce, or difficult to produce in mass numbers, it will have inelastic supply. If the price goes up, the producers cannot increase the amount supplied. An example is an antique item. No matter how much the price rises, no more can be produced.

Price Controls

Dissatisfaction with market-determined prices has often led an overactive government to impose price controls such as a "price ceiling" or a "price floor".

A price ceiling is a maximum legal price which often leads to a shortage resulting in:

> Fewer exchanges than at equilibrium, more units sold and bought at equilibrium price than when there is a maximum price charged.

> The use of non-price rationing devices, price is not allowed to adjust with demand and supply and naturally rationing goods which are ration by government allocation. This non-price rationing is less efficient than using market price. Market price rations the goods to the consumers who are willing and able to pay the most for them. Non-price rationing will not ration the goods to the consumers who are willing and able to pay the most.

> Non-price rationing produces illegal transactions at prices above the imposed ceiling. Buyers and sellers will break the law to reap the mutually benefits.

Price controls are economically inefficient. A free market generally produces the most efficient quantity of output. A price control, whether a ceiling or a floor, reduces the quantity of transactions.

Third Party Costs and Benefits

When a business transaction takes place, there are two parties: the seller and the buyer. The transaction takes place between the two parties and no one else. Sometimes, however, a third party, someone that was not involved in the transaction is either hurt or helped by the transaction. This is called "third party cost", or a "third party benefit".

An example of a third party cost would be a pack of cigarettes: There's the drug store owner as the seller, the smoker as the buyer, and the people who are offended by the smoker's smoking are the third party that are hurt by the transaction, even thought they had nothing to do with it.

A third party benefit would be the nicotine patch: There's the seller of the patch, the smoker that buys the patch, and the third party that benefits are the people who no longer have to breathe the contaminated air.

Gross Domestic Product (GDP)

The Gross Domestic Product is the total value of all goods and services produced in the United States in a given year regardless of the nationality of those who produced them. In computing the GDP, only the value of the final goods and services are included. This means that only the value of the final product is included and not all the individual supplies that went into making the product. A house, for example, would only have its own value included in the GDP, and not the lumber, brick, wire, glass, cement, and shingles that went into building it. Exclusions in calculating GDP are intermediate goods, nonproduction transactions, nonmarket products (do-it-yourself), underground (unreported) productions, leisure, used goods, financial transactions, and government transactions which continue to be an ever growing percentage of GDP.

In 1930, the federal government spent 3.4 percent of GDP. In 1937 and 1939, in the midst of the Great Depression, federal expenditures consumed 8.6 percent and 10.3 percent of the GDP, respectively. During 1943 and 1944, in the midst of World War II, expenditures were 43.5 percent and 43.6 percent. In 1948, after the war, the percentage dropped to 11.5 percent. Throughout the 1950s and 1960s, federal expenditures as a percentage of GDP hovered between 15 percent and 17 percent. During the 1970s and 1980s, these numbers ranged between 17 percent and 19 percent. In the 1990s, the percentage varied 15 percent and 19 percent. By 2000 and 2001, there was a small drop to 14.8 percent in both years. Starting in 2009, the percentage reached 21.1 percent-the highest percentage of federal spending since 1946. And in 2010, federal expenditures jumped to 24 percent of GDP.

At the end of 2008, the federal debt as a percentage of GDP was at 40 percent. In 2010, it jumped to over 60 percent. For 2011, the Congressional Budget Office (CBO) has projected and it has obtained 70 percent of GDP, the highest level ever and it is expected to exceed 100 percent of GDP in the future. This growing imbalance between revenues and spending, combined with the spiraling interest payments, will swiftly push debt to higher and higher levels.

Historical Tabled, budget of the U.S. Government

Furthermore, the most recent estimate of total unfunded obligations in dollar terms-for which no resources are currently available and will never be available-is $61.6 trillion, or $528,000 per household. This includes $25 trillion in unfunded obligations for Medicare, $21.4 trillion for Social Security, and $9.4 trillion for servicing debt.

As a country we are certainly on the wrong road and spending will have to come under control as revenues from taxing can never accommodate this ever-growing debt and GDP productivity cannot possibly keep up and in fact will begun to decrease, inflation will spiral, and unemployment will be rabid.

Gross National Product (GNP)

Is the value of what's produced by a country's residents, no matter where they live. So if a U.S. resident earns money from an investment overseas, that value would be included in GNP (but not GDP). And the value of goods produced by foreign-owned businesses on U.S. land would be part of GDP (but not GNP).

As for which is the better indicator of economic health, GDP is the primary measure used by the U.S. Department of Commerce's Bureau of Economic Analysis.

CHAPTER FIVE

INFLATION

"Inflation is when you pay fifteen dollars for the ten-dollar haircut you used to get for five dollars when you had hair."
Sam Ewing

Inflation and Unemployment

Inflation is very unpopular. The dictionary defines inflation as a substantial and continuing rise in the general price level. The words "general price level" in the definition is very important. They mean that the term "inflation" applies only to a rise in the average cost of all the things we buy, and not to an increase in the price of only one item or class of items. Of course, a large increase in the price of one item can sometimes lead to rapid inflation—that is to a rapid increase in the price level. For example, a very rapid rise of oil prices could lead to a rise in the general price level, because oil plays a key role throughout our economy.

Inflation is when the cost of goods and services in the marketplace all go up at once, an increase in the price level.

The price level in an economy depends on the relationship between the quantity of money spent and the quantity of products purchased. If the quantity of money spent increases relative to the quantity of products purchased, the price level will increase. If the quantities of money spend decreases relative to the quantity of products purchased, the price level will decrease.

There are two main types of inflation: **Demand-Pull** inflation, and **Cost-Push** inflation.

Demand-pull inflation happens when people's incomes rise, but the amount of goods and services in the marketplace remain the same. Since people have more money to spend, they are willing to pay more for goods and services. In other words, the total demand will go up, which will cause prices to rise. Demand-pull inflation has been described as "more money chasing the same amount of goods."

Cost-push inflation happens when the cost of producing the goods and services goes up. This means that the total supply for an item goes down, and again prices rise.

Demand-pull inflation can be represented by the equation MV=PQ.

M is the amount of money available to spend.

V is the velocity that the money is spent, in other words how many times one dollar is spent as it circulates through the economy.

P is the price of an item.

Q is the quantity of items available in the marketplace.

If money (M) rises, then mathematically either the price (P) must rise, or the amount of goods (Q) must rise, or the velocity of spending (V) must go down. If the money supply (M) increases, and the amount of goods (Q) and the velocity of spending (V) stay the same, prices (P) will go up.

Inflation results when there is too much money and credit around in relation to the amount of goods and services. By "money" we mean cash in circulation and the amount that people and businesses have in bank accounts. "Credit" refers to the amount that banks and other lenders have lent.

What's wrong with inflation anyway? After all, if prices go up, people who sell things will receive more dollars than they did before. That means that incomes go up too. What's wrong with that?

One answer is that not everyone's income goes up as much as prices do. People whose income rise less than prices-or don't rise at all-are hurt by inflation. They are unable to buy all the things they used to with their income.

In general, inflation hurts people. When price rises, people can't buy as many things with their money. People on a fixed income (an income that doesn't increase when the cost of living goes up) are especially hurt, since the things they need to survive have increased in price, but their incomes don't increase. Businesses are hurt, since they can't invest as much in the business, and it's difficult to plan for the future if you don't know what the value of the dollar will be.

Inflation also reduces the value of people's savings when price increases are larger than the interest rates that people receive on their savings accounts. Because inflation reduces the value of savings, it gives people an incentive to spend rather than to save before their money is even further eroded. By discouraging saving, inflation can harm the U.S. economy. That's because the economy needs a supply of savings to provide the funds for people and businesses to borrow so that they can invest in the things that help the U.S. economy. Inflation also gives people an incentive to invest in ways that don't help the economy grow (gold, silver, jewelry).

When people realize that they have overbought out of fear of a value-declining dollar to beat anticipated price increases, they will cut back on spending, and the result can be a **recession,** a downturn in economic activity that brings a decline in production and an increase in **unemployment.**

Some people are helped, however, and those people helped are people in debt (people who owe money). If someone borrows money, and inflation causes the value of money to go down, then the money paid back won't be worth as much as when they borrowed it. They are essentially paying less money back then they borrowed.

Macroeconomics focuses on overall economic behavior; Microeconomics focuses on the components of that behavior. Society has three overall macroeconomics goals as it deals with the basic economic problem of scarcity.

1. Price level stability

2. Full employment

3. Economic growth

Achieving these goals will contribute to the basic goal of producing as much consumer satisfaction as possible with the limited resources available.

In pursuing the goal of price level stability, the primary concern is to avoid inflation or to keep the inflation rate low.

The price level does not refer to the price of only one good. The price level refers to the weighted average of the prices of all goods and services.

Inflation is an increase in the price level resulting in the devaluation of money.

Effects of Inflation

Some will gain from inflations and others will lose. Among the effects of inflation are:

1. **Inflation decreases the buying power of people who hold money.** This effect is minor as long as the rate of inflation is low and people don't hold money for very long. But if a person holds money for an extended period of time or when the inflation rate is high, that person will lose significant buying power.

2. **Inflation reduces the real interest rate earned on savings.** The real interest rate is equal to the nominal interest rate minus the rate of inflation.

3. **Increasing inflation benefits borrowers and hurts lenders.** The interest rate agreed to between a borrower and a lender will reflect their expectations of the future rate of inflation. If the rate of inflation increases, the borrower will benefit because the real rate of interest that the borrower is paying will be lower than expected. Likewise, the lender will suffer because the increase in inflation will lower the real interest rate the lender is earning on the loan.

4. **Inflation increases uncertainty and discourages investment.** Changes in the rate of inflation change the real interest rate. The higher the rate of inflation, the more unpredictable the inflation rate tends to be.

Higher inflation increases the uncertainty faced by both savers and investors about what the real interest rate will be. The increasing uncertainty discourages investment. A lower level of investment means a lower rate of long run economic growth.

The Price Level, Money, and Production

The price level in an economy depends on the relationship between the quantity of money spent and the quantity of products purchased in the economy. If the quantity of money spent increases relative the quantity of products purchased, the price level will increase. If the quantity of money spent decreases relative to the quantity of products purchased, the price level will decrease.

Consumer Price Index

The price level in the economy is measured by constructing a price index. The most widely reported price index is the consumer price index (CPI). The CPI is based on the price of a market basket of goods and services.

Broken down into categories, the market basket consisted (as of 12/10) of housing (41%), transportation (17%), food (15%), medical care (7%), education and communication (6%), recreation (6%), apparel (4%), and other (3%).

Computing the Rate of Inflation

The CPI index is used to compute the rate of inflation. The rate of inflation is the percentage annual increase in the index. The percentage annual increase in the index is calculated by dividing the annual change in the index (current year minus previous year) by the previous year's index.

e.g. CPI for 1945 was 18.0; CPI for 1946 was 19.5 therefore:

(19.5—18.0) divided by 18.0 = 1.5 divided by 18.0 = .083 or 8.3 % inflation rate.

Unemployment

*"Economics is extremely useful as a form
of employment for economists."*
John Kenneth Galbraith

Reminder: the basic economic problem is scarcity. The basic goal in dealing with the problem of scarcity is to produce as much consumer satisfaction as possible with the limited resources available. The total production that society can achieve will be reduced if some of the limited resources are **not** employed, such as one of the factors of production **labor.** Unemployed labor reduces total production and reduces wages earned is the primary source of income for most households (recall the circular flow).

Measuring Unemployment

The Bureau of Labor Statistics gathers information to determine the size of the labor force and the number of unemployed workers determining the unemployed rate. This calculation only includes people 16 years old and older. No one under 16 is included no matter how much money they may make or what job they may have lost. Accordingly, those under 16 can neither be employed nor unemployed in this determination. Those older than 16 are classified into one of three categories:

> **Employed**—those with paying jobs; the job does **not** have to be full-time, and during hard times like a recession often it is not. Therefore someone laid-off from a high-paying job and now working in a low-paying part-time job is counted as employed.

> **Unemployed**—those without paying jobs who are still actively seeking employment; An individual without a paying job who has become discouraged, surviving on government assisted unemployment, and quit seeking a job is **not** counted as unemployed.

> **Not in the Labor Force**—anyone not in the above two categories is not considered in the labor force and has no effect on the unemployment rate.

Therefore statistically the Labor Force is the sum number of people employed plus the number unemployed. The unemployment rate is the percentage of the labor force that is unemployed. It is calculated by dividing the number of people unemployed by the number of people in the labor force.

Labor Unions

Labor is a factor of production. The labor market tends to be highly competitive. Workers find that they are in competition with many other workers for the available jobs. To help stem their unemployment and provide bargaining power when negotiating with a potential or existing employer, they often join a labor union.

A **Labor Union** is an organization of workers. The union represents all of the eligible workers in negotiating with management over wages and other issues. This is called **collective bargaining**. The union gives the workers a monopoly in selling their labor. According to the antitrust laws, monopolies are illegal in the U.S. However, unions have been specifically exempted from antitrust law by the Clayton Act of 1914 and by judicial interpretation of the National Labor Relations Act of 1935; an example of government regulation impacting business.

Types of Labor Unions

Craft Union—a union made up of workers who practice the same craft, such as actors, carpenters, electricians, mechanics, pilots, plumbers, etc.

Industrial Union—a union made up of workers in the same industry, such as autoworkers, steelworkers, etc.

Public employee union—a union made up of workers employed by the government.

Union membership has been declining in the United States. In the 1950s, around one-third of the labor force was unionized. According to the Bureau of Labor Statistics, the percentage of wage and salary workers who were union members had fallen to 20% by 1983, and had fallen to 11.9% by 2010.

Two opposing views of unions are:

1. Unions hurt productivity due to; strikes, unnecessary staffing requirements, and keeping willing employers and employers apart.

2. Unions increase productivity by; providing a collective voice for union workers, and attracting higher quality workers.

Taxes, Deficits, and the National Debt

The basic economic problem is scarcity.
Human wants are unlimited.
Resources are limited.

"Government's view of the economy could be summed up in a few short phrases: If it moves, tax it. If it keeps moving, regulate it. And if it stops moving, subsidies it."
Ronald Reagan

Taxation transfers limited resources from the private sector (households and businesses) to the public sector (government).

Classification of Taxes

Taxes can be classified as proportional, progressive, or regressive. A **proportional tax** imposes the same tax rate on all levels of income. A **progressive tax** imposes higher tax rates on higher levels of income. A **regressive tax** imposes higher tax rates on lower levels of income.

Most taxes imposed in the U. S. are regressive. Two of the largest taxes, the social security tax and the federal corporate income tax are both regressive taxes. Sales tax and property taxes are also regressive.

Over 90 percent of the federal government tax revenues come from the three largest federal taxes: Personal Income Tax, Social Security Tax, and Corporate Income Tax.

Personal income tax is not a regressive tax but is a progressive tax.

Deficits and the National Debt

"I, however, place economy among the first and most important republican virtues, and public debt as the greatest of the dangers to be feared."
Thomas Jefferson

A budget deficit occurs when government expenditures are greater than tax revenues. Years of budget deficits have led to a huge national debt (about $16 trillion as of September 2012). The National debt is the total amount the federal government owes its creditors.

When the federal government pays for current expenditures by deficit spending (by borrowing), the current generation receives the benefit of the current government spending and passes the burden on to future generations. But a part of the burden of deficit spending also falls on the current generation to the extent that private consumption is crowded out by increased government use of resources. The basic economic problem is scarcity. Deficit spending allows the government to use a larger share of the limited resources. This leaves fewer resources for the private sector (consumption and investment). Deficit spending increases the government's demand for loanable funds. To the extent that consumption is crowded out, the current generation shares the burden of deficit spending.

The burden of deficit spending falls on future generations in two ways. Deficit spending drives up interest rates. The higher interest rates will reduce investment. The reduction of investment in the present will lead to slower economic growth in the future; Future generations will experience a lower standard of living because deficit spending reduces current investment.

The second way that deficit spending creates a burden on future generations is if the deficit spending is financed by **foreign creditors.** Presently (as of 8/11) the deficit is about 31% financed by this external borrowing (69% by internal borrowing from American creditors). When the external borrowing is repaid, fewer resources will be available to the domestic economy.

"An economy that robs Peter to pay Paul, can always count on Paul's support."
DRH

CHAPTER SIX

BUSINESS

*"It's just paper—all I own is a pickup
truck and a little Wal-Mart stock."*
Sam Walton

Business Entity—an entity (firm, organization) that employs resources to produce goods and services generally (in private ownership) for a profit

Business entities are either business for profit firms or nonprofit firms. Business firms are owned by individuals; proprietors, partners, or stockholders. Business entities come in different legal types. The most common legal type of business is the proprietorship, but in terms of total sales, corporations are the most important type.

Most corporations are small businesses. But the small percentages of corporations that are large provide the majority of total corporate sales.

Forms of Business Entities

- Sole Proprietorship
- Partnership
- Corporation
- S Corporation
- Limited Liability Company

SOLE PROPRIETORSHIP:

Advantages

- Simple to create
- Least costly to begin
- Complete decision making authority
- Profit motivation
- Few legal restrictions
- Easy to terminate

The Sole Proprietorship is simple to create and to terminate. The business is owned, operated, and managed by one person. The business and the person are one and the same –alter egos. Most small businesses start this way, particularly life-style businesses. It is the least costly to form; the only formalization required is to obtain whatever license or permits that may be necessary from the local governments especially if doing business under a trade name (DBA).

The owner retains all profits and makes all decisions—he/she is truly their own boss, the main reason why most start a business. There is also little complication in terminating the business. The owner simply ceases activity.

Disadvantages:

- Unlimited personal liability
- Limited skills and resources
- Limited capital available
- Lack of continuity
- Isolation

The owner has unlimited personal liability as a result is personally responsible and obligated for all debts and taxes of the business. All profits flow to the owner and personal income tax must be paid on them. Not only are the assets of the business but also all personal assets are at risk in the event failure or business default.

The sole proprietorship suffers from limited skills, expertise, and resources relying solely on those of the owner. A business owner is usually very much isolated and is the sole source of management skills, business knowledge and resources both tangible and intangible. If such shortcomings cannot be filled by hiring the necessary talents then surely the business may fail.

Since the business is solely dependent on the owner, in the event of illness the business will certainly suffer without others to sustain it.

The sole proprietor is limited to capital from personal resources and credit only. There are no shares of stock to sell for capital and loans may be scarce due to the business sole dependency on the owner. Without the owner to continue the business activity due to illness or death, the business will not continue.

If the business begins to accumulate assets and employees, the owner would be best advised to incorporate to protect personal assets and limit personal liability.

PARTNERSHIP:

Advantages

- Easy to create
- Complementary skills and resources of partners
- Additional capital access
- Little government regulations
- Division of profits and subsequent taxation

Partnerships, like proprietorships, are also easy to create. When individuals require and seek out complimentary skills and resources, they may come together for mutual benefit and profit. By virtue of an agreement, either formal or informal (ill-advised), outlining terms and conditions of the partnership, they will decide upon the division of profits and responsibilities. As a partnership, the business may have access to additional capital then may have been available to a sole-proprietorship. The partnership may also attract capital from limited partners—persons who invest their money for a possible return but has no input in the operations of the business or shares in its liability beyond their investment.

Like a proprietorship there are few government regulations and simplistic taxation.

Disadvantages

- Unlimited liability of general partners
- Moderate ability to raise capital
- Difficult to transfer or dispose partnership interest
- Lack of continuity

- Conflicts of personality, authority, and decision-making

In a partnerships, general partners have unlimited liability as does a sole proprietor. As such proportional percentage of profits also flows to the partners to be taxed personally. Unfortunately, with some exceptions, a partner is also responsible and liable for the actions and obligations of the other partners in the course of the business activity.

The partnership has similar continuity difficulties as a proprietor and is compounded by the multi-ownership. If a partner becomes ill, incapacitated, bankrupt, incarcerated, or dies; the partnership ceases. Often a formalized partnership agreement can mitigate some of these concerns by specification as to how ownership portions can be redistributed. This same agreement may equally prove to be hindrance by imposing restrictions as to how ownership may be redistributed and/or acquired by surviving partners. Too often a surviving partner may find himself in partnership with people with whom he has no desire to so partner.

Without any sort of succession agreement the partnership dies with the death of a partner and the accumulation of wealth and capital must be dealt with in probate.

Even with the survival of all partners there is almost always the inevitable potential for authority, distribution of benefits, and personality conflicts as time passes and the interest and personal agenda of partners' changes.

CORPORATIONS:

Advantages

- Limited liability
- Ability to attract capital
- Perpetuity
- Transferable ownership

Corporations are a separate legal entity from their owners. They may, as any individual legal entity, engage in legal commerce, business dealings, contract, own assets and real property, sue and be sued by others. The Supreme Court in its 1819 ruling defined corporations as "artificial beings, invisible, intangible, and existing only in contemplation of the law".

A corporation doing business in state in which it is incorporated is known as a

DOMESTIC CORPORATION

A corporation doing business in a state other than the state in which it is incorporated is known as a FOREIGN CORPORATION.

A corporation formed in another country but doing business in the United States is an ALIEN CORPORATION.

Registration of a corporation requires the filing of its "Articles of Incorporation" which becomes its Charter. Shareholders hold a meeting to elect Directors. The Directors appoint the corporate officers.

A corporation provides limited liability for its shareholders in that their liability of corporate debt after liquidation is limited to each shareholder's interest. An ongoing corporation is responsible for its liabilities, not the shareholders.

Recent court decisions have pierced this corporate shield of limited liability with respect to environmental and pension related matters removing the shareholders immunity to such claims. Additionally any attempts to use the corporate entity to commit fraud or evade existing legal obligations will also pierce the corporate shield of limited liability.

Because a corporation can issue and sell shares, it has the ability to raise additional capital in the form of equity. Likewise it can borrow more easily as corporate assets are readily available to be encumbered by lenders as well as the pledge of the corporate stock itself enabling a lender to easily seize ownership for continued operations, or the sale or liquidation of the company. Principals and majority shareholders can also be required to personally guarantee the corporate debt effectively eliminated their limited liability and providing additional cushion for secondary repayment.

The perpetual continued life the organizers can and generally elect enables the separate legal entity enterprises to continue long after the existing and even the lives of the organizers and principals.

Ownership shares are easily transferable and can be sold to someone else. They can be gifted to or inherited by family and friends.

Disadvantages
- Cost and time of incorporation (depends)
- Double taxation (depends)

- Legal requirements
- Potential loss of control by founders

The cost and time of incorporation are always regarded as prohibitive. If the corporation is to be a large and complex one such expense could be considerable and should be undertaking to assure the proper formation of the company. However most start-up corporations are not complex and can be incorporated in a timely matter for minor cost often by the entrepreneurs themselves.

Double taxation is often cited as a distinct disadvantage to incorporation. It is true that because corporations are separate legal entities, they must pay taxes on profits, and if distributed to shareholders, then they too must pay individual taxes on them again. However the corporate tax rate is generally lower than the personal tax rate incurred by proprietorship and partnerships; and most often the corporate revenue subject to income tax is greatly reduced by operating expenses not available as tax deduction to individual owned businesses. With the exception of dividends paid to stockholders, which is truly double-taxed, often when taken the total into consideration the corporate and individual stockholders tax liability is considerably less than the individuals alone operating as a partnership or proprietorship. In such matters a tax consultant would be of great assist in ascertaining the potential of tax reductions in the overall scenario.

Unlike partnerships and sole proprietorships, corporations required more formalized records to be maintained. Corporate management must record and report decisions, actions, and financial information to government regulators, shareholders, and often to lenders. Annual meetings must be held and officers are required to advise and consult with a board of directors. All of which sounds very tedious and difficulty and is indeed a serious undertaking for a large company, particularly one that is traded publicly. However, for the majority of small low capital corporations with a limited number of shareholders, such presents little problems and are quite easily accommodated.

With the ease of transferring ownership especially if a company does go public; there is a real possibilities that the founding organizers can and will lose controlling interest. Such may actually be done deliberately in an exit harvesting strategy or such could occur in a hostile takeover. Depending on the life cycle of the company and its stage of development, such activities should be orchestrated by the founding entrepreneurs to realize their dreams and aspirations for the company and themselves; to not be diligent in this regard as a result of poor management or naiveté will have dire consequences.

"S" CORPORATIONS

Advantages and Disadvantages

- No different from the "C" corporation (normal corporation) from a legal perspective
- For tax purposes, however, an "S" corporation is taxed like a partnership, passes all of its profits or losses to individual shareholders
- All shareholders must agree to elect "S" status

Legally a business is or is not a corporation. The "S" corporation is little different from the regular "C" corporation other than how it chooses to be taxed. Upon reflection, if the organizers of a corporation determine that it would behoove them to be taxed as individuals and still wish to enjoy the benefits and protection afforded by incorporation, they can choose to avoid any possibility of double taxation by electing to be taxed in accordance with the sub-chapter "S" of the tax regulations having all profits pass through to the shareholders much like a partnership.

To elect "S" status all shareholders must consent and the corporation must file with the IRS within the first 75 days of its tax year. It must be a domestic corporation with no nonresident aliens as shareholders. The "S" corporation can only issue one class of common stock and cannot have more than 100 shareholders.

A distinct disadvantage of an "S" corporation over a "C" corporation is that all benefits paid to shareholders, even if also an employee, such as hospitalization, insurance, vacation, travel, etc. cannot be deducted as business expense and must be reported as taxable income to the shareholders receiving them. This means that reimbursement for meals, lodging, travel, and insurance for the shareholder and perhaps any family member is taxable income.

Also the marginal tax rate for individuals filing under an "S" corporation, sole-proprietorship, partnership, and limited liability company is currently higher at 38% than the maximum rate for a corporation at 35%. The maximum corporate rate is exclusively the purview of those very successful high earning companies. Smaller corporations average an approximate tax rate of 15%. Be mindful that for a "C" corporation, the taxable income is greatly reduced via operating expense which is not available as deductions for an "S" corporation, proprietor, partnership, and limited liability company.

It would appear that from a tax viewpoint any form of business entity other than a "C" corporation would be most advantageous for those companies that are losing money which can be passed to individuals who can use the losses to offset other sources of income.

LIMITED LIABILITY COMPANY (LLC)

Advantages and Disadvantages

- LLC resemble an "S" corporations without some of the restrictions
- Two documents are required: the articles of organization and the operating agreement
- An LLC cannot have more than TWO of the four corporate characteristics:

1. Limited liability

2. Continuity of life

3. Free transferability of interest

4. Centralized management

The Limited Liability Company (LLC) was recently formed as a hybrid to offer some benefits of a corporation with the benefits of a partnership particularly as relating to the flow of taxable revenues and limited liability. However, as most businessmen soon discover, the LLC does neither well for a growing profitable business. This form of business ownership does serve well those companies that are losing money, have no intentions of growing, and in fact is a life-style business. Sometimes, in the grand scheme of tax planning, there is a place for an LLC as a real-estate holding company or as an affiliate owned by a "C" corporation.

Similar to an "S" corporation, profits and losses from an LLC flows through to the owners who are not shareholders but members. The members pay their own taxes as individuals.

Unlike an "S" corporation or a "C" corporation, the LLC can only have TWO of the four corporate features as enumerated. Members inevitable want and seek limited liability, after all this form of ownership is known as a limited liability company. But too often, inadvertently, the members by exercising one of the other features unintentionally violate the most desired limited liability protection. The very protection they seek is easily cast aside by attorneys and courts in the event of financial difficulties or law suits relating to negligence or fraud by a member. The courts are proving especially onerous to LLC for they are regulated differently from state to state and the limited liability provision has yet to be permanently established.

Corporations are organized for perpetuity because it is vital for a growing business. LLC are not so organized. Most are of a short duration and usually are no longer than 20 years with the maximum in some states of perpetuity similar to a corporation. By definition choosing to limit perpetuity indicates that the business has no long range growth plans.

If the LLC chooses or decides to readily accept new members or the sale of existing memberships to others, even family, this is often an accidental expiration of limited liability for it is usually done as a good thing to bring additional skills, knowledge, or capital resources into the company.

LLC are to be managed and governed by a majority vote of its membership who must meet for major decisions. If there is a management committee or a head managing member, that represent centralized management—one of the corporate features. Most LLC are casually operating with centralizes management, with free transferability of interest, with no thought toward or plan for cessation of activity, and still expect to enjoy the protection of limited liability. The members may very well be in for a surprise, much as they may at tax time.

One other small caveat about taxes—In the event the LLC, "S" corporation, or partnership is growing and earning profits and to sustain and support that growth the profits are retained in the company, the individuals will still pay personal taxes on those retained earnings even without personally taken any of it out of the company. Not so in a "C" corporation.

Proprietor Partnership "C" corporation "S" corporation LLC

Liability	Unlimited	Unlimited	Limited	Limited	Limited (perhaps)
Transferability	Fully	Consent of partners	Fully	Within "S" status	Consent of members
Continuity	Terminate by owners cessation or death	Dissolve upon death or incapacity of partner	Perpetual	Perpetual	Limited/ Perpetual
Raising Capital	Limited	Moderate	Very High	Moderate to High	Moderate to High
Tax Liability	Individual rate	Individual rate	Corporate rate Individual rate on dividends	Individual rate	Individual rate

Stocks and Bonds

When a corporation sells a piece of itself, that piece is called a stock. Selling stocks are a way that corporations raise money to invest in their company. When a person buys a stock, they become part-owner of the company. How big of a part of that ownership is determined by how much stock they buy. Since a shareholder is part-owner, they receive some of the profit of the company. Therefore, people invest in companies as a way to make money.

Common stock involves ownership in the corporation. Bondholders and preferred stockholders are viewed as creditors. Unlike bonds, common stock does not have a maturity date but exist as long as the company does.

Another way that corporations raise money is to sell bonds. When a company sells a bond to a person, they are really borrowing money from that person, with a promise to pay the money back, with interest, at a future date. A company that sells the bond must pay the value of the bond back at maturity, even if they lose money. A bond, therefore, carries a lower risk than stocks, which makes it more appealing to many investors.

There are two kinds of bonds: Bearer bonds and registered bonds. When a person buys a bearer bond, they are given a coupon that they can turn in when it is time to collect on the bond. A person could buy a bearer bond and give the coupon to someone else to turn in if they so desired. On the other hand, when a person buys a registered bond, the corporation keeps the bond on record so that only the person who bought the bond can collect on it. This adds a measure of safety against theft or loss.

The Stock Market

A stock exchange is a place for businesses to sell stocks, pieces of ownership of the company, and for people to buy and sell stocks from each other. As more people buy a stock, the more valuable it becomes to shareholders and the price of the stock goes up. As people sell stock, the price of the stock goes down. The primary goal of a stock buyer is to buy the stock when the price is low, and sell it later for a profit when the value of the stock goes up. When a stock can be sold at a higher price than it was bought at, it is called a capital gain.

Common vs. Preferred Stock

There are two kinds of stock, common and preferred. Owners of preferred stock are first in line for dividends, and have a fixed dividend rate. Common stock holders are last in line for dividends, and the dividend for a common stock holder is variable. Common stock holders are allowed to vote for company directors, so a common stock holder has a say in how the company is run. Preferred stock holders, however, are usually not allowed to vote for directors. In short, common stock holders bear the greatest risk, because they are last in line for dividends, and their rate of dividend can drop. Dividends payments to common stockholders must be declared by the board of directors. In the event of bankruptcy, the common stockholders, as owners of the corporation, cannot exercise claims on assets until the company's creditors, including its bondholders and preferred stockholders, have been satisfied. However, common stockholders' liability is limited to the amount of their investment.

Bull and Bear Markets

When people are optimistic and investment in the stock market is rising, it is called a "Bull Market". When people are pessimistic and investment is dropping, it is called a "Bear Market".

Buying on Margin

Buying on margin is when a person buys stock with borrowed money. A person buys stock on margin when he expects the price of the stock to go up. He can then pay back the loan out of the profit made on the sale of the stock.

What Determines Stock Price

A company's ability to generate cash flows now and in the future.

1. Any financial asset, including a company's stock, is valuable only to the extent that it generates cash flows;

2. The timing of cash flows matters-cash received sooner is better, because it can be reinvested to produce additional income or be returned to investors;

3. Investors generally are risk averse, so they will pay more for a stock whose cash flows are relatively certain than for one whose cash flows are more risky.

Therefore the company's stock price is enhanced by increasing the size of expected cash flows, by speeding up cash flows receipt, and by reducing risk.

U.S. Government Securities are debt instruments issued by the federal government. When a person buys a newly issued government security, that person is making a loan to the federal government.

The federal government issues a tremendous amount of debt securities (Federal Reserve open market operations) in order to finance deficit spending. U.S. government securities are classified as Treasury Bills (maturities up to one year), Treasury Notes (maturities beyond one year up to ten years), and Treasury Bonds (maturities greater than ten years).

Banks are huge purchasers of U.S. government securities for their own portfolio and for their customers.

U.S. government securities are attractive for banks for three reasons:

1. They pay interest. The interest rate is usually low, but banks earn even lower interest on their excess reserve. Purchasing U.S. government securities are a safe investment of excess reserves until an opportunity to make a more attractive investment (loan) comes available.

2. They are a low risk safe investment. The federal government has historically and hopeful will continue to pay its debts when they come due. However, recently, Standard's & Poor's credit rating agency has downgraded long-term U.S. government securities from AAA to AA+ primarily due to deficit spending and a spiraling overall deficit.

3. They are highly liquid. U.S. government securities are considered a liquid asset because they can be converted quickly into cash with low transaction cost.

THE FINANCIAL SECTOR:

To "finance" something means to pay for it.

Since money or credit is the means of payment, "financial" basically means "pertaining to money or credit."

Recall that the financial system has five parts:
- Money
- Central Bank
- Financial Instruments, like stocks, bonds, and loans
- Financial Markets, where those instruments are bought and sold
- Financial Institutions, which bring people and firms into contact with financial instruments and markets

The Financial Sector plays a vital role in the economy because it helps money be efficiently channeled from savers to prospective borrowers, making it much easier for firms to obtain financing for profitable investment in new capital and for individuals to borrow against their future income.

Without financial markets and institutions, borrowers would have to borrow directly from savers. Probably not much borrowing would take place at all, as most would-be borrowers would tend to have a hard time finding individual able and willing to loan them money. (Recall the double-coincidence of wants with barter.)

Without much borrowing or finance, the economy would be a lot less developed, as few businesses would be able to raise funds to invest in new plant and equipment, products, and expand markets. Likewise, few individuals would be able to own their own house, car, consumer goods, or even to go to college.

Therefore—**A well-functioning financial sector is necessary for a well-functioning economy.**

FINANCIAL INSTRUMENTS:

A Financial instrument is a financial asset for the person who buys or holds one, and it is a financial liability for the company or institution that issues it.

Financial Asset: any financial claim or piece of property that can be owned. Financial Assets usually have no intrinsic value of its own, but they entitle the bearer to a stream of income or a share of assets from the issuer of the asset.

Financial Liability: the obligation that the issuer of an asset has to the owner/buyer of that asset.

A SECURITY is a tradable financial instrument, like a bond or a share of stock.

The payments promised to the holder of a financial instrument are more valuable if they are:

- Larger
- Sooner to be made
- More likely to be made (less risky)
- Made when they are needed most (e.g., when the holder is poor, retired, or otherwise in need of money like an insurance policy.)

Financial Assets have two main uses:

1. Store of value—financial assets like stocks and bonds are mainly valued for their high rate of return.

2. Trading risk—financial assets like insurance policies allow you to transfer certain financial risks to another party.

Financial Liabilities are useful as a means of raising money and, for issuers like insurance companies which charge premiums, as a means of income.

"Regular" financial instruments are called *underlying financial instruments,* debt and equity instruments, which are the type described so far and involve basic transfer of money or assets from one party to another.

A more complicated type of financial instruments is *derivative financial instruments,* which are based on an underlying (regular) financial instrument (i.e., Stocks are underlying, regular, financial instruments). Stock options (e.g., to buy shares of a stock at a particular price on some future date) are derivative financial instruments.

Debt Securities (tradable financial instruments that pay interest) are broking down into two categories according to their maturity length:

Money Market Instruments

—Short-term, maturing in < 1 year

COMMERCIAL PAPER—short-term corporate debt, similar to bonds in the sense of being formal, short-term IOUs promising that a certain sum of money plus interest will be paid back

TREASURY BILLS—short-term debt issued by the federal government to help finance its current and past deficits

BONDS- A BOND is a formal debt (IOU) with a maturity of one year or more.

—Long-term, maturing in >=1 year;

Corporate Bonds issued by corporations

Treasury Bonds issued by the federal government to finance the national debt

Municipal Bonds issued by state and local governments to finance large, long- term capital projects.

CAPITAL INVESTING

Capital Investments are long range decisions that usually involve large sums of money and have uncertain outcomes at best. Should we purchase a new piece of equipment? Should we invest in a long-term advertising contract? Should we do some leasehold improvements? All are questions which can involve capital investments. The significance of the investment is directly related to the expected outcome and its potential impact on the business. An equipment purchase that may be considered a minor investment for a large company may be tremendously significant for a small to medium size company. For this and many other reasons it is important that capital investments be analyzed prior to implementation.

Most people view capital investments as tangible projects related to facilities, machinery or equipment. However a capital investment can be a long term project that is expected to yield benefits over time. Examples of this may be marketing campaigns, and research and development programs. Any investment representing significant capital expenditures and yielding benefits over an extended period should be considered as a potential capital investment.

In practice, capital investments generally emphasize asset purchases (equipment, land, machinery and furniture). The criteria for identifying a capital investment are:

- **They are long-term in nature**
- **They require significant outlays of funds**
- **They are expected to yield benefits over time**

When a business makes a capital investment it expects to recover the initial cash committed plus additional cash in the future. Because capital investments involve significant outlays of funds with benefits expected to be yielded over time they commit companies to a course of action over a long period. Capital investments also affect product cost. Because of these factors capital investment project need to be analyzed in the context of a company's overall capital strategic direction, long-term financial objectives, and business plan.

One important step in the implementation of a capital investment is the identification and classification of cost. This classification is important because generally accepted accounting principles (GAAP) require a matching of the cost of an asset whose benefits extend over time with future outcomes.

Expenditures incurred in the acquisition of a capital asset are capital cost. These costs are capitalized on the balance sheet and systematically charged against operating income over the useful life of the asset (depreciation). Therefore, it is critical that cost in any capital investment be identified as those to be capitalized and those to be expensed.

The determination of whether to implement a capital investment project or not involves a number of considerations.

- **Identify relevant cash flows**
- **Financial analysis of the investment**
- **Identify and assess the risk**
- **Do a "What If Analysis"**
- **Consider any other qualitative factors**

What is cash flow?

A cash flow is the cash that enters and leaves the business. Cash inflows are sales, cash savings and cost reduction. Cash outflows are cost for acquisition of machinery, inventory, and operating expense. Several cash flows to be considered in a capital investment analysis are:

- **Initial investment**
- **Inventory**
- **Operating Expense**
- **Disposal of Existing Equipment**
- **Future Disposal Cost**
- **Depreciation of new equipment**
- **Book Value of existing equipment**

After all relevant cash flows have been identified the attractiveness of the investment can be evaluated from a financial perspective. Acceptance of the capital investment is generally defined in terms of time (how much time will it take to recover the initial investment?) and money (how much additional cash will the business earn from this investment?). There are several methods that can be used to analyze the financial return of a capital investment which involve measuring inflows of income from the investment and outflows of cash associated with the investment.

Risk factors should be identified as part of the capitalization process. Four types of risk factors should be considered:

- **Economic Risk or the cost of doing business**
- **Commercial Risk or competitive actions**
- **Technological Risk or failure to meet technological goals**
- **Implementation Risk or failure to meet project plans due to human behavior**

The final steps in evaluating a capital investment involve qualitative factors such as employee moral or customer goodwill. These factors cannot necessarily be assigned a dollar value but are important in any decision making process.

TEN THINGS TO KNOW ABOUT BUSINESS FINANCIAL STATEMENTS

"Financial statements are like fine perfume:
to be sniffed but not swallowed."

- **Rules and Standards Matter**—Financial statements are prepared using generally accepted accounting principles (GAAP)
- **Exactness is always strived for but Estimates are Key**—The balance in the cash account is exact, but virtually every other number is based on an estimate. The amounts of expense, revenue, assets, and liabilities are calculated down to the last dollar, but they're based on estimates, and estimates never turn out to be accurate down to the last dollar.

  Estimates are unavoidable in accounting. A prudent business chooses estimates toward the conservative.

- **Financial Statements Fit Together like pieces of a Puzzle**—The three primary financial statements: the balance statement, the income statement, and the statement of cash flows appear on separate pages and may seem to stand alone, but in fact they are intertwined and interconnected.
- **Accrual Basis Is Used to Record Profit, Assets, and Liabilities**—The accrual basis must be used to reflect economic reality. Examples—Credit sales creating Account Receivables, Depreciation of an asset over its useful life, Expense recordation now even thought it will be paid later.

To record the expense a liability is increased; later, when paid, the liability is decreased.

If a business does not sell on credit, does not carry inventory, does not invest in long-term assets, and pays bills quickly. It may use the Cash Basis of Accounting instead of the Accrual Basis. Basically all it does is maintain a checkbook.

- **Cash Flow is not the same as Accrual Basis Profit**—Accrual Basis causes one point of confusion; bottom line profit in the income statement does not increase cash for the period. Cash flow almost always differs from the amount of bottom line profit reported in the income statement.
- **Profit and Balance Sheet Values can be Manipulated**—Business managers can "massaged the numbers" to make profits or the financial condition of the business look better.
- **Financial Statements May be Revised Later to Correct Errors and Fraud**—This annoying practice makes all financial statements tentative and conditional.
- **Some Assets Values are Current but others may be Old**—for example, inventory at FIFO or LIFO, and Fixed Assets original cost and current replacement value.
- **Financial Statements Leave Interpretation to the Reader**—The financial statements reports the facts but don't interpret what they mean. The assessment and forecast of the business's financial performance and condition is left for the reader to analyze.
- **Financial Statements tell the Story of the Business, Not its Owners (Shareholders).**

CHAPTER SEVEN

BANKING

Condensed History of American Banking

Banking has changed in many ways through the years. Banks today offer a wider range of products and services than ever before, and deliver them faster and more efficiently. But banking's central function remains as it has always been. Banks put a community's surplus funds (deposits and investments) to work by lending to people to buy homes and cars, to start and expand businesses, to put their children through school, and for countless other purposes. Banks are vital to the health of our nation's economy. For most of us, banks are the first choice for savings, borrowing, and investing.

EARLY AMERICAN BANKING HISTORY

There were no banks in early Colonial America. England not only prohibited forming American banks but also limited the amount of English currency and coins that could be brought to the colonies. Colonists were forced to barter.

The Massachusetts colony issued its own paper money in 1690 and soon other colonies did as well. England stopped this practice in 1741. Consequently American Banking began with the achievement of independence from England in 1776.

America's first banks were almost always temporary, informal, an early experimenters with their own paper money. Colonial banks were not banks as we know them today. They did not receive deposits from the public and did not regularly make loans. Their main purpose was to issue paper money.

At that time lending was generally handled by merchants and other wealthy individuals. When men of wealth wanted to deposit their money, they still choose to keep it in England.

Alexander Hamilton, Secretary of the Treasury, convinced the newly formed Congress to form the first permanent American Bank, in 1781. In response to the new revolutionary government's need for funds, the Bank of North America was federally chartered in 1781.

While the Bank of North America was important for the services it rendered to the Revolutionary War effort, it was also an important step forward in the development of our money and banking system. The population and business were growing and with it came the need for more credit. In 1784, the Massachusetts Bank and the Bank of New York were organized; by the turn of the century additional state banks had been established, most of them in New England. In 1787, the Bank of North America was again chartered by the State of Pennsylvania because of doubts over Congress' authority to grant banks which was granted as a State's authority. Being a privately owned bank with an original federal charter acting as a central bank, it received much opposition and was closed in 1811.

When the new Government was firmly established in 1789, financial problems were of predominant concern. These included the question of what to do about the indebtedness incurred during the Revolution and how to provide adequate credit for commerce.

A national Bank of the United States that Hamilton proposed, would provide a much needed paper currency since under the provision of the Constitution, the states were forbidden to issue paper money after 1789. The federal bank would benefit government and business by providing sound credit. In addition, it would act as the Government's fiscal agent and provide a facility for the safekeeping of government funds. Congress approved this Federal Central bank, the Bank of the United States, in 1791 (the first Bank of the United States, there was to be a second). The first Bank of the United States was chartered for a term of 20 years. It was essentially a private bank operating under a Federal charter as opposed a State charter. The Government however was a part owner. It subscribed to one-fifth of the Bank's $10 million capital; the rest was raised by the sale of stock to the public.

The Bank of the United States had eight branches. The main office was in Philadelphia; its branches were in New York, Boston, Charleston, Baltimore, Norfolk, Savannah, Washington D. C. and NEW ORLEANS.

The Bank of the United States operated very successfully and was a great benefit to the country. The loans made to the business community contributed to the development of the economy. The Bank also served the newly-formed Federal Government by strengthening the market for bonds issued by the Treasury and acting as revenue agent. Most important was the Bank's provision for a sound and stable currency.

But the Bank of the United States had its opponents from the start. Opposition arose similar to that of the Bank of North America from the state banks, now numbering about 88—100, who shared Thomas Jefferson's belief that control over banking should be in the hands of state government. When the proposal to renewal the Bank of the United States charter in 1811 was advanced, it was defeated. The bank was liquidated and its assets sold to Stephen Girard, The Girard Bank of Philadelphia, which is today the Philadelphia National Bank.

Due to economic problems after the War of 1812, and the financial impact of the closing of the first Bank of the United States, the second Bank of the United States was chartered. It operated successfully for several years but met with the same opposition. President Andrew Jackson so hated the "Federal Central Bank" that he refused to put Government money in it and scattered over several state banks. He regarded the Bank as a dangerous monopoly. The second Bank of the United States, with capital of $35 million and 25 branches in 20 states, and over 500 employees, charter was also not renewed and it closed.

The arguments for and against the Federal banks were political as well as economic. The first and second Banks of the United States and most of the branches were located in the East where the country was more develop. The financial community there favored sound money and therefore deter state banks from issuing their paper money restricting the state banks lending opportunities. In the West, the frontiersmen needed loans to build farms and to buy more land. These needs were met by state banks not the federal bank. Therefore support was growing for state banks to oppose the limits placed on them by the federal bank.

With the country expanding westward, the money and credit needs of the country were diverse, and no single bank could supply them. The demise of the second Bank of the United States brought to an end the policy of regulating bank credit and the nation's currency through a Federal Bank. From then on, until the Civil War, banking was a mess. It was left to the state banks to meet the country's needs for paper money and different banks issued different currency.

By 1860 more than 10,000 different bank notes circulated throughout the country. Commerce suffered as a result. Counterfeiting was epidemic.

Hundreds of state banks had failed due to depositors withdrawing their funds until there was no cash left. Throughout the country there was an insistent demand for a uniform national currency acceptable anywhere without risk. In response, Congress passed the National Currency Act in 1863, revised in 1864 as the National Banking Act.

Full Federal control over commercial bank credit was not to reappear as a concept of national policy until the establishment of the Federal Reserve System in 1913 to avoid another cash shortage.

BANKS

Modern banking has its origins in the ancient past. In its very simplest forms, banking was practiced by the Assyrians, Babylonians, and Athenians. It achieved a higher development in ancient Rome and medieval Europe. The word *bank* is derived from the Italian word *banca*, which refers to the "table, counter, or place of business of a money changer." In fact, banking functions have been performed ever since people started to use money. It is difficult to conceive of an advanced society without some kind of banking.

The chief basis for banking has always been the lending of money. While moneylenders have been with us for a very long time, banks as we know them today are of comparatively modern origin. Among the forerunners of modern banks were the Bank of Venice (1171), the Bank of Genoa (1320), and the Bank of Amsterdam (1609). In England, the oldest banking business still operating on its original site is Martins Bank, established by Sir Thomas Gresham, a goldsmith, in London in 1563.

Banks in one way or another influence each of us in our day-to-day living; they also play a significant role in the economy.

FUNCTIONS OF MODERN BANKS

"The business of banking, in its widest sense," an early American writer noted, "is to collect the capital of a community, that which is either money or can readily be turned into money, and upon this capital to build up, by proper management, a credit which will extend and enlarge its usefulness to the community."

In conducting their business, banks have long performed three basic money and credit functions:

1. Acceptance of funds for safekeeping

2. Provide a mechanism for making payments

3. Putting deposits to work by lending or investing.

Banks as depositories for safekeeping:

People put money in banks for safety and convenience; the funds are subject to withdrawn upon the customer's request as checking accounts (demand deposits). Customers also deposit funds into savings accounts (time deposits). Such funds are left in banks for longer periods of time than are demand deposits.

Mechanism for making payments:

Money is the basis of our modern economic society. Recall that the bulk of the nation's money supply today consists of checking accounts in banks (checkbook money).

Today checks are the chief medium of payment.

Banks also play an important role in meeting the public's lesser need for currency (paper money and coins).

Putting deposits to work:

Banks put deposits to work by making loans and investments. Bank credit has been of great importance to America throughout its history. The use of bank credit permits expansion of production and the creation of jobs. Individuals also borrow for homes, automobiles, and other personal use. Borrowing permits bank customer to make expenditures sooner than they could otherwise do.

COMMERCIAL BANKS

A commercial bank is a private corporation that is a financial institution, chartered either by a state or the federal government (dual banking system), that accepts deposits and makes loans. Originally, accepting deposits and making loans were the only activities associated with commercial banking. Since the 1960s, most commercial banks have expanded to full-service "financial department stores" serving both consumer and business markets, and deriving earnings not only from loans, but also from financial investments and financial services.

Most of the nation's commercial banks now offer time and savings deposits accounts, rent safe deposit boxes, exchange foreign currency, maintain automated teller machines (ATMs), issue credit and debit cards, and sell traveler's checks, in addition to accepting demand deposits (checking accounts) and providing businesses and individuals with loans. Some of the largest banks also operate trust departments.

A striking feature of the U.S. banking industry is the very large number of banks. Most of these commercial banks are very small, state chartered, privately owned financial institutions. Over half of all U.S. banks have assets of $100 million or less. Approximately 10 percent of the banks have asset of $500 million to $1 billion. A few very large, over $1 billion (5 percent of the banks), commercial banks are global corporations with hundreds of branches and thousands of employees. These banks are concentrated in the nation's money centers—New York, Chicago, and San Francisco—and they hold a relatively large share of the banking system total deposits. Presently, the largest U.S. bank, Citigroup (Citibank), is the largest bank with over $1.5 trillion in assets.

In other countries, four or five large banks dominate the industry, controlling the vast majority of bank assets. The U.S. banking industry has lately been moving in that direction fairly quickly. While the number of banks has fallen considerably since 1935, the number of bank branches has more than quadrupled to between 75,000 and 100,000. Technology and online banking has also made it unnecessary for you and your bank to be in the same town.

In all, the U.S. has about 10,000 commercial banks, plus approximately 10,000 thrifts (smaller depository institutions, mostly credit unions, also savings & loan associations and mutual savings banks specializing in mortgage and consumer loans).

The primary role of commercial banks remains to make loans. This activity creates the demand deposit dollars that serves the nation's principal form of money. About 40 percent of commercial bank loans, by dollar volume, are made to business firms; about 25 percent to consumers; and another 30 percent are for mortgages, many on residential properties, but most on commercial properties.

More than 65 percent, by dollar volume, of demand deposits, and nearly 30 percent of time deposits are owned by businesses.

Money Creation

Banks are able to create money due to the **fractional reserve system** in which they operate. Money creation is increases in checkable deposits made possible because banks hold reserves only equal to a fraction of their deposits enabling them to employ the balance in other loans which are subsequently deposit into the banks creating more excess reserve to again be lent out.

Required reserves are the minimum amount of reserves that a bank is legally required to hold against its deposits. Only two types of assets are counted as reserves; vault cash and deposits with the Federal Reserve. Excess reserves may be loaned out for creation of money in the form of new deposits. The loan may result in spending which results in new deposits within the lending bank or into another bank. In this way, the amount of checkable deposits in the financial system increases. The initial deposit sets off a chain of lending and depositing, which leads to multiplied increases in deposits.

THE "Cs" of CREDIT

Historically banks adhere to the "C's" of credit in evaluating loan request and establishing credit policy. They are: Character, Capacity, Capital, Conditions, and Collateral; to this the entrepreneur should add Communication.

Character: The foundation of all lending is the basic character of the applicant rather individual or business owners. Often borrowers have the ability to repay a loan but are simply not willing or determine to do so in the face of some difficulty. Character is simply the willingness and determination to repay the loan.

How is it possible for a lender to know if the borrower has good character or not? The applicants past payment history and credit records revealing a willingness and determination to pay in the past are a good indicator particular if analyst reveals that repayment was made even through hard times. Adversity will truly indicate the applicant's character. How have you managed other loans with the bank both business and personal will have an impact. It has been said that good character is easy when everyone is watching and times are good, but how one behaves in private during hardship is a true indicator of character.

Capacity: While character may be considered of the utmost importance, pragmatically capacity is essential. Character is the willingness to repay; Capacity is the ability to repay. No matter how good and decent a person is, and how determined to make repayment; if the business does not have sufficient cash-flow payments will not be made when due and repayment will not come. Capacity is more than willingness, a very willing borrower may be totally unable to repay because the business is not producing the necessary cash. It has been said that "Sales may pay interest, but profits are needed to pay principal." Banks look for positive cash-flow with profitability to follow for complete repayment. This reflects upon the feasibility of the business, its market, the execution of the plan, and the strength of management. Both the lender and the borrower would be wise to consider if the purpose for which the loan is requested will in fact generated repayment.

Capital: Capital represents the paid-in money and retained earnings of the business; the part of the business owned by the owners as opposed to that of the creditors. It is the leverage of the business and should always reflect that the owners are well-vested and committed to the business providing a comfort level for the bank. Banks never want to have more money in your business than you do making the business more theirs than yours.

Conditions: While Character, Capacity, and Capital directly relates to the borrower; Conditions relate to the market, the industry, and to the economy in general. It may very well reveal a management weakness if the owners are not able to read these factors. The lender will and if they are unfavorable it will not be conducive to an approval of the loan request. Adverse conditions of the economy, industry, market, location, and the facility itself can diminish character, capacity, and capital.

Collateral: Collateral will assist by helping to make the loan safe but not sound. It is no substitute for the other "C"s". Collateral must be marketable, assignable, and of sufficient margin for quick liquidation without lost. A borrower may mistakenly think that collateral will supplement a weakness. It is viewed only as a reluctant secondary source of repayment, as added incentive for the borrower to repay, to encourage willingness and determination to make payment. A loan paid this way is a failed loan and usually the result of a failed business. Collateral is never a substitute for good character and capacity.

Communication: How do entrepreneurs, potential borrowers, and bank customers communicate with the bank and the banker? Good communications goes beyond the occasional coffee or lunch, or even the friendly greeting on bank visits. It behooves the small business owner to establish a rapport with the bank; in fact it would be recommended that more than one bank relationship be established.

Simply keep the bank aware of your progress and familiar with your business. Even if not now a borrower supply financial statements regularly to start your credit file. Definitely if a loan has been obtained keep the bank informed on a timely basis prior to being asked. They should already have your business plan and updates as adjusted, interim financial statements both internal and CPA prepared, and tax returns. Make your contact person aware of changing in your organization, market place, and industry. Since it is a fact of banking today, bank representatives tend to move quite frequently, so such advisement should be done formally with a memo to your bank file—request it.

Effective communications in this matter will improve your business relationship and enhance your professional image. It also prevents you and your business from being a stranger to the bank with documentation beyond your relationship with the local bank

BANK HOLDING COMPANIES

A bank holding company is a corporation that owns or controls one or more banks. About 7,500 bank holding companies in the nation own or control one or more banks, and these banks hold about 85 percent of bank deposits. The significance of this corporate structure is that bank holding companies may engage in financial activities through their nonbank affiliates that banks themselves are not allowed to engage in. Such activities range from selling economic information and data processing services to brokering gold bullion, providing investment advisory services, and underwriting many forms of insurance. During the period prior to deregulation when banks could not branch beyond state, county, and parish lines, holding companies allowed banks to expand statewide or national.

THRIFTS

The U.S. thrift industry consists of mutual savings banks, savings and loan associations, and credit unions. The role of thrift institutions has traditionally been to lend people's savings to individuals who wanted to buy homes. However, new payment and deposit-related powers granted to thrifts in the 1970s and 1980s effectively eliminated most of the differences in deposits and sources of revenue between banks and thrifts.

Many thrifts found that this expanded powers did not guarantee increase business or profits but for many their demise. The rapid rise in interest rates of the 70s and 80s accelerated the shifting of funds into these new types of volatile short-term interest-earning transaction accounts and savings accounts that were sensitive to market rates from their traditional source of funds- stable, low-interest-earning, long term passbook deposits. The impact was a sharp increase in interest expense and a resulting squeeze on profits. The income of many thrifts—generated mainly from fixed-rate mortgages—failed to keep pace with the rising cost of funds.

The Federal Reserve System

You're probably familiar with a bank in your neighborhood. Perhaps you or someone in your family has a checking or savings account at a local bank, or perhaps someone in your family has recently taken out a loan at a bank…to buy a car, for example.

The Federal Reserve System (known as the Fed) is the nation's bank much like your neighbor bank is your bank. It doesn't provide services to individuals the way your bank does, but it does perform a variety of tasks to help the U.S. economy function smoothly and meet the nation's economic goals.

The Fed is best known for its handling of **monetary policy**, which consists of influencing money and credit conditions in the economy in order to help the U.S. economy experience strong growth in output and income, high employment, and stable prices.

The job of making monetary policy often is a balancing act, as the Fed has to make sure that money and credit don't grow either too slowly or too rapidly. If they grow too slowly, funds won't be available for loans, and people and businesses will find it harder to borrow to make major purchases. Insufficient money and credit growth can lead to a **recession**, a period in which economic activity (such as production and spending) declines and unemployment rises. On the other hand, when money and credit grow too much, the result can be **inflation**—a sustained and rapid increase in the price level.

So to try to prevent both recessions and inflation, the Fed has three main monetary policy tools: **Open Market Operations, Reserve Requirements, and the Discount Rate.**

Open market operations are purchases and sales by the Fed of U.S. government securities (bonds), which are large IOUs of the federal government. When the Fed buys securities, it pays for them by crediting the amount of the purchase to the account that the seller's bank has at the Fed. The bank, in turn, credits the seller's account. This open market operation provides the banking system with additional funds to lend. In that way, open market purchases tend to lower the **federal funds rate,** the interest rate that banks charge each other on very short-term loans. A drop in the federal funds rate can also lead to a decline in the rates that banks charge on loans and pay on deposits. And, when interest rates fall, spending in the economy eventually increases.

The opposite occurs when the Fed sells government securities. The Fed collects payments for the securities by subtracting the amount of the sale from the account that the buyer's bank has at the Fed. The bank, in turn, subtracts the amount from the buyer's account. Banks now have less to lend, the federal funds rate may rise, and some borrowing may be discouraged with higher rates. That means people may buy fewer cars and businesses may buy less new equipment or hiring new employees.

Reserve requirements are another, thought far less frequently used, tool of monetary policy. Reserve requirements are the percentages of certain deposits that banks must have either in their own vaults or on deposit at the Fed. For example, if the reserve requirement is 10%, a bank that receives a $100 deposit must have $10 in its vault or at its Federal Reserve Bank. One reason the Fed rarely changes reserve requirements is that frequent changes would make it hard for bankers to plan.

Still another tool of monetary policy involved the **discount rate**, the interest rate the Fed charges banks on short-term loans. Changes in the discount rate can influence other interest rates.

The Federal Reserve also affects the U.S. economy when it intervenes for the U.S. monetary authorities—the Treasury Department and the Fed—In the foreign exchange market, in which dollars are exchanged for foreign currencies such as the Japanese yen and the euro.

The Fed also provides banks with services that help the economy function smoothly. For instance, the Fed provides banks with cash to meet their customers' needs. On the other hand, when banks have more cash than they need, they ship the excess to the Fed for credit to their account. While cash is used for some transactions in the economy, checks are used for many others, and the Fed processes about one-third of all checks written in the United States. And, although cash and checks are used for most transactions, the dollar volume of electronic payments processed by the Fed is much larger than that of checks and cash combined.

Another responsibility of the Federal Reserve (one that it shares with some other government agencies) is to supervise and regulate banks in order to make sure they operate safely and soundly, and are sensitive to risks.

The Federal Reserve System is headed by its Board of Governors which is in Washington, D.C. The Board of Governors consists of seven members, appointed by the U.S. president and confirmed by the U.S. Senate. Governors are appointed to a 14-year term. These terms are much longer than those of the president, senators, or members of the House of Representatives. Also, the 14-year terms are staggered. That means they don't all expire at the same time. One term expires every two years. The staggered 14-year terms reduce the influence of politics on the Fed.

In addition to the Board of Governors, the Fed consists of 12 Federal Reserve Banks spread around the country. The Reserve Banks provide financial services for the U.S. government, supervise banks in their districts, and provide banks with services, such as the provisions and storage of cash, loans, and check processing.

Fiscal Policy—changes in government expenditures and taxation to achieve macroeconomics goals.

Changes in fiscal policy affect the federal government's budget. The federal government's budget could be balanced, with tax revenues equal to government expenditures. However with unwise and wasteful spending the government expenditures can (and has been) excessive beyond with a society is willing to pay in taxes. Therefore, typically, the federal government's budget is in a deficit. It is possible for it to be in a surplus if tax revenues were to exceed expenditures.

Budget deficit—when government expenditures are greater than tax revenues.

Budget surplus—when tax revenues are greater than government expenditures.

There are four potential problems with attempting to use fiscal policy to stabilize the economy:

1. Politics; there may be a political bias toward expansionary fiscal policy

2. Crowding out; increase in government spending lead to decreases in private spending

3. Mistiming; fiscal policy may be activated inadvertently due to normal business cycle lags

4. Error; the fiscal policy action may be miscalculated as to its outcome

Continued deficit spending (expenditures beyond revenues) does and has led to a growing federal government, which has and does lead to higher marginal tax rates. High tax rates reduce incentives for businesses and individuals. Thus reducing all commercial activity and leads to recession.

Lower tax rates would increase incentives, production, and commercial activity. Lower marginal tax rate might actually increase tax revenue as a result of the increased activity as demonstrated by the Laffer curve (economist Arthur Laffer).

Functions of the Federal Reserve

1. **Control the money supply;** This is the most important function of the Fed.

2. **Supervise and regulate banks;** Regulations, such as the required reserve, Supervision, such as audits of lending policies, is carried out by the Federal Reserve Districts Banks.

3. **Lender of last resort;** A bank in need of reserves can borrow from other banks through the federal funds market or from the Fed. However if there is a general shortage of reserves and there are no other banks with excess reserves to lend then reserves can be borrowed directly from the Fed. In this way a financial panic can be avoided.

4. **Holder of banks' reserves;** Banks are required to hold fractional reserves to back up their checkable deposits either in their vaults or with the Fed.

5. **Supply the economy with currency;** Currency, produced by the Treasury department, is put into circulation through banks by the twelve Federal Reserve District Banks.

6. **Provide check-clearing services;** Many payments are now conducted by electronic transfer, however the Fed remains the

large provider of check-clearing services in the U.S. economy handling about 20 billion checks per year.

Independence of the Federal Reserve

The Federal Reserve is intended to be an independent central bank. Other nations have created central banks that are relatively independent but many are more politically influenced by government officials. It is a fear that the United States central bank may become politically influenced. It is established that the more independent a central bank is the more successful it will be in avoiding inflation and positively controlling the economy.

The Fed is independent as its decision does not have to be approved by the President or Congress. The boards of governors of the Fed are required to submit bi-annual reports to congress on the state of the economy as they see it and on the conduct of their monetary policy enacted. This independence is intended to allow the Fed to make policy decision free of political influence.

The Fed's political independence is strengthen by its financial independence. The Fed is not dependent on Congress for its funding. In fact, it has earned a profit each year (unique for a government agency).

CHAPTER EIGHT

MONEY

MONEY—(anything that is generally accepted as payment) is more efficient than **BARTER** (trading goods/services for goods/services); BARTER requires a DOUBLE COINCIDENCE OF WANTS (you want the goods/services offered by someone and they want the goods/services offered by you); money does not require a double coincidence, because everyone can find a use for money.

Three Functions of Money –

1. Medium of Exchange—a financial asset (money) is used to trade (exchange) real assets (goods/services).- Primary Function

2. Store of Value—money serves as a means of storing purchasing power.

3. Unit of Account—prices are denominated in terms of the monetary unit, such as the dollar.

Concept of Money—anything generally accepted as a medium of exchange—formally Commodity Money such as rocks, tobacco, cattle, etc., presently- currency, coins, and checkable deposits (checkbook money) at banks and other financial institutions. Credit cards not a medium of exchange but a deferred payment system.

Bank Deposits, followed by Cash in Circulation, are the main form of money in our society.

A BANK is a financial institution that accepts deposits and makes loans.

Money eliminates the inefficiencies of a barter economy and enhances the growth of the economy.

Money encourages specialization and division of labor.

FIVE PARTS OF THE FINANCIAL SYSTEM

1. MONEY—anything generally accepted as payment—Main types: bank deposits and cash

2. FINANCIAL INSTRUMENTS—formal obligation that entitles one party to receive payments and/or share of assets from another party

3. FINANCIAL MARKETS—places where financial instruments can be sold quickly and cheaply

4. FINANCIAL INSTITUTIONS—firms that provide savers and borrowers with access to financial instruments and financial markets

5. CENTRAL BANKS—large financial institution that handles government's finances, regulates the supply of money and credit in the economy, and serves as the bank to commercial banks—The Federal Reserve of the United States, the European Central Bank for countries using the EURO

FIVE CORE PRINCIPLES OF MONEY AND BANKING

1. TIME has value—a dollar today is worth more than a dollar next year.

2. RISK requires compensation

3. INFORMATION is the basis for decision

4. MARKETS set prices and allocate resources

5. STABILITY improves well-being.

Acronym—TRIMS—Time, Risk, Information, Markets, Stability

MONEY: The dictionary has several definitions of money. In ordinary conversation we commonly use the word *money* to mean income (he makes a lot of money) or wealth (she has a lot of money). In this course (and in macroeconomics), we use a different definition, namely the one given in the previous notes:

Money = anything that is generally accepted as payment.

This is the economist's usage of the term *money*.

Money is not the same thing as Income or Wealth.

Q: If money is something generally accepted as payment, then what counts as money today?

A: Obviously, cash—dollar bills, coins—is a form of money.

Q: Is there anything else that counts as money?

A: Checks and all other types of negotiable accounts as well.

Q: Are credit cards money?

A: No. They are not legal tender. What a credit-card purchase represents is an extremely convenient, pre-approved loan. It is a deferred payment system that must be paid with money.

AGAIN recall the Three Main Functions of Money:

1. Medium of Exchange (means of payment)—Because money is a generally accepted form of payment, you can use it to buy things.

2. Store of Value (an asset in its own right)—stores purchase power, while cash earns no interest (unless deposits into an interest bearing account which may or may not be negotiable and readily liquid); cash is perfectly liquid and has no default risk.

3. Unit of Account (unit of measurement)—You can use it to price things in dollars and cents. Quoting prices in terms of dollars, the American unit of account, is a lot easier than quoting prices in terms of other goods—e.g., my cell phone bill is 300 Big Macs per month.

Money is FUNGIBLE in that any dollar is interchangeable with any other dollar.

Money has value because it is generally accepted as a medium of exchange. Money is not valuable in itself. We do not want money to keep. We want money to trade for what we really want.

Since we use money as a measure of value, we tend to think that money makes goods valuable. It does not; it is the other way around. The goods we produce and purchase makes our money valuable because we trade our money for them.

THE EVOLUTION OF MONEY

Many diverse items have served as money such as: cattle, furs, bark, cloth, tea, salt, fish, and anything else that ancient civilizations may have regarded as valuable.

COMMODITY MONEY

The earliest monies were mediums of exchange that were also useful commodities with intrinsic value. Commodity Money was made up from precious metals or other commodities that had intrinsic value (value in their own right). The inherent value of the commodity itself supported its use as an exchange medium for goods and services. Gold was the world's longest-reigning commodity money which was universally accepted throughout the ancient world whereas other commodity may or may not have been so accepted. Unfortunately, most commodity monies lack the physical characteristic necessary to assure their performance as uniform standards of account and good stores of value. Even gold lacks the easy divisibility and portability necessary for a truly efficient and practical exchange medium. The role of gold today is primarily that of a fluctuating store of value.

REPRESENTATIVE MONEY

The impracticality of commodity money quickly became apparent. Tradesmen and merchants began to deposit their gold with goldsmiths (the earliest bankers). The goldsmiths gave receipts. Soon the receipts were being exchange as a more rapid, practical, and safe method of payments.

These receipts, the precursors of our modern currency, were **representative money;** they represented claims on gold or other items of value held at a central depository (goldsmith) functioning as an effective medium of exchange.

FIAT MONEY

Fiat money represents the third major stage in the evolution of money. **Fiat Money** is money by decree—a medium of exchange mandated by a government and backed by the law and power of the state. Virtually all of the coin and currency used today is fiat money issued by governments and central banks of the nations of the world.

The Value of modern money is based what it can buy in the market place— its **purchase power.** The value of one U.S. dollar is the same whether that dollar takes the form of a metal coin, a currency note, or a check drawn on a bank account.

Although checks are the preferred means of payment in the United States today, they carry no status as LEGAL TENDER. **Legal Tender** refers to money items designated by the government and the courts as acceptable payment for goods and services or settlement of debt. Some advantages of **Checkbook Money** are: ability to spend small or large amounts with the same instrument, deterrence to theft or counterfeiting because of signature requirement, ability to stop payment after a transaction has been made, written proof of payment, an audit trail through the check collection process, which allows for identification of transaction errors, and extended time for use of funds (float) due to the check collection process.

In today's economy, the lack of Legal Tender status of checkbook money has been supplanted by public confidence in the strength, safety, and soundness of the American Banking system. This confidence has been bolstered by ongoing government supervision and inspection of banks.

Today the acceptability and value of money are not rooted in money's intrinsic worth, but in its purchasing power.

The Money Supply is equal to the cash in circulation plus checkbook money in depository banks.

A BRIEF HISTORY OF U.S. CURRENCY

Today currency in the United States is issued by the U.S. Treasury and circulated by the Federal Reserve Bank. This has not always been the case. During the Colonial period, the British colonies were prohibited from printing their own currency. Barter was commonplace, and other exchanges occurred using various Commodity Monies. To help finance the Revolutionary War, the Continental Congress issued a new kind of currency called the "Continental". Since the Continental Congress had no taxation power, the Continental was backed only by a promise and was rapidly depreciated giving rise to the phrase "not worth a continental".

The first privately owned bank in the United States, the Bank of North America, was chartered in Philadelphia in 1782. From the earliest years of banking until the Civil War, banks issued their own currency called "Banknotes". Banknotes were redeemable in gold, circulated as money and dispersed when loans were made. Banks soon began to issue more notes than their gold reserves and ever fearful that the notes would not be able to be redeem; note-holders would endeavor to rush to the banks. The result was that banknotes often circulated at a discount and banks often failed. The period from the late 1830s until the Civil War became known as the "Wildcat Banking Era". Banks that were unable to redeem their notes would relocate to the woods where it was difficult for even a wildcat to find them.

During the Civil War, the government issued "Greenbacks" to finance the war. In 1863 and 1864, Congress passed the National Banking Acts, which established a network of federally chartered National Banks and created a uniform currency. In addition, the acts levied a ten percent tax on the banknotes issued by state chartered banks. Subsequently these state chartered banknotes disappeared and the new uniform national banknotes circulated at full value. The National Banking Acts were successful in providing a sound and stable national currency for the first time since the birth of the nation.

Money is such a routine part of everyday living that its existence and acceptance are taken for granted. One may sense that it must come into being either automatically as a result of economic activity or as an outgrowth of some government operation. But just how this happens all too often remains a mystery.

As you have seen, many things—from stones to cigarettes—have served as money through the ages. Today, in the United States, there are only two kinds of money in use—*currency* (paper money and coins) and *demand deposits* (checking accounts). Since $1 in currency and $1 in demand deposits are freely convertible into each other, both are money to an equal degree.

The stock or supply of money (how much money is available to buy goods and services), then, have two components: currency and demand deposits held by private business and individuals (the public). It should be noted that Vault Cash held by banks is NOT considered a part of the stock of money available for spending by the nonbank public.

The collection of Monetary Assets the *Monetary Aggregate* as measured and monitored by the Federal Reserve is known as M1, M2, and M3.

M1 is Currency in the hands of the public plus checkable deposits, Money that is quickly and easily raised.

M2 is everything in M1 plus other highly liquid assets like savings accounts, money market accounts, mutual funds, and certificates of deposits, Money that may take a little more time to obtain than currency.

M3 is everything in M2 plus some less liquid assets, large time deposits, term repurchase agreements, and term Eurodollars.

M1 contains the monetary assets that we currently use in transactions, and what we have in mind when we refer to the *money supply*. All components of M1 are a means of payment. This is not true of M2 and M3; for example, large time deposits, a component of M3, cannot be used to buy groceries. Therefore only M1 is transactions money which functions as a medium of exchange.

Q: **Why should we care about the Money Supply?**

A: The Money Supply (M1) matters because it affects three very important things:

The price level, inflation, and economic recession:

1. Price Level—higher levels of the Money supply are a direct cause of higher price levels, increases in the money supply tend

to cause the general price level to increase which may result in—INFLATION.

Inflation (increase in the price level), which is often described as "too much money chasing too few goods", When the money supply increases faster than the productive capacity of the economy, inflation is the usual result.

2. Inflation—faster money supply growth rates tend to cause higher rates of inflation

3. Recession may be caused by steep declines in the money supply growth rate, in the past 50 years, there have been eight recessions, and every one of them was preceded by a notable decline in the M1 and M2 growth rate. (the reason the Federal Reserve rushed to lower the Fed rate recently).

Q: **Why does the Money supply need to be controlled?**

A: Because the prices of goods and services can be somewhat managed by controlling the amount of money available in the economy.

If TOO MUCH MONEY is available, prices go up—INFLATION

If TOO LITTLE MONEY is available, prices go down—RECESSION

All have an effect on employment and economic growth.

FIVE PRINCIPLES OF FINANCE

1. CASH FLOW MATTERS

   Positive Cash Flow, not profits, pays the bills and represents money that can be spent and reemployed to make more money. Consequently, it is cash flow, not profits that determine the value of a business.

   Recall from accounting that profits can and often does differ dramatically from cash flow.

   Also recall from economics that we and businesses make financial decisions from the marginal differences in alternatives. Therefore it is the marginal difference in cash flow, the incremental cash flow that determines our financial decision choices. This incremental cash flow is the difference between the cash flows that will be produced with and without the investment or choice being considered.

e.g.: Disney movies; not only does Disney make money on the movies, but it also increases the number of people attracted to the toys, theme parks, and rides. So, if you were to evaluate the value, cash flow, of the movies, you would want to include the incremental impact on related sales throughout the company.

2. MONEY HAS TIME VALUE

The most fundamental principle of finance is that money has a TIME value. Simply, a dollar today has more value than a dollar tomorrow (besides the effect of inflation). Why? Because we can reemploy, invest, the dollar today to earn more money.

e.g.: You have a choice of $1,000 now or one year from now. If you decide to receive it one year from now, you will have passed up the opportunity to earn more money, perhaps interest or a return on a profitable investment. Economist would call that opportunity cost. The gain you have given up if you had invested that money for a year.

Finance focuses on the creation and measurement of value. To measure value, we use the concept of the time value of money to bring the future benefits and cost measured by its cash flows, back to the present. If the benefits, cash inflows, outweigh the cost, cash outflows, the alternative should be accepted; if not it should be rejected.

The cost-benefit relationship is a key concept in finance.

3. RISK REQUIRES REWARD

Investors will only invest if they expect to receive a return on their investment. They want a return that satisfies two criteria:

$ A return for delaying consumption—no one would put off the use (consumption) of their money if they were not to be rewarded by earning more satisfaction (money) in the future.

$ An additional return for taken on risk—Investors don't like risk and seek to avoid it. Risky investments are unattractive, UNLESS, they offer the prospect of greater returns.

The risk-return relationship is another key concept of finance in valuing stocks, bonds, and proposed capital investments.

4. MARKET PRICES ARE GENERALLY RIGHT

An *efficient market is one where the prices of the assets traded in that market fully reflect all available information at any instant in time.*

Security markets for stocks and bonds are important in finance since these markets are the places where businesses can go to raise capital to finance their investments, expansions, and acquisitions.

The speed in which information is dissipated is relative to the decisions made. Too often that information may be erroneous and misunderstood causing for the human bias to react causing bad decisions. Equally harmful is that "perception" often becomes and is accepted as reality.

5. CONFLICTS OF INTEREST CAUSE AGENCY PROBLEMS

Agency problems may result from the separation of the management and ownership of the business. Management may act in their best interest even if contrary to the interest of ownership.

CASH FLOW

A "Cash Flow" poem reprinted from *Publishers Weekly,* by Herbert S. Bailey, Jr. (with apologies to Edgar Allen Poe).

92

Once upon a midnight dreary as I pondered weak and weary
Over many a quaint and curious volume of accounting lore,
Seeking gimmicks (without scruple) to squeeze through
some new tax loophole,
Suddenly I heard a knock upon my door,
Only this, and nothing more.

Then I felt a queasy tingling and I heard the cash a-jingling
As a fearsome banker entered whom I'd often seen before.
His face was money-green and in his eyes there could be seen
Dollar-signs that seemed to glitter as he reckoned up the score.
"Cash flow," the banker said and nothing more.

I had always thought it fine to show a jet black bottom line.
But the banker sounded a resounding, "No.
Your receivables are high, mounting upward toward the sky;
Write-offs loom. What matters is cash flow."
He repeated, "Watch cash flow."

Then I tried to tell the story of our lovely inventory
Which, though large, is full of most delightful stuff.
But the banker saw its growth, and with a mighty oath
He waved his arms and shouted, "Stop! Enough!
Pay the interest and don't give me any guff!"

Next I looked for noncash items which could add ad infinitum
To replace the ever-outward flow of cash.
But to keep my statement black I'd held depreciation back,
And my banker said that I done something rash.
He quivered and his teeth begin to gnash.

Though my bottom line is black, I am flat upon my back,
My cash flows out and customers pay slow.
The growth of my receivables is almost unbelievable:
The result is certain—unremitting woe!
And I hear the banker utter an ominous low mutter,
"Watch cash flow."

FIVE FUNCTIONS OF FINANCE

1. **Financing Function**—Raising capital to support operations and investment programs.

2. **Capital Budget Function**—Investing resources based on perceived risk and expected return.

3. **Capital Structure Decision**—Managing internal cash flow in it's mixed of debt and equity, and financial management to ensure payment of obligations.

4. **Corporate Governance Function**—Ensuring that management acts ethically in the interest of shareholders and other stakeholders.

5. **Risk Management Function**—Managing exposure of all types of risk, insurable and uninsurable to maximize shareholder value.

Financial Management:

Concept of complete control over the operations of the business:

The Entrepreneur is often alone, particularly, in a start-up, without the resources for sophisticated financial help, and even with, the ultimate decision is always his/hers. "In the final analysis, we are all alone."

Complete control is a demanding responsibility and the entrepreneur will wear all the hats of management, making decisions often alone. Therefore the entrepreneur must be aware of all facets of the business, and must understand what the numbers mean.

The necessities of meeting payroll, buying inventory/equipment, extending receivables, marketing, paying expenses, and implementing plans require financial resources often when such are scarce.

Financial Management is more than the all-important task of raising the needed cash. Beyond obtaining cash, the decision as how to apply, conserve, and generate more funds are diverse and all involve money or credit.

Financial Management is about managing money and credit, and about the analysis of and planning for the financial effects of all decisions.

Evaluating financial performance and position, and adjusting the plan when necessary to achieve objectives

Planning for the future and present needs to achieve the future goals

Managing the Assets and Liabilities essential for sustained business and profitably growth

Required is a working knowledge of:

- **Basic financial statements**
- **Cash Flow and Sources & Uses of Cash**
- **Financial Ratio Analysis**
- **Break Even Analysis**
- **Financial and Cash Planning**
- **Profit Planning with Pro-Forma statements**
- **Cash, Working Capital, Accounts Receivables & Payables Management**
- **Inventory Management**

Procedures to follow:

$ Keep track of trends—trends of sales, gross margin, expenses, available capital (cash, credit lines, account receivables), and profit & loss on a monthly basis, as soon after month end as possible. To do so you must have an adequate bookkeeping and accounting system.

$ Cash Flow equals survival—Cash flow must be positive. You need both positive cash flow and consistent operating profits to survive and grow. How accounts receivable and inventory is turning must be followed closely.

$ Businesses without budgets go broke—All expenses must be analysis monthly. Examine for deviation from planned budget, both in dollars and percentage of sales from month to month as well as same time last year.

$ You can never have too much capital—most growing

businesses don't have enough, however if available never leave it idle, put it to work.

$Sales and Marketing takes precedence over finance—this may sound contradictory but most financial management problems are ultimately marketing problems. All expenses are tied to marketing decisions. Revenues rise and fall with marketing efforts; capital is raised, depleted or denied in light of how marketing is effective. Cash flow problems are invariable not the problem but a symptom of the problem which is often related to marketing or ineffective expense, accounts receivable, or inventory controls.

The Three "Fs"

> *"He was a self-made man who owed*
> *his lack of success to nobody."*
> Joseph Heller

What is it that keeps some many from realizing the dream of self-employment, financial independence, security, and personal freedom? Too often what prevents an individual from taking the first step to realizing the dream are the initial start-up capital and the courage to abandon the false security of a paycheck.

A favored anonymous quote is "An action without thought is nothing and a thought without action is nothing-at-all."

An action without thought refers to "planning". Nothing sustainable will ever be achieved without a plan that is worked. Good fortune, good luck, influential contacts, even talent, will not carry an enterprise the distance to consistent success without persistent dynamic planning. More will be discussed on the subject of "planning" in the Business and Financial Plan chapter.

So where does the would-be entrepreneur and struggling enterpriser find the necessary capital to start, sustain, and grow a business? Beyond personal financial resources from the three "F's": Family, Friends, and with a weak attempt at joviality, other Fools.

This source is often the only outside availability of capital for the fledgling new business, the growing business, and the business struggling to survive. It is often that a business of many years in operation, because of lack of sufficient start-up capital, positive cash-flow, and/or poor management due to inexperience or a lack of overall expertise, is still having difficulty. The five, ten, or even twenty year old business has not matured but is still in the first year survival stage five, ten, or twenty times.

Whereas no institutional lender, for lack of a proven track record of success and progress, will consider a loan; one of the three "F's" may out of belief in you and your vision (friends), out of love for you and your idea (family), or simply out of greed with the vague possibility of untold riches to come (other fools).

Most entrepreneurs launch their dream business with the idea that money will come. Why not? There is a good product/service, there is a need/desire for that product, there is a market of eager customers, and the entrepreneur is a good person who will work very hard; besides the banks will provide any money for any worthwhile purpose that may be needed. They won't! Banks are not one of the three "F's".

Limited capital or even just ample initial start-up capital will quickly dissipate if the enterprise is fortunate enough to experience unanticipated success and sales growth. Bank financing will be limited to personal resources and capacity at best, not sufficient to satisfy rapid unplanned for success and growth. It is not the bank's function to underwrite risk. Theirs is a fiduciary responsibility. They do not lend their own money but that of their depositors. Therefore they only lend to those with a proven history of consistent successful and profitable operations. Collateral alone is not sufficient incentive for a bank—They are not moved by loans that are only safe but look for loans that are both safe and sound, able to be paid back without difficulty. Banks make loans that are safe and sound. It has been said that a banker is someone who lends you an umbrella when the sun is shining but as soon as it starts to rain, he wants the umbrella back.

As noted Capital is essential, the life-blood of any enterprise; Can it be more difficult to obtain the relatively small amount a business needs than it is for large corporations to raise millions of dollars or for third world countries to be granted billions of dollars? It is.

So where does the entrepreneur manager who is fortunate to have a well received good business with growing sales go for financial assistance when paid-in capital and internally generated cash flow has burned off (burn rate is how rapidly capital is being used before profits can catch up) if bank lending is not available? Besides exhausting personal resources most often the only relief is afforded by the three "F's"—family, friends, and other fools.

A word of caution—the three "F's" are certainly a viable source and one not to be taken lightly especially if it is the only source. Many businesses have been launched and sustained by such means, just be sure to treat it as a business transaction. Do realize that although the source may be very familiar, almost intimate, you will fare better if you keep it strictly-business. The relationship no matter how close or how friendly will fundamentally be altered. Now instead of inquiring about your health; "How are you doing?" they will ask "How is 'our' business doing? Made any money yet?"

Invariably the venture will encounter problems: the wonderful market reception will decline or continue to grow at such a rapid rate that the cash needs will begin to suffocate the business, time demands and operation and quality problem will surface, the burn-rate is accelerating and more capital, more time, more resources are needed; it is never, if you will have trouble, or if you will fail; but when. Now is the test of a true entrepreneur manager, any opportunist can take advantage of good fortune; but now is when flexibility, resiliency, and persistence are needed. Now is the time when your family and friends who have supplied capital become a problem; now when you are lest prepared to deal with them. The honeymoon is over and often so is the friendship or family love. They, well-intended and concerned for themselves, their money, and perhaps even for you, want to intervene. They want to help.

They now feel like equal owners (hope you didn't make this mistake) and want to have an input in management. Perhaps even draw a modest salary, after all there are no profits to reward them and you are drawing a salary—where is their compensation or pay-back?

No matter what the original relationship, and the fact that they did believe in you and somewhat shared your vision, they are not the entrepreneur, nor do they have an entrepreneur's mind-set.

They do not have the entrepreneur's, your, zest, persistence, determination, flexibility, and capacity for chaos. Therefore early on, realizing that their investment of capital is and was very important, do not take it lightly at the inception or on-going. To avoid any dilution of ownership, avoid any equity transfer or agreements and instead structure the capital injection as debt. Equity often appears attractive with the lack of debt service and accruing of interest, but in a well organized successful venture it may prove much more costly and even perhaps open the way for a loss of control. In a slow-track toward profitability or a not so successful venture, the disruptive and more than likely not helpful intervention into management and decisions of strategy, operation, and risk by the other "owners" may doom the business completely.

Structure the debt in a formal business like matter with a proper promissory note and formally drawn loan documents and/or contractual agreements that after careful and pragmatic deliberation by all parties spell out obligations, responsibilities, and duties. Keep the arrangement strictly-business with all the details spelled out and a payment schedule based on conservative pro-forma projections with provisions in the event of unrealized expectations that suit all parties.

If you have prepared a sound business plan (appendix A-5), and have the skills, expertise, and management ability to implement and adjust it when required which your "lenders", not co-owners or partners, have reviewed; it is that plan and you they had confidence in and they should allow you to work it. You may have to insist upon such and hopefully you have not structured your agreement in any way that may hinder your efforts. You may very well lose a friendship and incur family difficulties (hopefully not a divorce) but if the plan was sound, there is a market, and you have the right stuff to work the plan and reach the market, to accept adversity and allay self-doubt—all may work out.

Personal Resources

> *"The happiest of people don't necessarily have the best of everything; they just make the most of everything that comes their way."*
> Anonymous

No doubt before seeking out the three "F's", especially during the initial stages of the "Entrepreneurial Process", the enterprising entrepreneur manager must commit personal resources that are available and perhaps some that are not. In the concept stage and the beginning of the start-up, there is little to convince anyone else to assist in the idea, and whatever tangible picture is able to be presented, all potential parties will want to know that you are fully committed with your personal assets at risk before considering the feasibility of committed theirs.

There will always be an ongoing necessity to employ personal resources throughout the life of a struggling growing business. During the first stages of the fledgling business life cycle, those assets that are readily accessible such as savings, profit-sharing and pension accounts, cash value in life insurance policies, and home equity will be tapped. Then perhaps will follow the three "F's", loans from family, friends, and others. As the need continues it is quickly follow by attempts to obtain or even by obtaining personal loans from the friendly neighborhood bank.

A pragmatic word of caution about that friendly bank is in order. It, of course, always considered you a favored customer. After all throughout your career at the "whatever" corporation as a faithful employee for five, ten or more years, the bank was always there to accommodate your banking needs. It has maintained checking and savings accounts, granted personal loans for vacations, automobiles, tuition, home-improvements, and perhaps through a mortgage department a home loan. It will surely always be there as you launch your new business; you have a long and good relationship, and the bank is pro-business.

Don't be surprised if you discover as it pertains to a new credit request for that business, your long and good relationship with the banker you know and dealt with is not the same as a long and still good relationship with the bank. The individual you know as your banker in today's modern banking world is generally without relatively significant loan authority. He/she is but the friendly liaison, the public-relations helpful face of the bank; the care-taker and perhaps personal manager of your account; your personal-account-manager in a very superficial role. The credit banking relationship, particularly since your classification and status has changed, will rely upon the statistical standards and parameters adopted and established as credit policy for the entire banking organization. They are established much like an insurance company does in its risk-management with little if any regard toward the individual or personal relationship and history.

So what you may say. You have been a good customer; you have excellent credit and a superb repayment record on all bank loans. So what, your bank will be there. Will it?

Your relationship has been established, as has been your credit history on the strength of the years you have accumulated on the job with its measurable and predictable compensation. Now as an aspiring new business owner and entrepreneur you have bravely and boldly forsaken such job-security for this untried and new frontier. The bank will applaud and encourage this capitalist adventure. You will now be more valuable to them as a new business customer. Surely they will be most anxious to assist from the very beginning. **They will not** and in most cases you are no longer qualified for their credit consideration—too much of a risk for a non-speculative, conservative fiduciary financial institution.

Therefore personal bank loans may not be available and may remain unavailable for the duration until you have proven the new business venture as one with consistent and sustainable profits.

Credit Cards

After exploring family and friends, and the lack of positive cash flow and capital needs continue hopefully due to growing business, you will soon discover a source of working capital, albeit very expensive if not managed well, becoming ever increasingly more important to small business owners—credit cards.

Entrepreneur literature reveals this source to being utilized by 10% to 15% of start-up and growing businesses. Actually the number is more like 50% to 85% and still growing. As start-up capital burns off and business sales continue to grow, in fact the new business is actually "growing broke", pressures on operating capacity and inventory demands surface, personal credit cards increasingly become a most convenient way to meet these urgent demands. They will enable the purchase of office supplies and equipment, travel expense, and other necessities at a time when there is no other way to accommodate these on-going expenses.

It is true that formally personal credit card companies, in the fine print, only authorize expenditures for personal and consumer purposes not business needs. But they have long realized that such is unrealistic and unenforceable for who can ascertain what use a cash-advance is applied. Finally recognizing this growing usage all major card companies now issue business cards which has proven to be a most lucrative and growing business for them.

Even though many card issuing companies are owned by banks and it is a type of bank financing, they are not as restrictive in the access to credit offerings and offer relatively quick and easy availability which would usually be declined at a local bank. The credit advance is not made to the business nor is the business financial history or lack of usually taken into consideration, they are evaluated solely in the perceived ability and past history of the individual to repay. It is true that interest rates are substantially higher particularly with the fees for cash advance or convenience check usage, but if properly managed with matching of cost, cash-flow, and profit margins; credit card usage can be a most attractive answer to a most persistent problem.

Business and Corporate credit cards will not only enable a business to have the convenience and availability of capital doing times of strain on positive cash-flow but can also offer: the opportunity to establish and build a business credit record, help build the business image, afford time saving and security in making purchases with self-generated documentation, and even the opportunity to save money for many card companies offer specials on business and office supplies as well as the opportunity to take advantage of vendors discounts. Many card companies also extend special purchase warranties and discounts on travel, insurance, and other benefits.

There was mention of higher rates but as indicated the opportunity for many cost savings are available. The ability to take advantage of vendors and suppliers discount is certainly one to be employed. For example: typical terms of 2% 10 days net 30 days, will yield a savings of 36% annual (30 days minus 10 days = 20 days, divided into a business year of 360 days 360/20 = 18 X 2% = 36%)

The ease of obtaining credit card availability, the "teaser" rates (introductory short period rates often lower than bank prime), and potential low cost if managed well, will assure continued used of this type of debt financing by the small business entrepreneur manager.

Bootstrapping

Often a new business owner in order to fund the new venture must and will resort to "Bootstrapping". The idea of "pulling yourself up by your bootstraps" comes out of necessity. If the entrepreneur has a true vision, is driven, determined, and filled with self-confidence; he will use all of his ingenuity and creativity to sustain and grow the business. When the ability to borrow money is not there or used up, and being always hard for a new venture to obtain funding, this is when the resilience, flexibility, and persistence of the entrepreneur is most valuable and tested.

Bootstrapping is a combination of raising money and other resources, and of cutting cost in any way legally possible. Some examples are: Vendor credit—securing credit terms from your suppliers is essentially obtaining an interest free loan for 30, 60, or 90 days. The vendor, who is usually very much pro-sale, may even consider extending a special financing, loan with interest, for a year or more to penetrate the market you are addressing. You should have your business plan (appendix A-5) prepared to offer for the vendors consideration and review with specific emphasis on the marketing and management sections. If the credit accommodation is obtained, this will still allow the capacity for bank debt when available.

Often the customers themselves can be a source of working capital particularly when substantial cost or time and effort may be involved in the delivery of the goods or services. It is common in many industries to require down payments that will cover initial material cost and upfront expenses. The fledgling new business manager should not be bashful about requesting these terms unless it is not an acceptable practice in the industries and would be competitive prohibitive.

Often an enterprising business can partner with other businesses to share expenses such as delivery, advertising, or purchasing; as well as sharing office and warehouse space. A new business should always avoid unnecessary non-revenue producing expense such as large and lavish offices, furniture, equipment, and staff. Too often has a well-intentioned enthusiastic entrepreneur, perhaps a reluctant entrepreneur having been laid off after many years within the big corporate womb, can't seem to function without all of the amenities previously enjoyed in the former work life. He must learn that this is a new venture, requiring not only work adjustments but perhaps even life-altering adjustments, and those non-income producing luxury are not affordable. He must always be mindful of the Hogan 1% rule (A-7) keeping the relation of cost and revenue in perspective with the impact that even a change of 1% in sales and expense will make. He must watch purchases and expense diligently—must always shop for the best deals and terms, and always consider leasing equipment and office space rather than buying. Too often is a business manager strapped for cash because it is all tied up in equipment, vehicles, or brick and mortar and not available as working capital.

Leasing may be more expensive than outright purchasing and there is no capital depreciation benefit, but it frees up money to used elsewhere producing profits and the entire amount of the lease cost reduces taxable income as an operating expense. When all is considered this off balance sheet type of financing produces increased profits and the opportunity for greater retained earnings.

Salary expense is another cost demanding close scrutiny and in any growing business should be tied to performance. Like cancer, this expense can grow unreasonably in a struggling cash strapped business. Those same family and friends that may have lent some money may very well end up on the payroll with their only contribution being that loan. Invariably close family always becomes employees with perhaps immeasurable work performance results. Often they don't regard themselves as employees and do not want to be treated as such until payday when they definitely want to be treated as an employee and receive a paycheck.

The new business owner may himself have to do with considerable less than previously compensated in a former job, and perhaps have a period when there is no salary at all. In fact, not being able to afford other workers, he will be wearing many hats as the sales person, bookkeeper, delivery driver, janitor, etc. This all contributes to the "Sweat Equity" the new business owner invests.

Commercial Finance Companies

"A hen is only an egg's way of making another egg."
Samuel Butler

A new or growing small business experiencing cash flow problems loan request are too often considered unbankable. There is no track record of success or progress for a traditional lender to consider; and the company may very well be now experiencing business credit troubles. In such a situation a cash-strapped small business with growing sales may find that a commercial finance company will accommodate its needs. This situation, known as "Growing Broke", is a cash flow problem. Even thought the business is profitable and will realize profits when the sales are complete, the business cannot survive for lack of the positive cash flow to sustain it. Its very success is choking it to death.

At the start of the business venture the cash needed for equipment, inventory, accounts receivable, staff, office and sales expense, etc. came from the owners, their resources and friends, and whatever short term assistance may be obtained from suppliers and the local bank. Collected sales are of course the most preferred source of cash. However as sales continue to grow, more and more cash is needed to sustain the growth. Often business expenses like staff wages, sales and travel expense, and inventory replacement must be paid immediately while sales collection may take 30, 60, or 90 days depending on the industry terms. A cash flow problem is when cash is flowing out faster than it is flowing in or no inflow at all. Often the only solution appears to be the generation of more sales, but this usually only makes the problem worse. The expense to grow more sales, salaries, inventory, additional equipment, and market planning and promotion may have to be paid before any sales are realized and collected. To offset this dilemma, a business must actively engage in dynamic cash flow planning, and an essential tool in that planning is the commercial finance companies.

Commercial finance companies are considered asset-based and income statement lenders. These finance companies are not banks, but many larger bank holding companies have a commercial finance lending company subsidiary. Like banks they take a business past experience and profitability into consideration to evaluate the market and management ability, but unlike banks they place more emphasis on current quick turning assets and projected sales to new and existing acceptable customers. They will, after being satisfied that the business can perform and has delivered, look past the business to its clients for the credit quality assurance and financial strength that may be lacking in the business financed. The lender is not as interested in the business receiving the money as it is in the companies that owe the money via the invoices. An asset-based lender will not ignore the balance sheet, but will go beyond it to tangible collateral and/or funds due the business. After a new and small business has exhausted all of the owners personal resources and bank credit is the time when commercial secured financing with the growing business assets become necessary. Such financing becomes self-evident when the business working capital needs far outstrip its net worth.

Commercial finance companies enable a business to use its assets like accounts receivable and inventory as a collateral base. They will more readily finance new business and those businesses with spotty or poor profitably than traditional bank lenders. Such financing enables a company that is rapidly growing and no doubt highly leveraged to use its limited working capital multiple times to continue to find receivables and inventory for future sales. As capital is spend to produce sales and create accounts receivable, it becomes an additional lending base to produce more sales to generate more profits. Financing should only be done by a business when the return produced by the financing well exceed the cost of that financing.

To take advantage of an asset based loan the business must have consummated sales to credit worthy customers creating a receivable that is available as collateral. The receivable often combined with inventory becomes a source of collateral and the ultimate source of repayment. The commercial finance company lends at a 75% to 90% margin depending on conditions—quality of the customer, term of sales, cost of material, or the industry norms. At the time a loan is extended interest begins to accrue; as soon as it is paid back be it 30, 60, 90, or 120 days interest stops. Even thought the rate of interest is considerably higher than that charged by a bank, with astute management of cash flow, attention to details, and rapid repayment, much like the management of credit card usage, the interest cost is kept from being prohibitive; and if it enables a business to realize a 50% to 100% profit margin. Consequently what does it matter what the loan interest cost if it enables such profits is 5%, 10%, or 20% above that cost.

Commercial finance factoring companies calculate interest on a per diem rate as opposed to a per annum rate- to convert to an annum rate the business multiply the per diem rate by 365 (days) i.e. per diem of 1/30 of 1% converts to 365/30 of 1% equals 12.17%

An example of factoring pricing is as follows:

$1,000,000	acceptable invoices
80%	margin—advanced to business
800,000	loan proceeds enabling other sales
12%	interest expense per diem—average (instead of per annum)
96,000	cost of interest per month

Invoices outstanding 30 days—Interest cost $96,000 now 12% of loan proceeds

Payment received	$1,000,000	received from customers directly into lenders lock box
Minus	800,000	to pay the loan back
Minus	96,000	interest on the loan
	104,000	net to the business

If the profit margin was 20% (200,000); after interest expense, which is a tax deduction, net profit now 10.4% (104,000); 10.4% that would not have been made without the loan. If no financing was available instead of making this profit, there would have been none, no sale, 0%. If no financing the business would be out of business unable to make payroll or acquire inventory for additional sales.

Another example of factor pricing common in the market place is:

$1,000,000	acceptable invoices
80%	advance rate
$800,000	proceeds to business
1.5%	discount on acceptable invoices
$ 15,000	cost of factoring

Invoices outstanding 30 days—Factoring cost of $15,000

$1,000,000	Payment received
800,000	to pay back advance
15,000	to pay factoring charges
$ 185,000	net to business

While the cost is much higher than a bank loan, the business knows that if their customers pay in 30 days, its cost is $1.50 for factoring a $100.00 invoice for 30 days.

In addition to the advantage of professional credit and collection services afforded the business from the factor, often the amount of accounts receivable the business must carry to support their increased level of sales is reduced by the rapidity that the receivables turn over thus reducing the amount of money the business needs to borrow resulting in lower interest cost.

To assure that more expensive receivable financing and factoring is right for a business, it must be aware of its own cost structure. If it operates on a very low margin of profit, this type of financing may be too expensive. However it is ideal for high-mark up products and companies with low overhead. The business must realize that there is a difference between the cost of money and the stated interest rate. This cost is only for the amount of loan proceeds and only for the time outstanding with no related cost of required compensating balances in a checking account; in fact a commercial finance companies does not even care where a business banks. Minimum balance requirements in a bank can add another 2% to 3% to the loan rate. A commercial finance company may average 6% to 10% above prime rate and a bank 1% to 3% above prime rate but considering the actual cost of money and the services performed saving additional operation expense (credit department) and often completely eliminating credit risk, it is value added.

Factoring is when the lender takes ownership of the receivables with or without recourse back to the business in the event of default of the sales customer, as opposed to simple accounts receivable financing when the receivable is used as collateral but remains a pledged asset of the business. Both methods will utilize the business's customers mailing payment directly to the lender's lockbox to affect quicker payment rather than being forwarded to the business for repayment by it. This additional expense plus the extensive hands on management and all the credit investigation to approve acceptability of the business's customers as credit worthy receivable is the reason for the higher cost. When a small business with limited resources is able to partner with such a commercial finance company, it not only allows it to realize sales and profit goals, but gives it access to a virtual credit department that it could ill afford. Due to this administration and higher risk commercial finance companies charge higher rates than traditional bank lenders. If handled properly the risk is minimal and the expense to the business nominal. Much like credit cards the cost can be managed and in fact the commercial finance companies supervision assures it.

Accounts receivable financing, as offered by banks, is calculated in a more traditional matter of Interest = Principal X Rate X Time (I=PRT) on a per annum basis. It too may be 5% to 6% above prime but as simple interest.

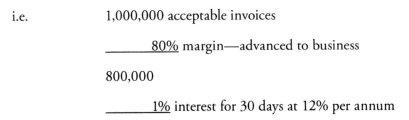

i.e.   1,000,000 acceptable invoices

                      _____80% margin—advanced to business

                800,000

                      _____1% interest for 30 days at 12% per annum

8,000 cost per month (considerably less—that's why margins may be less than 80% and there may also be commitment and handling fees; and more difficult to obtain)

Whether a business has just started or has years of experience and is now expanding and growing faster than cash can keep up, a commercial finance company can provide the working capital needed to realize the business goals. A well established commercial finance company can help a business get where it wants to go, to grow and succeed, easily, efficiently and affordably.

Types of financing offered short and long term are:

Accounts Receivable

Receivables are created when a business extends credit to its customers and sells on terms which are the length of time per industry standards or on its own credit policy terms for the customer to pay the invoice. The business itself may always be looking for a friendly bank, but when it extends credit to its customers it is in fact banking them. So when a business extends credit it is losing the use of that money until it is paid. It denies the business access to this working capital which may be needed for other expenses and additional inventory, and if the customer exceeds the selling terms this tied up money can become critical with serious deficit cash flow. Accounts receivable financing and factoring can alleviate this situation by getting money as soon as the business ships and bills the customers. The business will receive its money before the customer pays the invoice and in some factoring situation the business receives its money even if the customer never pays the invoice. An additional benefit of receivable financing is that there is usually no credit limit; as fast as the business grows and the more it sells and bills, the more is available to enhance working capital and continue the growth.

Factoring and Financing

In factoring the business essentially sells its receivables to the lender at a discount. Factors are lenders who actually purchase the business's accounts receivable. The business receivables now belong to the factor. In most cases it is without credit risk recourse to the business with the factor (lender) assuming the credit risk. They also bear the credit research and analysis cost of qualifying the customer. The higher cost to the business is due to this assumption of risk and the expense involved in the investigation and maintenance of the accounts and collections. The customer pays the factor that in turn pays the business less the interest rate and fees. This credit service offered by the commercial finance factoring company is extremely valuable to a growing business with little experience in credit extension. They in effect becomes the business's credit department with vast experience in assisting the business in establishing credit policies, acting as the credit approval agent, monitoring the credit of customers, mailing statements and late notices, providing accounts receivable management and accounting, and most important acting as the collection agency. It is due to these services that factor cost are considerable higher than bank financing, and upon considering that the business has no need for bookkeepers and collectors salaries to staff an in-house credit department, it is very cost effective.

Financing the business receivables requires the business to pledge it receivables to the lender who will normally advance 75% to 80% of the value which will depend on the business financial strength and that of its customers and their credit worth. The business customers are usually notified that their accounts have been pledged as collateral and according to the conditions of the arrangement the business's customers may pay the lender directly or the business who then must pay the lender. The business own credit worthiness and financial strength are a larger consideration in financing as opposed to factoring. No lender, rather bank or commercial lender wants to bear the expense of collecting and liquidating accounts receivables if it had not been price accordingly nor had a decision in the credit approval particularly if the business customers are not of good credit caliber. Most accounts receivable lenders will not lend on receivables that are older than 60 days unless that is the normal terms, nor will they lend on a current receivable if a portion of it is considered delinquent.

Accounts receivable financing is borrowing from the lender using accounts receivable as collateral. Factoring is selling the accounts receivable to the lender. Factoring creates no debt on the balance sheet. Both are considered self-financing in that as sales grow, and the business grows, there is more money to fund that growth. Depending on the lending arrangement, the business customers may or may not have to be notified that the receivable is being used as collateral and to pay the lender directly.

Inventory Financing

When a business needs to go beyond the value of its accounts receivable, an inventory term or revolving loan may be used to extend the availability of capital. Such financing will supply working capital as the business waits to collect outstanding accounts receivable and inventory turnover from current sales. With inventory as additional collateral the accounts receivable advances may be allowed at 100% as opposed to 75% or 85%. A longer term loan based on acceptable inventory levels may be helpful as a permanent injection of working capital.

Inventory financing solely on its own merits is extremely hard to obtain due to its lack of liquidity, type of inventory, the industry and the market. Unlike accounts receivable which are one step from cash; it is two steps from cash. And if prior to any sale, which may be a quick liquidation sale for less than anticipated value, it will have to be stored, moved, protected, and insured. Flooring or floor plan of inventory is much like factoring whereas the lender buys the inventory and actually owns it until it is sold. As the inventory is sold the loan is paid. This type of credit facility is most often used by automobile and boat dealers, as well as heavy equipment sellers. Similar is warehouse financing where the inventory is stored at a public warehouse and the receipt for it is held by the lender until sold.

Equipment and Real Estate

Commercial finance companies are a good source of equipment financing with terms of two to five years or perhaps longer depending on the useful life of the equipment; often with a comfortable amortization and a balloon payment, a loan amortized for perhaps ten years on a three year maturity note with review of refinancing the balance at that time. Equipment financing may be on the equipment a business wants to purchase or on existing equipment as collateral. It can be new or used with the margin of credit granted depended upon it useful life and remarket value.

Commercial real estate with sufficient equity will enable a longer maturity of 10 to 25 years both as first and second mortgages, which may also be written with a balloon payment. Maturity period and amortization period are not always the same. A business may have a 25 year amortization with a five year maturity requiring the final balloon payment for the rest of the balance to be refinanced. Often a business will initially tie up too much or all of its working capital in expensive equipment or real estate, whereas this may not have been wise, the business does have a valuable asset that can be used as collateral to get that working capital back. It would appear to be a mistake for an entrepreneur to invest all or a large portion of capital into the brick and mortar of a business not leaving any money with which to work; however many business owners thinking of their own exit-strategy consider the building as an investment for retirement. In fact many life-style business do not appreciate in value as much as the building will, never-the-less, it is usually very restrictive for a cash poor business to survive with such an investment. It is true that real estate is easier to finance than other business assets because it retains its value and most often will appreciate with proper maintenance, easily identifiable and attached, and depending on location and purpose more than likely easily resold. Even with a failed business, the real estate will still hold its value and not be affected by the failed operation housed within it, making it excellent collateral in the event of foreclosure. Therefore if cash flow needs are being accommodated and rent is a large portion of a business expense, especially if a large outlay is required for leasehold improvements; it may behoove the business to pay rent to itself as opposed to making the landlord's property more valuable. Depending on circumstance, use of property, and location the loan to value could range anywhere from 75% to 90%. A start-up business may have difficulty in meeting the down payment requirement, in such situation consider requesting the seller to carry-back a portion, in this way a new business may realize 100% financing of an asset that will appreciate and assist in providing the very cash flow and profits that will pay the loan back.

Leasing

Basically leasing is a two party transaction where the finance company (lessor) purchases and owes the equipment, often per specifications of the business (lessee), and rents it to the business to gain income from the rental payments; the business (lessor) has use of the equipment at a fraction of the cost if purchases to put it to work earning other income and saving cash for other working capital needs. In traditional equipment financing the business has ownership of the equipment and pledges it as collateral at anywhere from 50% to 80% of its value. In leasing the lender has ownership of the equipment (100% of value) and rents it back to the business. Traditional financing creates a liability on the business balance sheet, leasing does not and the payments are completely expensed. Commercial finance companies, and sporadically banks, are offering this most attractive option to acquire needed equipment. It is one of the fastest growing methods of obtaining capital equipment today. Under a lease agreement a business can acquire necessary equipment without buying it, an off-balance sheet acquisition. Leasing will appear more expensive than buying equipment outright and the business accountant will be quick to point out that there is no depreciation benefit to the business. It passes to the lender who has purchase and owns the equipment and then leases it to the business at a monthly rate for the useful life term or shorter. However it enables the acquisition of income producing equipment that the business would not have otherwise to earn profits and the entire lease payment is an operating expense further reducing income tax liability somewhat offsetting the lack of depreciation. The leasing company will conduct the same credit research as would a bank, but their criteria is significant less with emphasis on business performance, customer base, cash flow, and profit potential as well as the experience and character of the business owners and managers. A source for such a lease arrangement is most often referred by the equipment seller.

Leasing will provide conservation of the capital of the business and offer 100% financing which would not be available from a lender. It will provide flexible long term payments which can usually be tailored to a requested pay back with realistic projection of sales. Lease companies being very much pro-sales with close relationships with the equipment sellers have less restrictive credit criteria and the pay back is usually tied to the useful life of the equipment which could be considerable longer than traditional equipment financing. Leasing does not create a liability on the balance sheet, it is off-balance sheet financing, and the lack of depreciation credit is more than recaptured by all of the lease payments and the related soft cost—insurance, maintenance, taxes, and shipping as tax deductions. For those business involved with high technology equipment which is ever changing, leasing provides protection against obsolescence by providing the ability to upgrade equipment as new technology is delivered.

Generally there are two types of leases: the operating, closed-end lease, and the capital, open-end lease.

In the operating lease the lender (lessor) owes the equipment and is responsible for its maintenance and repairs (this can be modified per agreement). The lessor has full benefit of depreciation and any available tax credits. This is a rental agreement of payments over a period of time.

In the capital lease the business (lessee) is responsibility for all upkeep, repairs, insurance, and taxes; all the obligations of full ownership. Capital leases have a term that extends to the full payment of the equipment plus interest, similar to traditional financing with the exception that it may be for 100% of the equipments value as opposed to a lesser percentage. At the end of the lease the business has the option to purchase the equipment by paying off the balloon payment if so structured. Capital leases are treated as loans on the balance sheet and depreciation credit belongs to the business.

Angel Investors and Venture Capitalists

"Do not let the enemy see your spirit."
Miyamoto Musashi

Angel Investors

So called Angel Investors are usually wealthy individuals who will invest in or lend to those types of businesses in which they have experience. They may be consider small personalized venture capitalists or as many like to refer to themselves in this informal venture capitalist market as adventure capitalists. They are always motivated by profit and return on the investment but are also enthused and excited about the thrill of the venture and the opportunity to be a contributor in perhaps a hands-on capacity.

To the enterprising entrepreneur starting a new business or to the struggling existing small business owner and manager, they will appear as angels from heaven when there are no other sources of capital available. But beware angels can quickly become devils particularly if the business does not progress as anticipated.

Angel investors look for those businesses with high expectations of growth in those industries they know, have experience with, and have networking ability within that industry and its related infrastructure. They generally always want part-ownership to share in that projected growth and will often structure a combination of debt and equity capital package. This type of financial assistance will be appropriate for both the new venture with no revenue stream yet established and the already existing business that was under-capitalized at inception and is now experiencing sales growth beyond cash flow capacity.

When accepting an angel investor's participation, the business owner must not only be comfortable with giving up some ownership, but must be prepared to surrender some control and perhaps management. Whereas the business owner's management ability is always an essential consideration in any funding transaction, the angel investors relies upon their own management expertise and looks for those companies with good products, delivery systems, and exceptional markets. Since angels like to be hands-on investors, it would behoove the business owner to have in the financing agreement areas of responsibility and an exit strategy for the investor usually within five years.

As can be expected since traditional funding is not available, and the three "F's" and credit cards have been exhausted; this type of financing is expensive. The part of ownership given up may range from 10% to 50%, perhaps even beyond 50% for controlling interest. There may also be monthly consulting/management fees and if there is a debt portion, monthly payments of interest from 3% to 8% with principal payments monthly, quarterly, semi-annually, annually or deferred until a maturity period.

Angel investors are hard to locate and won't be found advertising for candidates to do business. They will almost always be contacted by a referral or a networking source. Sources of such referrals are accountants, attorneys, bankers, business publications, investor clubs, internet, universities, regional and state economic development agencies, business associations, vendors, and other business owners. Angels are interested in small investments of $10,000 to perhaps $500,000 seldom larger with most averaging below $250,000. Arrangements with angels are always individualized and very much informal and personal; they have their own network and larger amounts of capital may be obtainable by working in concert with several of them.

Angels regard their value to the business to be beyond the capital provided to their experience and advice. They can be counted on to have extensive network contacts, marketing ability, business acquaintance, skills, and entrepreneurial experience. Often this proves to be a most valuable and welcomed contribution to the business owner. However, if things go wrong or not as well as expected, this very involvement may prove unbearable. That is why it is essential that there is a clear and professional agreement and that there is reasonable assurance of a good personal relationship to avoid interpersonal conflicts and unrealistic expectations. Do not believe that angels are so-called because of their benevolence or good intentions. They want profits whether in capital gains, fees, or interest as much as 20% to 40% return on the investment; and they may very well want your company.

Unlike a bank, angels are investing their own money and have business and financial knowledge to make a valued decision rapidly regarding the business chances of success. They will want to be satisfied that there is a growing target market for the product/service and that the product is competitive and able to capture that target market. They will want to know about present ownership and its management and sales ability. It is true that they will rely heavily on their own management and entrepreneur skills, but depending on the planned or initial involvement with the company's operations, will want to have confidence in the primary owners' abilities; their effectiveness, credibility, and previous track record with this venture or a previous one. They also always what to know what is the money specifically being used for and what will it do for the business. Of interest is also how much is the present ownership financially committed to the venture.

Venture Capitalists

"There is no question that irrespective of the horse (the product), horse race (the market), or odds (financial criteria), it is the jockey (the entrepreneur/ manager) who fundamentally determines whether the venture capitalist will place a bet at all."
Ian MacMillan, Wharton Business School

After a business has been established and is demonstrating a profitable growth trend; larger sources of capital can sustain that growth and enable a company to realize its potential in obtaining higher levels of operations. To do so an enterprising entrepreneur will turn to and attempt to interest venture capitalists. Venture capitalists make "informed bets" based on the information in the business plan and its presentation, the feasibility of the opportunity, and the strategy and credentials of those that will make it happen: the nature of the opportunity, the potential size of the reachable market, the strategy proposed to reach it, and the skills, drive, and ambition of the management team.

Venture capitalist can fund a company to the next level often to an initial public offering (IPO). In spite of the general consensus and with exception of the dot.com foolishness of the eighties when VCs and others motivated by greed and unrealistic expectations threw away the concept of a good business model, experienced management, and the laws of supply & demand—venture capitalists do not specializes in high risk ventures. Many may specializes in particular industry in which they have expertise and interest, but they do tend to safeguard their investment by close scrutiny of the management and marketing prospects.

As indicated sources of capital for new business ventures and growing existing companies are difficult to find. As friends, family, credit cards, and all other traditional financing sources and personal resources are exhausted, if the business has true growth potential and a talented management team, it may be attractive to venture capitalist type investors.

Venture capitalist groups are professionally managed organizations which supply funds to be investments on an equity basis to private companies. They seek substantial return on the investment as much as 50% to 75%.

Unlike other sources of capital, if the business is acceptable, they will supply 100% of the requested capital.

The professional money managers of the venture capitalist fund raises money from its investors to invest in companies of promise usually in the early stages of development. They will fund in various phases of a company's cycle from the start-up stage to the exit stage which may be an IPO stage. By advances in stages the venture capitalist can reexamine the business before committed to additional funds until agreed upon targets have been reached.

Venture capitalists will generally advance capital in the following stages rather than all at the beginning:

> **Pre start-up**—At this stage the focus is on product and market research and development. The business is not yet ready to need capital for employees and infrastructure. It has no sales and no positive cash flow; in fact with continuing expenditures at this stage the cash flow is negative. Initial financing is primarily by the founders with a lot of bootstrapping and perhaps early angels as individual small adventure capitalists.

> **Start-up**—At this time the business is buying equipment and hiring employees to begin producing, selling, and distributing the product. Cash flow and income is still negative as there is no revenue at this stage but increasing expenses for salaries, rent, supplies, etc. The Business Plan (appendix A-5) should be completed and refined and the management team in place. This could be the first round of funding by the venture capitalists.

> **Early Growth**—Cash flow is still negative but some sales are being generated producing accounts receivable and some income yet still below expenditures. Second round funding may be advanced provided there is progress toward achieving goals and established benchmarks.

> **Rapid Growth**—Cash flow is even more negative due to increased growth in sales requiring much financing to sustain the rapid percentage volume increase. Third round funding will assist this stage if growth is in accordance with planned project

Mature Growth—The target market is becoming saturated so that the still positive rate of sales growth is decreasing. Cash flow and net income has become positive. Internally generated funds are sufficient to cover ongoing working capital needs. The company is successful in selling to its market and the last round of funding is available to prepare the business for venture capitalist exit.

Exit—The final stage to harvest returns for the investors either by sale of interest to other investors, IPO or private, or to begin operating the business for optimum cash to flow as dividends to the investors.

Since the risk of a company losing value and failing is high, the venture capitalists usually purchase convertible preferred shares of stock in the company: Convertible to be transferred to common stock when it becomes more advantageous to do so in a sell out; preferred to afford additional comfort to the fund holders by its priority upon dissolution and distribution of any dividends.

Most venture capitalist funds look for a substantial return on investment by the profit obtained in the sale of the stock with an anticipated exit within a specific amount of time anywhere from five to ten years. Unlike banks and other lending institutions, venture capitalists want returns in the form of capital gains not in earned interest. They invest for the long term as much as ten years for the purpose of their capital is long term to enable growth in value and the investment is in assets that are not able to be converted into cash in the short term. Venture capitalists are not interested in the assets of a business as collateral, but are interested in that those assets will produce cash flow and profits. For this reason a business must qualify as to its market potential, management expertise, product acceptance, delivery system, and technology to reach its maximum potential and be accepted as an investment candidate.

Venture capitalist management being very competent and experience professional business and money managers, they will want to be involved in the management decisions of the invested business. They do however still look strongly at the business existing management. They will always, unlike angels, look to invest in a company with good management and a good product and never in one with a weak management no matter how good the product or promising the market. They consider themselves as an added value source of capital. They are excellent financial partners with connections in the capital markets if required with continued growth, and entrepreneur experience in developing companies to reach higher levels. As long as the venture capitalist organization believes in the company, its management, and the business ability to handle difficult times in achieving its goals; the VC will remain in the investment and may continue to provide additional support both financial and with business advice for a longer period than originally anticipated. After all it is in their best interest to do so in order to protect the investment and realize the expected return on the investment. In order to implement further control over the management of the business, they will have representation on the company's board of directors, require timely receipt of all financial and operating statements, have veto power over certain decisions, and input on executive hiring, firing and compensation.

Obtaining funding from a venture capitalist group is not always easy to obtain and equity will most certainly always have to be surrender. If a business is high growth with good management and great potential in a growing industry with a reachable lucrative target market capable of reaching 25 million in sales within five years; it will require high capital and a venture capitalist fund can help to achieve the company's goals.

Upon approaching a venture capitalist firm the business should have completed a business plan that is succinct and concise and in addition to the outline in appendix A-9 the plan should contain:

> Funding amount—The specific amount of debt and/or equity required and a time frame with benchmark goals for draw downs of funds.

> Duration—Even thought the investment may be equity without a maturity, the VC will still want to know how long their commitment and participation is anticipated.

> Use of funding—A clear summary of how and when the funds will be used with the trigger milestones for capital injection and what will the money do for the business.

> Exit strategy—An explanation of how the venture capitalist will get its money and the expected return on the investment

back; a realistic projection of financial pro- formas that should demonstrate the capacity to prepare for harvesting.

Founder's investment—There should be an indication of what capital has already been invested by the existing owners and how it was used.

Related parties—Supply a list with contact information of all who have been involved with the formation of the business: Attorneys, Accountants, Bankers, Consultants, etc.; the company's BAIL (Bankers, Accountants, Insurance, and Legal).

Alternative Funding and Public Offering

"Everything bows to success, even grammar."
Victor Hugo

Alternative Funding

As a business begins to develop and emerge as a viable entity with a definite positive trend of growth and success, with a destination of fulfilling its mission and the entrepreneur's vision of becoming a substantial company; the largest source of funds to achieve the goals of becoming a major company will be through equity. Fast growing and high growth ventures are not a good fit with the constraints of a loan agreement's negative covenants and regular interest cost of debt. Such limitations will most often retard the very rate of growth of such a fast "gazelle" like enterprise.

Considerable debt may have enable the business to reach this stage and the founding entrepreneurs may not be enamored with any dilution of ownership and management control; but if high-growth is truly the destination such may have to be entertained. To enable those entrepreneurs that have started and grown a business to be eligible for and now needs larger considerations of financing but has not yet reach the mindset to accept equity dilution (which often comes in the next generation of ownership), all debt instruments must be couched to be nonconvertible (not convertible from debt to equity at maturities) where only principal and accrued interest will be repayable. Debt financing does not relinquish any ownership or management control, and interest expense, for the most part, is always a tax deduction. The entrepreneurs that have started a successful

121

venture and are able to find the needed increased debt funding and are willing to live with and handle the negative covenants in loan agreements will much prefer this type of financing. However for most enterprises to reach the highest levels of ultimate funds for growth, equity funding will usually be required.

As we have seen the entire network of commercial bank lending is to avoid risk and speculation. Both are present in taking a company public. Investors will look for capital gains to be enjoyed as a company grows; willing to undergo higher risk in expectation of higher returns. While the commercial bank lender will only have the opportunity to earn a relatively small percentage of interest if the company succeeds and a rather large loss of all principal and potential interest earnings if the company fails.

If qualified and growing sufficiently with a progressive trend of upward positive cash flow, a company may seek larger loans from major insurance companies and pension funds. These loans are most always tied to real estate as collateral and are frankly best used for the purpose of real estate acquisition and construction and not for working capital to support growth, expansion, and possible research and development.

Direct Public Offering

A business that is emerging into the market place as a major entity will find it most advantageous to obtain needed funds by selling common and preferred shares of stock in the company. Beyond the venture capitalists and those angels whom have taken equity to realize their returns, the company now requires more funds and wishes to regain some-what total management control by exiting the venture capitalist with a public offering.

A company may determine that one million dollars or less is required and that the cost of some equity will be tolerable, if so, it may sell directly to the public itself with completed Securities and Exchange Commission (SEC) registration. This is known as a Direct Public Offering and in this information age is most often offered to existing customers and acquaintance over the internet, by mail, and telephone contact. Investment bankers, who would normally represent the company and underwrite securities offerings, consider such inner-company efforts as amateurish and inferior to serious sales attempts. It is true that the majority of such attempts are unsuccessful as the company's sphere of influence is limited and unknown inquiries from random internet searchers to purchase are usually rejected. However it is a method by which an entrepreneur can perhaps raise relative cheap capital and retain majority control of the company. The business owner can also be sure who is purchasing by being very selective as to who will have a piece of the equity. From the investors standpoint such a purchase carries considerable risk as they are solely dependent upon the majority ownership and management for the ability to operate the business effectively to realize anticipated returns and upon their decisions regarding dividend policies.

Initial Public Offering

For those aggressive, high-growth companies, whether a start-up or an existing venture outpacing its own Business Plan, an initial Public offering may be appropriate.

An IPO is the sale of equity in a company, generally in the form of common stock, through an investment banking firm. These shares will trade on a recognized stock market such as: the New York Stock Exchange (NYSE) having it origin in 1792 it is the oldest, largest, and the main exchange in the United States. The companies listed on the NYSE are considered the strongest and must be valued at least for $18 million, the American Stock Exchange (AMEX) is the second largest and is more active in trading foreign stocks, value of listed companies must be at least $3 million, and the best known over-the-counter (OTC) trading exchange, the National Association of Securities Dealers Automated Quotation System (NASDAQ) started in 1971 was the first electronic stock market resulting in more shares being traded than any other exchange in the world. The minimum valuation of companies listed is $1 million which is probably best for smaller emerging companies as they tend to accommodate many small capitalized (small caps) companies and are heavy with high tech and biotech firms. In 1998 the AMEX and NASDAQ markets merged and took the name NASDAQ-AMEX Market Group. To give some perspective of size, at the time of the merger the total market value of all companies listed on both markets was $2.2 trillion, compared with $11.6 trillion for the NYSE. *(Chicago Sun-Times,* November 3, 1998, p45)

Start-up companies must demonstrate in a convincing fashion the potential to become a profitable, positive cash flowing business that will produce substantial increases each year in sales and profits.

Established companies should be building on an existing trend of increased sales and earnings, and demonstrated how it will sustain that trend and continue to grow significantly.

In both scenarios a minimum earnings growth of 20 percent annually will be expected, and the company's stock valuation should grow to be at least $100 million to be considered a truly successful publicly held corporation.

Whereas there may not be any cost of debt service in an equity offering; the cost of an initial public offering is high. Not only will a large portion of the company's equity, at least 25 percent and perhaps more, will be sold; but fees and expenses related to the sale will add up to approximately 20 percent of the offering. The typical smallest IPO is for five million dollars; therefore fees can be as much as one million dollars.

The success of an IPO is not assured and many do not succeed in raising the desired amount by selling all of the offering yet they still incur all of the expense. About 1000 companies go public each year in offering underwritten by investment bankers, and many fail to succeed in the process.

Strategic reasons why a company should undertake the process and consider an initial public offering are:

- A company needs to raise five million dollars or more
- A company needs substantial permanent capital it won't have to pay back or have interest to pay
- A company is attempting to grow through acquisitions
- Have access to capital markets to raise more money in a secondary offering and will be able to borrow more easily from institutional lenders
- Be able to use stock options and ownership to attract top management and key employees
- A public company enables the founding entrepreneurs to better harvest their interest and plan an exit strategy for selling ownership
- Public companies are worth more than private companies and are more prestigious.

THE DESIGN AND SYMBOLISM OF THE U.S. ONE DOLLAR BILL

The motto **"In God We Trust"** was added in 1957, prior to that it was not on the bill; however it was in use on coins long before that.

This so-called paper money is in fact a cotton and linen blend, with red and blue silk fibers running through it. A special blend of ink is used which is secret. The bill is starched to make it water resistant and pressed for a crisp look.

On the front of the bill is the United States Treasury Seal. The scales do not represent a balanced budget (although it should) but actually justice. There is a chevron with 13 stars representing the 13 original colonies. Underneath is a key that is a symbol of authority.

On the reverse there are two circles reflecting the two sides of the Great Seal of the United States. The left hand circle contains an unfinished pyramid. The pyramid represents strength and duration. It is unfinished to denote that the country is not yet finished. The pyramid is lit but the Western side is dark perhaps indicating that the West has not yet been explored. Inside the capstone there is the all-seeing eye, and ancient symbol for divinity.

The Latin above the pyramid, **"Annuit Coeptis"**, means "God has favored our undertaking." The Latin below the pyramid, **"Novus Ordo Seclorum"**, means "a new order for the world." At the base of the pyramid is the Roman numeral **MDCCLXXVI** for 1776.

The right hand circle there is an Eagle whose head represents the Executive (Presidential) branch of government, the shield represents the legislature (Congress) branch, and the tail feathers represents the Justice (nine feathers, nine Supreme Court Judges). The symbol 13 for the original 13 colonies is prevalent throughout—13 Olive branches represent peace, 13 arrows representing being prepared for war, 13 stars above the head, and 13 bars in the shield. The eagle is facing the olive branch to denote a preference for peace. In the eagle's beak is a banner reading **"E Pluribus Unum"**, "one nation from many people".

The colors of the shield's bar is taken from the American Flag; Red represents hardiness and valor, white represents purity and innocence, and the blue represents vigilance, perseverance, and justice.

CHAPTER NINE

INTERNATIONAL TRADE

The basic economic problem is scarcity.
Human wants are unlimited.
Resources are limited.

International trade is an important part of the U.S. economy and the U.S. economy is an important part of international trade. The U.S. is the largest international trader in the world. The U.S. is the world's largest importer and one of the world's largest exporters. In recent years the U.S. has had large trade deficits. A **trade deficit** occurs when a nation's imports exceed its exports.

Other major trading nations are Germany, Japan, the western European nations, and the Asian economies of China, South Korea, Taiwan, and Singapore.

People in different nations trade with each other to benefit themselves. Trade between nations is beneficial to both if there is a difference in opportunity cost. This is the free market system as outlined by Adam Smith in "the Wealth of Nations" working on a grand scale.

Instead of restraining trade, nations should behave as prudent individuals in the pursuit of their own self-interest, Quoting Adam Smith in his 1776 book:

"It is the maxim of every prudent master of a family, never to attempt to make at home what it will cost him more to make then to buy...what is prudence

in the conduct of every private family, can scarce be folly in that of a great kingdom. If a foreign country can supply us with a commodity cheaper than we ourselves can make it, better buy it of them with some part of the produce of our own industry, employed in a way in which we have some advantage."

In a free market, profit-seeking will lead to production and trade according to the advantage received. Therefore in order for international trade to achieve a beneficial result, the governments of the nations involved need to do nothing.

Free international trade:

1. Extends markets, which allows for economies of scale

2. Increases competition

3. Increases technological advances

4. Gives consumers access to more variety

5. Improves efficiency of production and distribution

6. Enhances international relations.

Though nations benefit overall from free trade, domestic producers facing increased competition from imports may suffer losses. This competition requires that they strive for improved efficiencies and operations to the benefit of consumers. However in opposition to constricts to produce in a more efficient manner, or if the ability to do so is prohibitive; they may seek governmentally imposed restriction to trade, such as a tariff (a tax on an imported good) or a quota (a legal limit on the quantity of a good that may be imported).

A trade restriction will allow domestic producers to sell a greater quantity at a higher price thus producing greater profits. A trade restriction will cause domestic consumers to buy a lesser quantity of goods at a higher price, thus receiving less consumer satisfaction. The consumer loss caused by trade restrictions often exceeds the producer gain which results in a net loss to the nation imposing the restriction. Therefore it is never conducive to impose such restriction in the stead of requiring domestic producer to improve their efficiencies and operation to meet consumer desires. Such restrictions benefit a few producers while harming many consumers.

These restrictions will also impose a loss to foreign producers by limited their access to the domestic market place. The nation of the injured foreign producers may also retaliate with trade restriction of their own. Creating a trade war in which no one benefits.

Trade barriers take the form of protective tariffs, quotas, nontariff barriers, and export restriction. Analysis reveals that protective tariffs and quotas increase the prices and reduce the quantities demanded. Sales by foreign exporters diminish; however, domestic producers gain higher prices and enlarged sales all at the expense of the consumer.

Common argument in support of trade restrictions are:

1. National Defense

2. New industry protection

3. Unfair foreign competition

4. Low foreign wages

5. Saving domestic jobs.

In spite of these, nations that practice free international trade generally experience more economic growth and consumer satisfaction than nations that restrict trade. In recent years there has been a movement toward freer international trade resulting in the U.S. benefiting greatly from reduced trade barriers.

Upon deciding to enter the international market place, whether point-of-sale or via the internet, a business must select a means of entry. Four general options exist: (1) Exporting, (2) Licensing, (3) Joint Venture, and (4) Direct Investment.

Exporting

Exporting is producing goods in one country and selling them in another country.

Indirect exporting is selling domestically produced goods in a foreign country through an intermediary. This is ideal for the business that has no foreign contacts but wants to market abroad. The intermediary is a distributor that has overseas contacts, the know-how and resources necessary to market the product.

Direct exporting is when a business sells its domestically produced goods overseas without an intermediary. A company becomes involved in direct exporting when the volume of sales is sufficiently large and easy to obtain making the expense of an intermediary unnecessary. Direct export involves more risk but can provide increased profits.

Twelve common export mistakes most fledgling business make in attempting to enter the international market:

1. Failure to obtain qualified export counseling and to develop an international marketing plan.

2. Insufficient commitment to overcome initial difficulties and financial requirements.

3. Insufficient attention to details in obtaining overseas distributors.

4. Chasing orders from around the world instead of a target market and establishing a base for profitable operations and orderly growth.

5. Neglecting the newly formed exporting business when the U.S. market is booming.

6. Failure to trust international distributors that was selected with proper due diligence and care.

7. Assuming that a given marketing approach will automatically be successful in all countries and cultures.

8. Unwillingness to modify products to meet regulations or cultural preferences of other countries.

9. Failure to print service, sales, and warranty messages in locally understood languages.

10. Failure to provide readily available servicing for the product.

Licensing

Licensing, much like some franchises, offers the right to a trademark, patent, trade secret, or other valued items of intellectual property in return for a royalty. The advantage to the licensor, the company granting the license, is low risk and the chance to enter a foreign market at no or little cost. The licensee, the company obtaining the license, gains value information that allows it to have a competitive advantage in its market (the foreign market).

The licensor, however, gives up some if not all control of its product. And, it is possible for the licensee to modify the product and profit with knowledge gained at the expense of the licensor. Also if the licensee proves to have been a poor choice and not able to properly market the product, the licensor's name and reputation could be damaged.

Joint Venture

When a domestic company and a foreign firm invest together to create a separate business entity it is called a joint venture. These two companies share ownership, control, and profits of the new company.

One company may not have the necessary financial, physical, contacts, or managerial resources to enter the market alone. But together, with one or the other providing what is lacking to enter the market, they can proceed.

Direct Investment

The biggest involvement and commitment a company can make to enter the international market is a direct investment. This entails a domestic business actually investing in creating and owning a foreign subsidiary.

The advantages to direct investment include cost savings, better understanding of market conditions, and fewer restrictions and bureaucracy; all which could outweigh the larger financial commitment and risks.

Nations that practice free international trade generally experience more economic growth than nations that restrict trade. In recent years there has been a movement toward freer international trade which has greatly benefited the United States.

"The world has become small and
completely interdependent."
Wendell L. Wilkie

PART TWO

ENTREPRENEURSHIP

CHAPTER TEN

ENTREPRENEUR PLANNING

OPPORTUNITY

"To open a business is easy; to keep it open is difficulty."
An Ancient Chinese Saying

It is a hard fact that more than half of businesses started are not existing three years later and only 20 percent will still be here in ten years. The process of identifying and creating a business consist of answering at a minimum two questions: "Do I have what it takes to successfully start and manage a new business?" and "Have I identified where a real and lasting opportunity exist?"

"Mismanagement" is the primary reason for most business failures. For the most part failed entrepreneurs always blame their demise on other factors like too much competition, no market for their product or services, high interest rates, lack of cash, inflation, recession, government regulations and other factors which all may have contributed but they are generally not the cause but the symptom of inadequate preparation and research. Lack of managerial experience, financial acumen, and market knowledge accounts for almost 90 percent of new venture failures.

In most cases:

They entered a market that was already crowded with competition.

Did not offer what people wanted to buy.

Failed to make changes in the business as market conditions changed.

And

They lacked sufficient knowledge of the legal, financial, purchasing, accounting, employee relations, or marketing aspects of the business.

(These are some of the reasons franchises are so popular)

To succeed you must know what to do, how to do it, and when to do it. If thinking of starting a business, consider getting a job in that type of business first. There is no substitute for experience and it will afford you the opportunity if such a business is a good fit for you. Experience eliminates some of the surprises a new business owner will encounter. Experience as an employee, however, is not the same as managing that type of business. That why the entrepreneur should learn as much as possible beyond the scope of employee duties and strive to actually become part of management before venturing out on his or her own.

Experience will help, but education and formal training also are important. Just because you have done it before is no guarantee that you were doing it right or that it was the best way to do it (a reason to consider your own business). Education and formal training in the technical fields of business (the business of the business), such as accounting, finance, marketing, law, and interpersonal skills are important.

Successful entrepreneurs exhibit eight qualities:

1. They Are Opportunity Seekers. "Within every problem lies a disguised opportunity." They are always looking for areas where people aren't having their needs met completely if at all.

2. They Are Future-Oriented. They have a vision of what is possible and are willing to invest time and money in transforming that vision into a business. "The best way to predict the future is to invent it." They don't live in the past, nor dwell on failure. Just because something has not been done before does not mean that it cannot be done. To quote **Star Trek:** They are prepared "To boldly go where no man has gone before." Or, as it has been updated "To boldly go where no one has gone before."

3. They Are Committed to Being the Best. They have contempt for the status quo. They avoid the words of failed businesses "But that's the way we've always done it." They are good learners and good listeners; they know that creating and running a business is a continuous process of learning, experimenting, and changing.

4. They Are Market-Driven and Customer-Oriented. They know that they are successful only to the extent that they are able to create and maintain customers for a profit. They are aware that their customers are the lifeblood of the business. They know that they are not in the business of selling goods and services (product-oriented); but are in the business of providing customer satisfaction (market-oriented).

5. They Value Their Employees. They recognize that the business will only be as good as its employees; dedicated, knowledgeable employees may be their only competitive advantage. They are keenly aware that the quality of customer-relations is related to employee-relations.

6. They Are Realistic. They know the difference between a dream and a solid business opportunity. They know that a new venture cannot be launched without an objective thorough business plan. "If you fail to plan, you are planning to fail." They also know that success comes from good management not good luck.

7. They Are Tolerant of the Tedium. They know that being an entrepreneur is not really glamorous. It also involves mundane activities and thankless task. Starting a business involves blood, sweat, and tears, as well as time, money, and perhaps an imbalance in lifestyle. The entrepreneur must be prepares to wear "many hats".

8. They Are Resilient and Persistent. They know that business is not a 100 meter sprint but a marathon. There are few overnight successes. "It may take two years to know if your business is a lemon and five years to know if it is a pearl." Success is not just the result of having a great idea or identifying an opportunity; it takes patience and persistence. Most entrepreneurs experience

one or two failures before they experience their first success. They learn from the experience and improve for the next one.

Starting a business is not a casual undertaking like starting a hobby. If you are going to undertake the venture, then you must do all you can to improve your chance of success.

You will need a solid business plan, good business opportunity, the necessary skills and abilities, and sufficient funds to start and operate until the business can be self-sustaining.

To quote Will Rogers: *"Know what you are doing.*
Love what you are doing.
Believe in what you are doing."

The Business Plan

"An action without thought is nothing, and a thought without action is nothing at all.

Now that you have identified the type of business venture you want to pursue it is time to begin preparing your business plan. A pragmatic outline is located in the appendix (A-5).

Even thought you have a general idea of the type of business to start, numerous questions remain unanswered. Is there a market, how will you reach it, who are your suppliers, what is the cost, what is your selling price, Is it competitive, what is your distributing method, do you have the resources, money, people, facility, what is your break-even point and how will you be sustained until it is reach? The business plan will provide a basis these questions and other decisions still to be made.

You may feel that you do not need a formal business plan. Completing the process may have taken a lot of time, effort, and thought, but a lot still needs to be determined. Preparing a business plan will help to identify questions (Appendix A-6) you need to answer. It also provides a framework and timetable for implementation.

The probability of being successful in starting a new business is directly related to the extent your business plan is accurate and complete. Some believe they do not need a business plan if they are not borrowing money or seeking investors. This is a mistake. A business plan is not the same as an application for financing; it is your road-map, blueprint for building a successful business.

It is true that a business plan is instrumental in obtaining financing, but it is also a reflection of your ability to manage. It identifies to all interested and to you the: who, what, when, where, how much, why, and how of your venture. If you do not have the patience, perseverance, skill, and information to prepare a plan, then you probably lack the ability to start and manage a new business. If you can't put your ideas into words, dates, and dollars, then you don't know what you are talking about and should forget it rather than waste your time and money.

Most small business owners do some sort of planning and if asked they may reply that it is in their head. This form of informal planning "in their head" is not planning at all. The plan should and must be more systematic, and must be written. No business will follow the plan exactly and conditions will not exactly materialize as projected. But a written plan, a dynamic ever-changing plan as condition warrants, will assist in focusing efforts and direction. Since there is ever present uncertainty in the marketplace that the business is attempting to grow and become successful within, there is a stronger need for more formal flexible planning to meet the many challenges ahead. A written plan will assist in staying on track toward desired objectives and goals; and if that track appears too ambitious or unobtainable following the existing action plan, then a period of rolling-revision to the plan is in order. At the appropriate time, perhaps a quarter or two, with the careful evaluation and analysis of results, a revision of the plan, resources, efforts, and its targeted objectives may be in order. The plan, like the business, is dynamic and is subject to change with constant monitoring.

The sole purpose of planning and preparing a formal written business plan is not just to raise capital as most fledgling new business enterprisers seem to believe. It is true that every lender, investor, and even trade creditors will want to see one to ascertain the ventures probability of success and the entrepreneur's ability and experience. In spite of the fact that a business plan is essential in raising money, it is not the paramount reason an entrepreneur contemplating a venture and an existing small business owner should invest the time, energy, and resources in completing one.

Planning involves the setting of the organizational visions, objectives, and goals. It creates a vision based on values. The vision is the encompassing explanation of why the organization exists and where it is trying to head. It is a process that tends to follow a continuous pattern. It answers the fundamental questions of:

What is the situation now and where do we want to go?

How can we get there from here?

Would you consider a road trip to an unknown destination without consulting a roadmap? Some would and those that would will have more difficulty than those that would not. It has been determined that with ten years nearly 75% of all small business ventures fail due to lack of planning and proper management. Management functions are defined as planning, organizing, controlling, and leading; all are essential throughout the life cycles of the business with planning important in all functions. Too many entrepreneurs have great difficulty in transitioning from entrepreneur and business founder to on-going entrepreneur business owner and manager. They forget or discount the planning aspects of running and growing a business and instead concentrate on sales, networking, technical and operational parts of the business, all the fun parts which were the reasons they went into the business to do what they like rather than learning to like what they must do to add sustainable value to the business. The entrepreneur must soon learn that for the business to survive it must be ran like a business with attention to details and not ran like a hobby. A good business owner must become a good business manager not only for himself, but also for customers, employees, investors, and creditors. Those entrepreneurs that are quick to point out that they are too busy building and working in the business to survive today rather plan for tomorrow will discover that the business is not being worked on, not being developed and nurtured, and that there is no tomorrow. These business owners will usually state that there is no time for planning, much less to put a business plan in writing, besides "the plan is in my head; I have no time for fairy-tale projections into the future, or action plans that I won't ever have the time to implement," will soon find that there is no future. This is a typical attitude and outlook of a business owner who is more of an opportunist than an entrepreneur. An entrepreneur is not simply a person who starts a business and takes reckless risk. A true entrepreneur starts, grows, and manages a business after due deliberation of accepting the calculated risks in exploring the business concept, and creates a business model that capitalizes on the identified market opportunities in a for-profit venture. Without the discipline of planning, forethought, anticipation of expenses and realistic expectations of sales and cash flow, the would-be entrepreneur is like a child learning to ride a bicycle, frantically striving not to fall by pedaling faster and faster. Fall they will. It usually is not will they fall, but when they will fall.

Inadvertently those opportunistic enterprisers that lack the entrepreneur's internal locus-of-control, "If it's going to be it is up to me," and are not purpose commitment to a specific venture will blame the failure on outside forces beyond their control such as, lack of capital, lack of sales acceptance, too much competition, a poor location, and not enough help; all management planning functions. All are not the cause but the symptom of lack of planning and management ability resulting in business failure. Therefore while the formal written business plan is definitely needed and used to raise capital, it is first and always used as a dynamic planning tool for the entrepreneur himself as a feasibility plan for the business concept. An idea for a business is not a concept of a business model but only the beginning of one.

Launching a new venture does have elements of risk. The new business alone may not be inherently risky but the unprepared and uninitiated entrepreneur is the risk. The prepared new business owner would have first planned to minimize the risk to a calculated one that, with effort and persistence, is feasible. A written business plan for the purpose of establishing and determining the feasibility of the venture would have assisted in answering such questions as:

- Does the entrepreneur have the personal skills, knowledge, expertise, perseverance, desire, and mindset to launch a new venture
- Is there a target market for the proposed product, service, and business being contemplated
- Can the market be reached and how and what resources will be needed
- What resources are available to sustain the business until it can surpass the breakeven point and sustain itself
- Where will those resources come from
- How long will it take to reach breakeven

- Will others be needed, when and with what skills and abilities
- From where and how can the business attract them
- At what price will the product or service be offered, is it competitive
- Will the contribution margin be sufficient to support overhead and produce a profit
- Who will be the business's vendors and suppliers, and at what cost and terms will it be able to purchase
- How dependent will the business be upon those vendors and trade creditors and are there other sources available in the event of interruption?

These and the 77 Questions Every Business Plan Should Answer (refer to appendix A-6) when appropriate will better prepare the entrepreneur to achieving success in the endeavor.

Depending on the industry and the entrepreneur's background and personal situation, there could be many other different questions which a thorough business plan will help to determine before personal and others resources are mistakenly invested into a venture with little practical expectation of success. Be mindful, that a plan that determines a venture to be unwise and not feasible would have serve its purpose and done the job of advising and forewarning the entrepreneur. It could very well reveal other entrepreneurial opportunities that would work and pay that are more reasonable to pursue.

The new business owner may be from the legion of reluctant entrepreneurs; those many thousands that for various reasons have found themselves out of a job. Too many have been laid off, downsized, outsized, fired, who feel displaced and are anxious to get back into the game. The desire may be strong but the motivation could be misdirected. If they were fortunate to have been separated from their employment with a pension or savings to invest; the very ease of entry which these funds may allow to embark on a new venture may be a downfall and lead to the lost of invested funds. A thorough study and a plan will be necessary to reduce the possibility of loss and to determine the reluctant entrepreneur's expectation and fit for the undertaking. The attraction of being independent, the freedom of being one's own boss, the drive to work for self and reap the rewards of your own efforts is strong and, in fact, is the main reason most seek the religion of self-employment. And, with no other job opportunities forthcoming, the appeal can be very appealing to a still energetic and talented individual with many good years left and a desire to again be relevant in the workplace.

Planning can make it so; planning at the inception to determine feasible, upon opening to assure initial capital requirements until breakeven, during operation to sustain growth and viability, and even an exit strategy for the founder to reap the value added.

Many relative new existing small business owners having lost their jobs are fond of saying, "I wish I would have been fired years ago. It is the best thing that has happened to me." That is wonderful and is no doubt the result of planning efforts. They have worked hard and smart, perhaps in a related field of their previous employment and experience, and are now enjoying the fruits of their labors. But, unfortunately, they are in the minority as far more without proper planning have gone the other way.

It is at this most vulnerable time of conception that a business plan will truly serve well. At this stage it is extremely important to exercise personal introspection in learning what are the actual characteristics and expectations of the entrepreneur as well as the feasibility of the marketing opportunity and practicality of financial resources. If the fledgling business owner is truly a reluctant entrepreneur having just been ejected from the shelter of a corporate womb, he may be little prepared for the realities ahead. There is much that may have been taken for granted in a former work-life that would not be available or so easily obtained in the new venture. The strain to provide them may be the very straw that will overwhelm the business and cause its failure. Perks like benefits, comfortable compensation, staff, office and infrastructure, expense account, company automobile, paid travel, vacation, hospitalization and insurance; all, and perhaps more, will have been supplied by a former employer which now is unaffordable to the new business venture. The entrepreneur himself may be in for a culture shock for it will be he who must provide those benefits if affordable at all; and it will be he who, for some time, will be wearing all the hats necessary to the business like: salesperson, bookkeeper, promoter, delivery, and even janitor.

For all these reasons the personal characteristics and abilities, and business expectations and feasibility are of vital importance and may be discovered by preparing a written business plan. The enterprising new business owner should first strive on paper to determine the venture's feasibility and fit before investing life-savings or home equity into a business that perhaps does not have a strong likelihood of success or that they do not care for or one that cannot deliver the comfort level and security that a job has for many years.

The personal criteria of job security, money, lifestyle, insurance, personal health and age, and family are all factors equally important as product, market, and cash-flow management to be considered before entering into the guerilla warfare of entrepreneurship. The very years of work experience may diminish in their mind the need for such planning. Often the ten, twenty, or more years of experience in an isolated corporate world is really one years experience twenty or so times which actually arms them with a cavalier attitude of "someone with my experience can certainly handle this little venture, let's do it." This is not to advocate not to explore a new venture, but to simply encourage that it is done right with proper planning.

Personal questions to be answered are as follows:

- Will the business generate sufficient money to meet business expenses and the owner's personal minimum needs
- What does your spouse and family think of this venture and do you have their support
- How much debt will the business need, can it be raised and services, and what is your tolerance for debt, how debt adverse are you
- Are you willing to give some ownership and control for an equity investment
- What are the legal requirements and regulations, if any, for the business and its location?

For these and other questions a wise entrepreneur will want to prepare, first and foremost for himself, a business plan to determine if the venture is feasible for him and him for it.

Having established the feasibility of the business concept from the viewpoint of personal planning; now, the business plan will take on a new audience and should be written accordingly for the different purpose. The entrepreneur has proven to himself the potential of the venture, now, he must pragmatically prove it to others and sell the concept to investors, lenders, key employees, vendors, and perhaps family and friends. The business plan will now perform the function as detailed in appendix A-5 and should strive to answer the applicable questions outlined in appendix A-6. It is now a true planning tool in which the business model can be refined.

Prior to presentation to interested parties, the business owner can think and make mistakes on paper rather than actually in the business avoiding wasting real money, resources, and time. Once the business is operational the plan will prove itself truly as a dynamic management tool to evaluate, manage, and monitor operations, sales, profit goals, and the all important cash-flow. As the business progresses and actual performance is compared to projection, deviations are analysis. The business plan can be rewritten to adjust tactics, activity, and goals to reflect new realities. Such monitoring and financial management by percentages and ratio-analysis against projections, past history (if any), or benchmark companies initiate adjustments to the plan's goals and projections which have now become the planning budget, can be called "rolling revisions" and are most effective if done quarterly. Any time sooner would not indicate a true trend or given time for a conscientious persistent effort to implement the original conceived well thought out plan. Any time longer, semi-annually or annually, will have been too long to effectively initiate corrective action.

A business plan serves three vital functions:

1. It is a tool for the entrepreneur to develop the idea and concept and determine if it is right for him

2. It is a retrospective planning tool to compare actual performance against projected performance and goals in order to implement corrective actions if necessary, and

3. It is an essential tool for raising money, both debt and equity. Most investors and lenders will not put capital into a venture without seeing a business plan that shows that the concept is well thought out, has a good product and delivery system with a reachable target market, good cost and profit structure, and most importantly, a good management team.

In the role of a presentation to investors and lenders to raise capital, the business plan becomes a sales tool. As such the written plan, and if fortunate to make a visual and oral presentation, must be factual and not wildly exaggerated but yet convey a sense of positive conservative optimism and excitement. If there are any negative risk or adverse competitive issues, they should be acknowledged but not with undue emphasis. The business plan should be written objectively realizing that in the role of raising money, the first role is to the entrepreneur and it is better not to get funding for a bad risk. If the business plan shows that it is not a good venture then the plan has done its job and saved the entrepreneur from a costly mistake.

Planning is both an organizational necessity and a managerial responsibility. Through planning companies choose goals based on assumptions and projections into the future giving direction to the concerted efforts of employees. The purpose of planning is twofold: to determine appropriate obtainable objectives and goals and to prepare for the unremitting, uncertain changing future. No organization is free of adaptive and innovative changes from within and without, so effective dynamic planning is necessary for survival and growth in order to gain a measure of control and influence over its destiny.

Planning is defined as the activity by which managers analyze present conditions to determine how to reach a desired condition. It embodies the management skills of anticipating, influencing, and controlling the nature and direction of change. Planning is a pervasive and continuous function involving processes of perception, analysis, conceptual thought, communication, vision, decision and action. A process rather than a behavior at one given point in time; it is the thinking that takes place prior to decisions and subsequent action. Its central concern is with the future, therefore planning is anticipatory decision making.

> *"If you fail to plan, you will plan to fail."*
> Norman Vincent Peale

There are five fundamental activities that are basic to the planning process:

The evaluation of present situation and condition

The time factor

The problems with forecasting and assumptions

The collection and analysis of data

The coordination and implementation of plans

Evaluation:

An important task in planning is to recognize present inadequacies that indicate a need to change. Dissatisfaction with a lack of progress of current goals, programs, and activities generates the desire of planning to achieve improvement. It is not always obvious when conditions warrant change and the need for planning. Ineffective and unproductive situation are often so gradual that only after a problem has emerged is the cumulative impact recognized.

Recurring problems can be subject to standing plans which continue to meet an enduring need, such as, a customer-service plan detailing policies and procedures for assuring customer satisfaction. It is not known what specific problems will arise, but the plan recognizes the need for attention when they do occur.

Plans to accomplish a particular purpose are generally major, single-use plans that are broad and inclusive, such as a new job evaluation system. They may also contain a set of related standing plans.

Contingency plans look into varying time spans in the future and attempts to prepare and take into account the possibilities for rapid, major changes. Through contingency planning, managers monitor current conditions and map probable alternatives of varying risk and benefit. The purpose of contingency planning is to consider and plan for alternative futures. Such plans require great flexibility and are often altered or discarded before actual use.

Time Factor:

For analytical purposes, planning may be viewed as both short-run and long-run; however, planning is a continuous process.

Short-run, tactical, plans are concerned with the near future; the next month or even the next couple of years. Long-range, strategic, planning attempts to foresee conditions, situations, and courses of action for perhaps five, ten, twenty-five years, or even longer into the future. Long-range plans focus on the organization's basic goals and strategies for growth and development.

As the time span increases, the accuracy of planning tends to decrease. The greater span of time affords more probability for unanticipated events to occur. The more remote the future, the more difficult it is to foresee and forecast.

Forecasting:

"The best way to predict the future is to invent it."
Alan Kay

Forecasting embodies assumptions, procedures, and techniques for predicting conditions or events that are expected to prevail in the future. It may apply to any relevant aspect of the future, but most focus is on the general level of conditions in the economic, governmental, and social sectors in which the organization operates.

Since uncertainties abound, forecasting is not an exact science and will always remain something of art. There is no economic geiger counter to identify right decisions or policies; but managers are always trying to rely less on judgment and make forecasting more of a science than an art by employing economist and other "experts" to make careful and detailed plans. Large firms may have as many as 100 economists with planning and forecasting responsibilities to reconcile technological innovation, population growth, mega-trends, and expanding physical facilities are interrelated. Small organizations also have access and attempt to use a great deal of economic and business data from consultants, industry and trade associations, universities business and economic research, as well as information from federal and state agencies.

Data Collection and Analysis:

"The journey of a thousand miles starts with a single step."
Chinese proverb

Effective planning depends on the quality, timeliness, and quantity of data available to the planners. The information must be organized, evaluated, and disseminated to those who need it; and data storage and retrieval systems must be established for the various groups or individuals involved in the process. Information is perceived and evaluated differently by different groups or individual.

Data for both internal and external plans will be accumulated. Internal data may consist of costs, production, sales, labor, and other matters pertain to the ongoing situation. Vital internal information will also include knowledge of organizational targets, objectives, quotas, goals, expectations and projections, and the overall strategic plans for operational activities. Internal data is provided systematically by periodic reports and statistics compiled from records. External information on industry, community, governmental regulations, and general economic trends and conditions are obtained from news sources such as papers, periodicals, trade publications, bulletins, newsletters, commercial research organizations and the government data, as well as the electronic media.

Coordination and Implementation:

"You can't direct the wind, but you can adjust the sails."
Anonymous

Coordination problems occur because seldom is one plan being activated at a time, but often there are multiple plans each related to the other vertically and horizontally. Plans range from those of strategic, broad, long-term scope which are the responsibility of senior management, to tactical, short-term oriented toward day-to-day operations of lower management. Effective planning must be integrated throughout the organization. It is surprising how many organization plans fail due to lack of commitment and coordination of all concern. Obstacles to effective planning and its successful implementation are grouped in two broad categories: administrative difficulties and the human element.

Administrative Difficulties:

A corporate culture and organizational climate must be created that encourages planning to thrive. The principal problems lie in the flow and timing of information, allocation of responsibilities, and the overall cost incurred in planning.

The time available to obtain information on which to base a decision is generally limited. A balance has to be struck between acting on inadequate information or not acted at all while waiting for complete information. Experienced managers know how to judge when there is enough information for a useful plan and when there is not. They are able to avoid analysis paralysis, but yet are still able to decide if missing data can be obtained within a timely matter to enable effective planning.

An oversupply of unanalyzed or unorganized information can be equally disruptive in the planning process. This may occur when a corporation, to achieve economies of scale and limit cost, centralizes computers and other data information systems in the headquarters. Although there may be advantages to centralization, branch offices and subsidiary units may receive much unwanted data and be forced to exert a redundant effort in reprocesses information to find and organize what is needed. Also with information specialist and researchers housed at headquarters, there is a tendency not to use them at lower levels or at other offices where there may be a great need for them. Once the planning process and the principal planners and decision makers are identified; the information flow problems can be worked out as part of the total management planning system to assure that relevant data get to who needs it when it is needed.

A further administrative difficulty is that effective planning is costly. It requires capital, time, information, and human resources including the costs of false starts that will result when data is incomplete or incorrect. Planning is generally regarded as a worthwhile effort with ample return on expenditures, but when economic conditions deteriorate it is usually the first activity to be curtailed as a waste of money. Plans under way or about to commence may be canceled or delayed. It should be realized that planning cost are a part of overhead and should be budgeted as any other fixed cost.

Even after plans are fully developed, officially approved, and activated, opposition may occur from resentful participants who may impede its progress by blocking or failing to carry out the plans. This is where the leadership and management skills of the planners will prove most valuable in properly communicating the plan and the benefits to all concern in motivating complete compliance.

Human Element:

"The human mind treats a new idea the way the
body treats a strange protein—It rejects it."
Peter Medawar, Nobel Laureate

Resistance to change is common. Planning often depends on the recognition and implementation of change that many involved would prefer to ignore. For example, in planning a merger of two companies, the very planners charged with the responsibility know that their jobs may be at jeopardy. The involvement of those affected and full communication with them will help reduce this agency problem. Planning that lacks consideration for the human factor and their relationships with all affected, managers and workers will have difficulties.

All planning connotes change and change produces anxiety.

A further human difficulty is that planning is essentially an intellectual activity. The final plan to activate is the tangible evidence of that intangible thought process. Thought requires effort and often involves the painful contemplation of previous unfortunate and undesirable events. The mental process require to plan is by necessity a passive activity. Managers used to action called upon to produce new changes are not favorable inclined to sit at a desk and think, to consider the manipulation of a complex array of variables in various combinations.

A final obstacle is when plans once made, adopted, and implemented are not accepted and acted upon. The investment of time, effort, and money seemed wasted, and senior management responsible appear impotent and ineffectual. Further when plans create changes they should be kept flexible and current to prevent them from being abandoned or scrapped. When a plan cannot be successfully implemented for unanticipated and unexpected reasons, those reasons should be clearly explained and communicative to assure acceptable of revisions to the original plans.

Effective planning requires senior management direction and support, and an appropriate organizational culture in which planning and constructive changes meaningful at all levels. The pragmatic question of effective planning is: does it lead to an action plan that moves the organization forward toward objectives? To answer this question the following factors are important:

- Objectives must be clearly defined, reachable, and properly selected
- Simplicity is preferable to complexity
- Reward and recognition motivates better planning efforts
- Flexibility should be built into the plan to allow revision and adjustments when warranted
- Acceptance and commitment of all participants is essential
- The plan should be in writing; writing the plan sharpens and focuses thought, enhances preparation, provides valuable learning experience for the planners, and aids in the communication, dissemination, and follow-up processes with those involved.

Because some elements and data are more important and relevant to resolving the situation or problem, the planning process should answer crucial questions like:

- What is the time factor before definite action must be implemented
- Have we tried anything like this before
- What makes this problem so urgent
- Why are some participants reluctant to cooperate
- What resources and who is available to help resolve this
- Have we defined the real problem
- Where can we get more information
- What is the potential gain and possible loss from this action

The entrepreneur manager must be aware of the **"Six P's of Business— Proper prior planning prevents poor performance."**

Strategic Management

"I have often heard it said that big companies, the corporate giants, are the ones that need to think about their business strategically. Smaller, more entrepreneurial companies, by contrast, do not need strategy; they can pursue other routes to business success. In my view, that is exactly backward. Unlike the giants, small businesses cannot rely on inertia of the marketplace

for their survival. Nor can they succeed on brute force, throwing resources at problems. On the contrary, they have to see their competitive environment with particular clarity, and they have to stake out and protect a position they can defend. That is what strategy is all about."
Michael E. Porter, Harvard Business School

A strategy is a course of action, a plan, that entrepreneurs take in an effort to attain and sustain superior long-term performance of their organization. The formulation of a "plan" is actually not as important as the "planning" process itself. The ongoing process with the necessary ramifications is all about planning for profitability, growth, survival, and achieving and maintaining a competitive advantage.

Five tasks of strategic management are:

1. Developing a strategic vision (what do we want to become) and mission (what is our business)

2. Setting objectives and goals (Goals are the broad, long-term accomplishments an organization wishes to attain; Objectives are the specific, short-term accomplishments to achieve the Goals.)

3. Crafting a strategy—formulation of the plan

4. Implementing the strategy (plan)

5. Evaluating performance and initiating corrective adjustments if required

These tasks are aimed at answering:

Where are we now?

Where do we want to go?

How will we get there?

Establishing this strategy is certainly of interest and the primary responsibility of the business owners, the entrepreneur manager, but if the key executive manager is not the business owner, the plan is more effective if that operating person and other employees have an input in the formulation, implementation, and evaluation of the strategy.

The Strategic Management Process consists of:

Formulation:	Develop the Mission and vision Statements
	Perform an external analysis
	Perform an internal analysis
	Establish long-term goals and short-term objectives
	Generate and select strategies
Implementation:	Implement strategies
	Marketing
	Pricing
	Production
	Finance
	Accounting
	Research & Development
Evaluation:	Measure and evaluate performance
	Revise and repeat all if necessary

EXTERNAL ANALYSIS:

For a company to succeed, its strategy must either fit the industry environment in which it operates, or the company must be able to reshape the industry environment to its advantage through its choice of strategy. Companies typically fail when their strategy no longer fits the environment in which they operate.

The typical SWOT (strength, weakness, opportunities, and threats) analysis applies. Whereas Strengths and Weakness are internal; the Opportunities and Threats are external.

Opportunities arise when a company can take advantage of conditions to formulate and implement strategies that enable it to become more profitable. Threats arise when conditions endangers the integrity and profitability of the company's business.

Michael Porter's Five Forces Model describes forces that shape competition within an industry and helps to identify strategic opportunities and threats. They are:

1. The risk of entry by potential competitors

2. The intensity of rivalry among establishes companies

3. The bargaining power of buyers

4. The bargaining power of suppliers

5. The closeness of substitutes to a company's products

INTERNAL ANALYSIS:

A business must identify its internal strengths and weakness in order to establish its distinctive competencies based on resources and capabilities. These competencies enable a firm to create superior value for customers by achieving competitive advantage, efficiency, quality, innovation, and responsiveness to customers.

A company has a competitive advantage when its profit rate is higher than the average for its industry.

Resources refer to the financial, physical, human, technological, and organizational resources of the business.

Capabilities refer to a company's skills at coordinating its resources and putting them to productive use.

Depending on the size and sophistication of the business, there are three main levels of management planning and implementing strategy. In a new small business, particularly a start-up venture, these levels may very well be centered in one or two people.

1. The Corporate Level—consists of the CEO, Board of Directors, and corporate executives, and in a small business

the ownership. They define the mission and goals of the firm, determine what business the firm should be in, and allocate resources.

2. The Business Level—consists of the department heads, managers of business units (divisions). Their role is to translate the intent of the corporate level into concrete workable strategies for the business.

3. The Functional Level—consists of managers of specific operations. They develop and implement functional strategies that achieve goals.

Mission Statements and Vision Statements

To best answer those three questions of: Where are we now? Where do we want to go? How do we get there? A well thought out mission statement will prove most helpful. It is first constructed for the entrepreneur manager to ascertain the right track to be on in achieving desired goals. Next, perhaps in more specific enumeration as a vision statement, it will assist and assure that all team members are in synch with tasks and objectives. It is the foundation for job descriptions, assignments, and management responsibilities and objectives. Further, it will be helpful in describing to customers and suppliers the nature, desire, and purpose of the company.

The mission statement is a dynamic belief and goal statement which should be establish at the organization inception and play a guiding role in the business plan. It is the outline of the fundamental purpose of the organization. The statement is subject to revisions, but, if carefully thought-out, it will not require frequent changes. An annual review should be sufficient to learn if it is still serving the purpose.

The mission statement will also be an integral part of numerous documents such as: loan request, customer service agreements, employee's literature and training documents, supplier's negotiations, and of course the business plan itself. It is always found in annual reports and should always be prominently displayed for customers' and employees' viewing.

It would appear relatively easy to determine what business an organization is in, yet in the course of continuing to do what was always done, often management and ownership lose sight of the reality. Some years ago there was a major fan company shipping fans of all sizes, commercial and residential, all over the country and beyond. Because they thought themselves in the "fan" business, after-all it was now a four generation family business, and not in the comfort, air-condition business; they are now out-of-business for failing to convert to modern air condition technology manufacture and sales.

> *"A business is not defined by its name, statues, or articles of incorporation. It is defined by the business mission. Only a clear definition of the mission and purpose of the organization makes possible clear and realistic business objectives. That business mission is so rarely given adequate thought is perhaps the most important single cause of business frustration."*
>
> Peter Drucker

Five keys to designing a Mission Statement

1. ***Keep it short.*** It must be understandable and memorable for all who come in contact with it. While principally written to guide employees, the statement also speaks to customers, vendors, stockholders, and creditors.

2. ***Keep it simple.*** It has to a statement that everyone can learn and understand. A mission statement that is not shared or poorly communicated has little value to the company.

3. ***Keep it straightforward.*** It has to be able to guide everyone in the company every day. It has to be actionable, something that helps the employees make active decisions without having to refer everything to a superior. It should guide everyone in the company to the goals that the owner has set; it helps to ensure that all are headed in the same direction.

4. ***Keep it clear.*** It has to tell everyone exactly what you do and conversely it will tell them what you do not do.

5. ***Keep it measurable.*** There should be a benchmark for every part of the statement to determine if the goals of the statement are being met.

EXAMPLES:

American Red Cross—The American Red Cross is a humanitarian service organization, led by volunteers, that provides relief to victims of disasters and helps people prevent, prepare for and respond to emergencies.

Apex Elevator—To provide a high reliability, error-free method for moving people and products up, down, and sideways within a building.

Avis Rent-A-Car—Our business is renting cars. Our mission is total customer satisfaction.

Chrysler Corporation—Chrysler Corporation is committed to providing our customers with the

World's highest level of satisfaction with our products and service

Concordia University Wisconsin—Concordia University is a Lutheran higher education community. Committed to helping students develop in mind, body, and spirit in the church and the world.

Hogan Financial Corporation—Organized to assist entrepreneurs with the skills, knowledge, and financial resources to start, grow, and manage a profitable business; and to assist individuals with the realization of financial dreams and aspirations.

Josephson Drug Company, Inc.—To provide people with longer lives and higher-quality lives by applying research efforts to develop new or improved drugs and health-care products.

Loyola University New Orleans—A Jesuit and Catholic institution of higher education, welcomes students of diverse backgrounds and prepares them to lead meaningful lives with and for others; to pursue truth, wisdom, and virtue; and to work for a more just world. Inspired by Ignatius of Loyola's vision of finding God in all things, the university is grounded in the liberal arts and sciences, while also offering opportunities for professional studies in undergraduate and selected graduate programs. Through teaching, research, creative activities, and service, the faculty, in cooperation with the staff, strives to educate the whole student and to benefit the larger community.

McCormick & Company—The primary mission is to expand our worldwide leadership position in the spice, seasoning, and flavoring markets.

McDonald's—To satisfy the world's appetite for good food, well-served, at a price people can afford.

Nunez Community College—Nunez Community College is a comprehensive community college offering a general education and occupational technologies curriculum that blends the arts, sciences, and humanities leading to associate degrees, certificates, and workforce development.

Salathe Oil Company—Salathe Oil Company's mission is to provide the highest quality petroleum products, coupled with the best service possible to its many diversified customers, thereby increasing its customer base, customer satisfaction, and improving profitability.

Starbucks—Establish Starbucks as the premier purveyor of the finest coffee in the world while maintaining our uncompromising principles while we grow.

Southwest Airlines—The mission of Southwest Airlines is dedication to the highest quality of customer service delivered with a sense of warmth, friendliness, individual pride, and company spirit.

Wal-Mart—To offer all of the fine customers in our territories all of their household needs in a manner in which they continue to think of us fondly.

SWOT ANALYSIS

Key to planning and ultimate prosperity and survival is an awareness of the external conditions in the market place and with competitors, and the internal strengths, talent, and resources to meet them. SWOT analysis is a planning tool used to analyze an organization's Strengths, Weakness, Opportunities, and Threats. Strengths and Weakness are internal to the organization. Opportunities and Threats are most often external to the organization and cannot always be anticipated.

For a company to succeed, its external analysis must yield a strategy that fits the industry environment in which it operates, or the company must be able to reshape the environment to its advantage. Companies will typically fail when their strategy no longer fits the environment in which they operate.

Opportunities arise when a company can take advantage of conditions to formulate and implement strategies that enable it to become more profitable. Threats arise when conditions endangers the integrity and profitability of the company's business.

Internally, a business must identify its strengths and weakness in order to establish its distinctive competencies based on resources and capabilities. These competencies enable a firm to create superior value for customers by achieving competitive advantage, efficiency, quality, innovation, and responsiveness to customers. An organization's internal resource refers to its financial, physical, human, technology capabilities, and its corporate culture and skills at coordinating these resources into productive use.

Michael Porter's Five Forces Model describes the forces that shape competition within an industry and helps to identify strategic opportunities and threats:

1. The risk of entry by potential competitors

2. The intensity of rivalry among established companies

3. The bargaining power of buyers

4. The bargaining power of suppliers

5. The closeness of substitutes to a company's products

Risk of Entry—the intensity of competition within an industry depends on the ease of entering that industry. There are several things that can make it harder for new competition to enter the marketplace: high investment of initial capital, difficulty or expensive for customer to switch, technology and service advantage, and superior and efficient work force.

Rivalry among existing competitors—utilization of tactics like competing on price, increased customer service, expanding geographical service areas, and increased advertising expenditures.

Bargaining power of buyers—buyers are powerful when they purchase a large volume relative to overall sales. They can exert influence for price concessions, discounts, and purchasing terms. They have considerable clout when there is low switching cost to purchase from a competitor.

Bargaining power of sellers—If a supplier is vital to your operation without any other convenient or inexpensive replacement vendor, they can be extremely powerful by threat of price increases, reduced quality, or availability and delivery of goods.

Closeness of substitutes—Intensity of competition also depends on the ease and availability of substitute products for your product; Products that perform the same or similar function at the same level of satisfaction and value at the same or better cost.

The **strategy formulation** portion of the planning process begins with specifications of an organization's mission, values, and goals. Next, an external and internal analysis is conducted to identify strengths, weakness, opportunities, and threats. In this step, information about competitors, products, processes, functions, the industry, and community conditions would be gathered and interpreted, resulting in detailed forecasts and estimates. Then, based on these first steps, appropriate strategies will be chosen. Decisions will be made about actions to be taken in the future.

Decision-making alone can be a difficult task; to assure the best possible decisions it is suggested to utilize the seven "D's" of decision making (Ch. 3).

The **strategy implementation** portion of the process consists of taking actions specified in the plans that are developed in the formulation phase. Then, the results of the implementation are monitored to ensure the intended consequences (**evaluation**). If the implementation achieves the desired results, no further action is necessary other than to continue with the plan. If the implementation fails to achieve the desired results, corrective actions must be chosen and implemented. Finally, the results of the process become input for the next cycle of the process (rolling revisions).

In this matter organizations are always formulating, implementing, and evaluating strategies in a never-ending process.

Too often entrepreneur managers who are busy running and operating the business to survive another day fail to plan for profit. They often sometimes don't even know if they are making profits or not. Because sales don't guarantee a net profit, it is essential to know the true cost of a product and the expense related to selling it and to set a fair profit margin in the selling price, budget with a realistic sales forecast and related expense and plan accordingly.

The business' financial position is not static. With every sale, money flows in, inventory is bought, expenses are incurred, and credit may be extended or obtained, assets and liabilities fluctuate. Managers must keep timely and accurate records of these transactions and pay attention to what the figures are saying.

To plan for profit there must be a profit target. To simply strive for break-even is a sure way to fall behind. Profit planning should include the following ten steps:

1. Establish the profit goal

2. Determine the required volume of sales

3. Estimate the expense for those sales

4. Determine the estimated profit with those sales

5. Compare the estimated profit with the profit goal

6. If unsatisfactory, determine alternatives to improve the profit

7. Determine the cost variables with changes in sales volume

8. Determine how profits vary with changes in sales volume

9. Analyze alternatives

10. Select an alternative and implement the plan.

CHAPTER ELEVEN

ENTREPRENEURS AS LEADERS AND MANAGERS

"The people who get on in this world are the people who get up and look for the circumstances they want, and, if they can't find them, make them."
George Bernard Shaw

Some 200 years ago the French Economist Jean Baptiste Say coined the term "Entrepreneur" from the French verb "Entrepredre", "To Undertake". It was derives from the French words "entre" meaning "between" and "prendre" meaning "to take." It originally describe those who "take the risk" between sellers and the buyers. The word "entrepreneur" has always eluded precise definition, but a pretty close definition is; "An Entrepreneur is someone who takes nothing for granted, assumes change is possible, and follows through; someone who is always thinking about ways to improve on the present reality; someone who believe that "A thought without action is nothing at all."

Leadership is the pivotal force behind successful organizations. Leadership is necessary to help companies develop the vision of what they can be, and to mobilize the company toward that vision. Leadership is the process of influencing and motivating people to work together to achieve a common goal by helping them secure the knowledge, power, tools, and processes to do so.

What is Leadership? The question is simple but the answer is not. Richard Barton, former CEO of Expedia, Inc. responds"

"I'll tell you what it is not. It's not management.

You have all these people with titles that have some kind of *manager* in it, and people talking about *management*. I hate the word. *Management is passive.* Management is minding the store. Management is something that you have to do, that you don't necessarily enjoy doing. *Leadership* is leaning forward, looking ahead, trying to improve, being fired up about what you are doing and being able to communicate that, verbally and nonverbally, to those around you."

Leaders don't lean back, leaders lean forward.

Leadership is concerned with pointing the way. It is focused far more on the destination than on the details of getting there. Entrepreneurs must convey their vision of the firm's future to others in the business so that all involved can contribute to the accomplishment of the mission.

Although leaders must engage in some of the more mundane processes of management, particularly as the business grows, their first job is to create and communicate the vision.

Entrepreneurs are generally thought of as "Risk-Takers". Whereas it is true they do accept risk; those entrepreneurs who have realized the most success have proven to be the most conservative businessmen who constantly "hedge-their-bets" with every new venture. It is not solely being perceived as taking risk that defines an entrepreneur, but his willingness, even eagerness, to accept full responsibility for his actions. That and the entrepreneur's vision of what can be and his strong faith in and persistent pursuit of that vision; coupled with the ability to motivate others to share in and work toward that vision. It is these attributes and traits that truly make an entrepreneur stand out as a leader.

Leadership skills were once thought of as a matter of birth. "Leaders were born, not made." This might be called the "Great Man" theory of leadership. A theory that even George Washington refuted stating: "There are no great men, only great deeds."

The Great Man theory sees power and leadership as being vested in a very limited number of people whose inheritance and destiny made them leaders. Either you had it or you didn't. No amount of learning, experience, or desire could change your destiny. The Great Man theory view has failed to explain leadership. And with apologies to George Washington, so does the notion that great events make leaders out of otherwise ordinary people. Was he, Washington, simply on hand when the colonies decided to overthrow England and form a country? No, he had previously established himself as a leader of men, as a man of vision with the ability to inspire others to share in that vision.

Entrepreneurs are almost by definition leaders. Those to whom we have graced as great leaders of the past: George Washington, Moses, Julius Caesar, Alexander, Winston Churchill, etc., would in today's world and economy posses the potential to be great entrepreneurs. They would still be leaders of men inspiring and motivating others to follow their vision.

Now, as in the past, problems cannot be solved without successful organizations, and entrepreneur types invariably start organizations and those organizations cannot be successful without effective leadership. A business short of capital can borrow money, and one with a poor location can move. But a business short on leadership has little chance of survival. At best it will be left to the controls of efficient clerks, accountants, the "bean-counters".

Businesses must be led to overcome their inbred inertia of trained incapacity and to adapt to changing conditions. The entrepreneur's leadership is what gives the business its vision and its ability to translate that vision into reality. Without this translation, an exchange between leaders and followers, the business has no pulse, no heartbeat, and no life.

The problem with many companies, and especially the ones that are failing, is that they tend to be over-managed and under-led. They may master the ability to handle the daily routine, yet never question whether the routine should be done at all.

There is a profound difference between management and entrepreneur leadership: "To manage" means "to bring about, to accomplish, and to have charge of or responsibility for, to conduct". "Leading" is "influencing, guiding in a direction, course, action, or opinion." The distinction is crucial. "Managers are people who do things right and leaders are people who do the right thing." The difference may be summarized as effectiveness—activities of vision and judgment versus efficiency—activities of mastering routines.

For this reason few managers are entrepreneurs and fewer entrepreneurs are managers. All entrepreneurs view themselves as leaders not bean-counters. They concern themselves with their company's basic purpose and general direction. Their perspective is vision-oriented. They see the forest not the trees. They do not spend their time with the nuts and bolts of the vision, but rather with accomplishing their vision, with doing the right thing.

A message published in the Wall Street Journal by United Technologies Corporation read:

"LET'S GET RID OF MANAGEMENT"

People don't want to be managed. They want to be led.

Whoever heard of a World Manager? World Leader, yes; Educational Leader, Political Leader, Religious Leader, Community Leader, Labor Leader, Business Leader.

They lead. They don't manage.

You can lead your horse to water, but you can't manage him to drink.

If you want to manage someone, manage yourself. Do that well and you'll be ready to stop managing and start leading."

Entrepreneur leaders and non-entrepreneur leaders (government, military, religious, etc.—all whom could no doubt be great entrepreneurs if they so desire) all possess the same four types of people handling skills:

- **Vision**
- **Communication**
- **Trust**
- **Positive Self Image**

Entrepreneurs have consciously or subconsciously realized and captured these skills that are possessed by many but used by few. The skills can be learned by anyone, taught to everyone, and are denied to no one.

Only a few of us will be world leaders, but many of us as entrepreneurs will lead companies.

Vision:

Vision is the creating of focus. All entrepreneurs have urgency, an agenda, and an unparalleled concern with outcome. They are the most results-oriented people in the world. And since results get attention, their vision is compelling and draws others to them. Intensity together with commitment is magnetic and it pulls others to them. Vision grabs. Initially it grabs the entrepreneur and his persistence, commitment, and intensity grabs others to follow. Ray Kroc, founder of McDonalds, defined his vision as "a combination of background, instincts, and dreams."

Communication:

Walt Disney said, "If you can dream it, you can do it." We all will agree that entrepreneur/leader Walt Disney's dream (vision) has become a reality. Yet Mr. Disney idea is incomplete. Believing in one's dream is not enough. There are many people with lots of dreams, visions, and intentions, but without communications none will be realized. Success requires the capacity to communicate the vision, to induce enthusiasm and commitment in others. The very capacities possessed by the successful entrepreneur.

Followers rely upon the leader to define the reality of the vision they are asked to commit. Without this clarity of meaning, they feel the vision is blurry and indistinct; and they will not commit to it no matter how much the leader believes in it. He must convince them to share his vision, to commit and believe in it. The vision is not a reality to the followers until the entrepreneur convincingly communicates it. Like the baseball batter asking the umpire—Is it a strike or a ball? The umpire replies, "It ain't nothing until I call it." The leader must call it for his followers. His call is not simply communicating the facts; facts have to do with technique, but of his philosophy, his thinking about the vision. He prepares them for what is to be accomplished, and what ought to be done to accomplish it. It conveys the "know-why" ahead of the "know-how".

The key to this communication is *integrity* and *credibility*. Communication creates meaning for people. It's the only way any group can get behind the overall goals and vision of a business. Getting the message across is an absolute key. It is what distinguishes the entrepreneur as a leader.

Trust:

Trust is the lubrication that makes it possible for a business to work. It's hard to imagine a company without some semblance of trust operating. Trust applies accountability, predictability, and reliability. It's what sells products and keeps companies alive. Trust is the cement that holds a company's integrity. We trust entrepreneurs who are predictable, whose positions are known, and who keeps at it.

An entrepreneur fosters and relies upon the trust of his followers for he will involve the company and them in taking risk. It is important that his followers share in his vision and stay the course taking the risk with him. The persistence and determination of the entrepreneur must be conveyed to the people he is leading. They must trust in him to follow where he leads.

Positive Self Image:

Leadership is essential a human business and entrepreneurs/leaders work through others to accomplish their vision. To lead others, the management of self is critical. Without self-management and self-awareness, the leader does more harm than good to him and to others. This conveying of self makes leading a very personal affair. Therefore a good feeling of self, a positive self-image is essential and all good entrepreneurs have it. Positive self-regard is not extreme self-importance or egoistic self-centeredness. A true leader is not possessed with self-worship or cockiness. But they know their worth. They trust themselves without letting their ego get in the way. They have self-respect. Leaders display an inner strength and a constant set of values that everyone knows and can rely on. They avoid self-aggrandizement, inspire others, and exhibit a combination of modesty and extraordinary competence.

The successful entrepreneur/leader achieves a positive self-regard by recognizing strengths and compensating for weakness. He does not seek constant approval and recognition from outside of himself. It does not really matter how many people like him, but the quality of work resulting from his collaboration with them does. It is part of the leader's job to take risk, and risk cannot be pleasing to everyone.

Entrepreneurs/Leaders simply don't think about failure. "A mistake is just another way of doing things." Harry Truman would say. "Whenever I make a bum decision, I just go out and make another one."

The successful leader focuses on success, the fulfillment of his vision. Mrs. Wallenda recalls that when her husband, the great tightrope walker Karl Wallenda, fell to his death; "All he thought about for three straight months prior was falling. It was the first time he ever thought about falling, always before he thought of nothing but walking the tightrope." It seemed to her that this time he put all his energy, his focus, into not falling rather than walking the tightrope.

Entrepreneurs/Leaders do not focus on failure. They even avoid the word—using instead such synonyms as: setback, mistake, false-start, and error, bum decision, etc. To focus on failure is to be destined to fail, to fall off the tightrope. Leaders focus on success, as do entrepreneurs.

When failure does occur, the successful entrepreneur uses it as a new beginning, an opportunity to regroup and refocus. "If you not falling down, you not learning."

Entrepreneurs quickly learn that successful leadership is a pull-style rather than a push- style. A pull style of influence works by attracting and energizing people to an exciting vision of the future. It motivates by identification rather than through rewards and punishments. They enroll themselves and others in the vision as attainable and worthy.

LEADERSHIP MYTHS:

In defining entrepreneurs as leaders, it might be helpful to <u>dispel some myths</u> on leadership. These beliefs could discourage potential entrepreneurs from taking charge of their vision and becoming the leaders they need to be.

Leadership is a rare skill:

Nothing can be further from the truth. While great leaders may be rare, everyone has leadership potential. While there are few that will become a world leader, there are literally millions of leadership roles available to entrepreneurs. Leadership opportunities are plentiful and within reach of most people.

Leaders are born not made:

The major capacities and competencies of leadership can be learned. This is not to suggest that it is easy to learn or that it will not require sacrifice. There is no simple formula, no cookbook to learn to be a leader. Instead, it is a deeply human process, full of trial and error, victories and defeats, requiring an entrepreneurial nature.

Leaders are charismatic:

Some are most aren't. Leaders are all human; short and tall, articulate and inarticulate, dressed for success and dressed for failure. Actually charisma is the result, not the cause, of effective entrepreneurial leadership.

Leaders are Doers, Not Thinkers:

Although it is true entrepreneurial leaders tend toward action, they are also thinkers. They are often very methodical, planning their moves carefully. The emphasis placed on the creation of a clear, concise, complete Business Plan (appendix A-5) is an indication thinking entrepreneurs are as important as doing entrepreneurs which makes for effective leadership.

Leaders control, directs, manipulates:

Leadership is not the exercise of power itself as it is the empowerment of others. Leaders translate their entrepreneurial vision into reality by attracting others to align their energy to fulfill a goal. Leaders lead by pulling rather than by pushing, by inspiring rather than by ordering, by enabling rather than by denying or constraining others experience and actions.

Leaders exhibit seven traits. They are seen as *authentic, decisive, focused, caring, coaching, communicative, and improvement-centered.* Leaders articulate a clear, compelling vision for high performance. As Ben Franklin said *"Well done is better than well said."* True leaders avoid letting talk substitute for action.

The Leaders of today are the Entrepreneurs. They are the shakers and doers, the dreamers and builders, the visionaries and motivators, the risk takers and standard bearers of our world. Together they command (lead) a larger army than any General in any war at any time.

Leadership:

"Weak leadership can wreck the soundest strategy."
Sun Tzu

The previous section indicated that corporate culture depends mainly upon the entrepreneur/founder, chief executive officer or the organization leader. The CEO or leader of the organization is not only the creator of the tangible aspects of the company but also of the cultural aspects.

Leadership is the ability to inspire confidence and support among the people who are needed to achieve goals; the art of influencing people by persuasion or example to follow a line of action.

To understand leadership, it is important to grasp the difference between leadership and management. Leadership is included in the functions of management. Those functions are planning, organizing, controlling, and leading. The best managers are always good leaders.

Managers must know how to lead as well as manages. An organization that is not well led as well as well managed will fail. Distinctions between management and leadership are:

- Management is more formal and scientific than leadership. It relies on the necessary skills of planning, budgeting, and controlling. Management is an explicit set of tools and techniques.
- Leadership, in contrast to management, involves having a vision of what the organization can become and where you want it to go.
- Leadership requires eliciting cooperation and teamwork from a network of people and keeping the key people motivated, using every manner of persuasion.
- Leadership produces change. Management is more likely to maintain status-quo and order.
- Leaders tend to transform their organizations, whereas managers just maintain organizations.

- A leader creates a vision to direct the organization. In contrast, managers implement the vision.

Effective leaders also manage, and effective managers also lead.

Leadership Roles:

1. *Figurehead.* Leaders spent some time engaging in ceremonial activities: entertaining clients, being available to outsiders as the organizational representative, official representative at gatherings outside the organization, and escorting official visitors.

2. *Spokesperson.* Emphasis on public appearance, answering letters and formally reporting to individuals and groups outside the organization.

3. *Negotiator.* Making deals and bargaining for needed resources.

4. *Coach.* Coaching team members.

5. *Team Builder.* A key role is building effective teams.

6. *Team Player.* Displays appropriate conduct and example; cooperates and displays loyalty to superiors.

7. *Technical Problem Solver.* Serves as a technical expert or advisor.

8. *Entrepreneur.* Have some responsibility for suggesting innovative ideas to further the business activity of the organization.

9. *Strategic Planner.* Setting direction for the firm, helping the firm deal with the external environment, and developing policies.

> *"If your actions inspire others to dream more, learn more, do more and become more, you are a leader."*
> John Quincy Adams

Leadership is an interpersonal influence exercised in a situation through communication to attain goals. These goals may be organizational, group or personal goals of the supervisor or the personal goals of the subordinate. The following conclusions define leadership further:

- Leadership is a relationship
- This relationship is based on position, power, ability, or some other factor
- The purpose of this relationship is to achieve some goal or objective
- The relationship involves individuals and groups
- In putting the relationship into practice, the organizational situation must be considered utilizing a variety of leadership styles

In general the term "leader" is interpreted by several meanings, but specifically in an organization, it means "management." The supervisory activity which is carried out by the person who oversees the problem solving and increases the productivity and progress of employees; It is the "management" role in business. To be an effective manager, one must have the leadership quality of self-confidence; confidence in decision making and also in the implementation and follow through of those decisions.

Effective leadership involves working with employees to establish suitable, measurable, and reachable goals, action plans, and time lines. A good leader will be able to motivate people with the desire to achieve the goals. The leader/supervisor delegates and provides ongoing guidance and support as the employees complete the desired action plan. Rarely can success be accomplished without the leader's consideration for other aspects of the employees' life, e.g., time dedicated to training, career preferences, and personal strengths and weakness, as well as a balanced personal life. Subsequently a leader is often confronted with a fine line between being a supervisor and a personal confident.

Becoming a Leader:

"The greater danger for most of us lies not in setting our aim too high and falling short; but in setting our aim too low, and achieving our mark."
Michelangelo

A universal theory of leadership contends that certain personal characteristics and skills contribute to leadership effectiveness. General personality traits associated with effective leadership include the following: Self-Confidence; Trustworthiness; Extroversion; Sense of humor; Warmth; and a High Tolerance for Frustration.

Some personality traits of effective leaders are closely associated with task accomplishment. Among them are: passion for the work and for the people; emotional intelligence; flexibility and adaptability; internal locus of control; and courage. Emotional intelligence is composed of five traits: self-awareness; self-regulation; motivation (joy of task); empathy; and social skills.

Certain motives associated with leadership effectiveness are closely related to task accomplishment. Among them are: the power motive, either personal or social; drive and achievement motivation; a strong work ethic; and tenacity and persistence.

Cognitive factors, including mental ability are also important for leadership success. Intellectual ability is closely related to the leadership requirements of possessing knowledge of the business or task, and to being technically competent. Insight into people and situations, including the ability to make effective judgments about business opportunities and problems, also contributes to leadership effectiveness. Farsightedness and conceptual thinking help leaders to understand the long-range implications of actions and policies, and to take an overall perspective.

The issue of whether leaders are born or bred frequently surfaces. A sensible answer is that the traits, motives, and characteristics required are a combination of heredity and environment and for most can be learned.

Leadership is often attributed to a person's charisma. *Charisma* is a Greek word meaning "divinely inspired gift." In leadership, charisma is a special quality of leaders whose purpose, powers, and extraordinary determination differentiate from others. Charisma is also a positive and compelling quality of a person, which creates a desire in others to be led by him or her. Charismatic leaders frequently manage their impressions to cultivate relationships with group members. (Think politicians who actually manipulate their impression to influence others).

Charismatic leaders have a vision (goal, agenda), masterful communication skills, the ability to inspire trust, and are able to make others feel capable and important. They also have an energy and action orientation, are emotionally expressive and warm, romanticize risk, have a self-promoting personality, and emphasize being dramatic and unique.

One does not have to charismatic to be effective. Many non-charismatic leaders are effective. A concern is that some charismatic leaders are unethical and devious; suggesting that being charismatic does not necessary help the organization but themselves. By behaving in a socially responsible manner, charismatic leaders can avoid abusing their influence over others.

Effective leadership requires the right behaviors, skills, and attitudes. Two major dimensions of leadership behavior have been identified: initiating structure and consideration.

Initiating structure is the degree to which the leader organizes and defines relationships by such activities as assigning tasks and specifying procedures.

Consideration is the degree to which the leader creates an environment of emotional support, warmth, friendliness, and trust.

The most effective leaders emphasize both initiating structure and consideration. The existing situation, however, often influences which should be emphasized more.

Leaders have been classified as production-centered rather than employee-centered. Yet, employee-centered leaders have been found to be most effective. Emphasizing both, employee-centered and production-centered, can lead to high productivity.

Many task-related attitudes and behaviors of effective leaders have been identified. Among them are:

1. Adaptability to the situation

2. Direction setting

3. High performance standards

4. Risk taking and a bias for action

5. Hands on guidance

6. Frequent feedback

7. Stability of performance

8. Asking tough questions

9. Strong customer orientation

Many relationship-oriented attitudes and behaviors of effective leaders have also been identified:

1. Alignment and mobilization of people

2. Concert building

3. Inspiration

4. Satisfaction of human needs

5. Making work meaningful for people

6. Emotional support and encouragement

7. Promotion of principles and values

8. Being a Servant Leader

Servant leaders are committed to serving others rather than forwarding their own goals. Aspects of servant leadership include placing service before self-interest, listening to others, inspiring trust by being trustworthy, and focusing on what is feasible to accomplish.

There are three basic explanation of how a person acquires leadership ability.

1. The Trait Theory: Some individuals have built-in leadership qualities in their personalities fostered in childrearing environment and experiences as evidenced in early behavior.

2. The Great Event Theory: A sudden event or crises gives the opportunity for a person to lead others and brings out the extraordinary leadership qualities.

3. The Transformational Theory: This is the most acceptable theory of leadership. Accordingly any person can become a leader through proper training and acquiring the necessary skills.

Leadership style is the consistent pattern of behavior that characterizes a leader. One of the earliest classifications of leadership style places the style on a boss-centered through employee-centered continuum. This suggests that leadership behavior is classified in terms of how much involvement leaders have with people-related versus work-related issues.

The leader selects a style by taking into account forces in the manager, the subordinates, and the situation, and also time pressures. For example, a more employee-centered style is appropriate if employees are independent, competent, and can tolerate ambiguity.

A leadership continuum has three key anchor points: autocratic, participative, and free-rein leadership.

Autocratic leaders retain most of the authority for themselves. Participative leaders share decision making with those concerned. The participative style can be subdivided into consultative, consensus, and democratic leadership. The participative style is well suited to managing competent people, eager to assume responsibility. Yet the process can be time consuming, and some managers perceive it to be a threat to their power; the free-rein leader turns over virtually all authority and control to the group for accomplishments of the goal.

Another important style of leadership is the entrepreneur. The entrepreneur style stems from the leader's personal characteristics, charisma, and circumstances of self-employment. The entrepreneurial style includes these elements: strong achievement drive and sensible risk taking; high degree of enthusiasm and creativity; acting quickly on opportunities; urgency and impatience; visionary perspective; dislike of hierarchy and bureaucracy; preference for dealing with external customers; and an eye on the future.

Male-female differences in leadership have been noted. Women have a tendency toward relationship-oriented leadership, whereas men tend toward command and control, militaristic style.

Rather than searching for the one best style of leadership, managers are advised to diagnose the situation and employees involved, and then choose an appropriate leadership style to match. To be effective, a leader must be able to adapt his or her style to the circumstances.

People are expected to and do respect a true leader. They observed what a leader does, not just says, and determines who he really is and that he is an honorable and trusted leader and not simply self-serving. A good leader must possess a respectable and selfless character to inspire others to follow.

Leaders usually demonstrate six traits which include drive, the desire to lead, honesty and integrity, self-confidence, cognitive ability, and knowledge of the business.

Leaders have drive. They are action-oriented with a high desire for achievement. They receive personal satisfaction from successfully overcoming difficult challenges. They are ambitious with much energy willing to work long hours and week-ends to accomplish their goals. They are persistent and readily accommodate obstacles and even temporary failure to reach the final destination.

Leaders want to lead. They feel compelled and uniquely suited to lead and motivate others. They eagerly accept the responsibility and authority.

Leaders are honest and have high standards of integrity. They must if others are to trust and follow them.

Leaders are self-confident. Again, they must, for if they are not confident in their decisions and actions others cannot be committed to the job and vision. Expecting success is confidence.

Leaders have cognitive ability. A leader must make the right decisions and pick the right path for others to follow for ultimate success. Therefore they must have the knowledge and decision making skills for achievement.

Leaders must know the business they are engaged in. They must know their company, its capabilities, and the industry they operate within. This knowledge assists in making informed decisions to accomplish goals.

Although corporate culture is an invisible and elusive concept, it significantly affects all aspects of corporate life and activities, ranging from the day-to-day routines to corporate strategy. How much mileage an organization can get out of this culture to achieve and maintain leadership and success in its business will depend on how it is nurtured and managed.

The purpose of managerial leadership is to integrate the interests of the individual and the organization. This parallel interest can take the form of translating organizational requirements into how they will affect the individual and the nature of the work to be done; setting the overall goals to be accomplished and the direction to achieve them is important to both the organization and the individual. Vital in this endeavor is also the personal rapport developed between the manager and the individual. The manager's genuine interest and commitment to the success and well-being of the individuals under supervision is essential to the overall job completion.

It should be noted that the leader and the manager may not be the same person. A manager may be a leader and a leader may be a manager; but neither may be the case. A manager is appointed to fill a particular position within the organization with the primary responsibility of attaining assigned objectives. It would certainly be helpful in that appointed if the manager had leadership skills.

A leader, whether appointed as the manager or not, is a uniquely personality phenomenon, in that followers define who is and is not a leader; if a leader has no followers, no leadership exist.

The major difference between leaders and managers lie in their sources of influence and authority. The manager obtains it from the organization and employs it to obtain results from subordinates to achieve prescribed objectives. The leader, who may also derive authority from the organization but not necessarily, exists in a relationship with followers and receives power directly from them. Both the official manager who may also be a leader and the informal leader who may not be the manager, in a well-ran and successful organization, control rewards and punishments appropriate to the purpose of the targeted goals.

The concept of managerial leadership is important because it brings together the roles for more effective task accomplishment, organizational effectiveness, and human satisfaction. A non-leader-manager can manager by fear and without consideration of the well-being of employees attempting to and perhaps meeting formal goals without human satisfaction and destroying morale for other task to be accomplished. But the leader-manager is able to clarify paths of organization and personal goal accomplishment that produces effective and efficient results while fostering a sense of personal and group worth, importance, and success as a functioning team realizing the company's vision.

Effective leaders are outstanding motivators and coaches, and the role of the modern leader and manager emphasizes coaching.

There are three major components of coaching and motivating which is referred to as the expectancy theory of motivation: valence, instrumentality, and expectancy.

The expectancy theory of motivation is based on the premise that the amount of effort people expend depends on how much reward they expect to get in return.

Valence is the worth or attractiveness of an outcome. Very high valences help explain why some people will persist in efforts despite a low probability of payoff.

Instrumentality is the probability assigned by the individual that performance will lead to certain outcomes.

Expectancy is the probability assigned by the individual that effort will lead to performing the task correctly.

Expectancy theory provides guidelines for leaders:
- Determine necessary performance levels
- Make the performance levels attainable
- Train and encourage people
- Make explicit the connection between rewards and performance
- Make sure the rewards are large enough
- Analyze factors that oppose the effectiveness of the rewards
- Explain the meaning and implications of second-rate outcomes
- Understand individual difference in valence
- Ensure that the system is equitable for everyone

Goal setting is a basic process of motivation:
- Specific and difficult goals result in high performance
- Goals must be accepted by group members
- Goals are more effective when they are linked to feedback and rewards
- The combination of individual and group goals is very effective

- A learning goal orientation is effective

Behavior modification is a widely used motivation strategy. Its key principle is the law of effect; behavior that leads to positive effect tends to be repeated, and the opposite is also true. The basic behavior modification strategies are positive reinforcement, avoidance motivation, punishment, and extinction (termination). A guiding principle is that you get what you reinforce.

Rules for effective use of behavior modification are:

- Target the desired behavior
- Choose an appropriate reward or punishment
- Supply ample feedback
- Do not give everyone the same size reward
- Find some constructive behavior to reinforce
- Schedule rewards intermittently
- Give rewards and punishment soon after the behavior
- Change the reward periodically
- Make the rewards visible and punishment known

A major purpose of coaching is to achieve enthusiasm and high performance. Coaching can be regarded as a paradigm shift from traditional management, which focuses on control, order, and compliance. Coaching is a partnership for achieving results. Coaching requires a high degree of interpersonal risk and trust on the part of both sides of the relationship.

Suggestions for improving coaching are:

- Communicate clear expectations
- Focus on specific areas that require improvement
- Listen actively
- Help remove obstacles
- Give emotional support
- Give some advice and gentle guidance
- Gain a commitment to change
- Applaud good results

Management should recognize and foster that each employee has a leadership role no matter their station within the organization. Every employee has the opportunity to demonstrate leadership ability in two major areas of responsibility:

1. The development of sufficient technical job knowledge and skill to satisfactorily perform a job

2. The development of the ability to produce job results by working with and through others.

A creative leader brings forth ideas or things that did not exist previously, or that existed in a previous form. The creative process has been divided into five steps:

- Opportunity or problem recognition
- Immersion (becoming immersed in the idea)
- Incubation (the idea simmers)
- Insight (a solution surfaces)
- Verification and application (idea is supported and implemented).

Distinguishing characteristics of creative people fall into five areas:

- Knowledge
- Intellectual ability
- Personality
- Passion for the task and the experience
- Social habits and upbringing.

Creative people possess extensive knowledge, good intellectual skills, intellectual curiosity, and a wide range of interests. Personality attributes of creative people include a positive self-image, tolerance for isolation, nonconformity, and the ability to tolerate ambiguity and chaos. Passion for the work is related to intense intrinsic motivation. Creative people also enjoy interacting with others. Many creative adults faced family problems during childhood. The right personal characteristic must interact with the right environment to produce creative problem solving.

A major strategy for becoming creative is to overcome traditional thinking, or a traditional mind set. Also, it is necessary to break down rigid thinking that blocks new ideas. A related idea is that creative people engage in lateral thinking in additional to vertical thinking. Lateral thinking, also called horizontal thinking, seeks many different answers to problems, whereas vertical thinking looks for the one best answer.

Specific leadership and management practices to enhance creativity include:

1. Provide intellectual challenge

2. Allow freedom to choose the method

3. Supply the right resources

4. Design work groups effectively

5. Have supervisors encourage creative workers

6. Give and obtain organizational support for creativity.

It is also important to provide loose leadership, and to allow people to pursue absurd ideas without penalty.

Coordination and Control:

> Alice said, "Would you please tell me
> which way to go from here?"
> The cat said, "That depends on where you want to get to."
> Lewis Carroll

Coordination and control is the process by which managers achieve integrated efforts of individuals and groups. To coordinate is to develop unity of action in common purposes. Coordination is one of management's leadership responsibilities. It is often confused with cooperation. No matter how much groups or individuals cooperate they will not automatically have a coordinated effort. Any degree of coordination so achieved is coincidental, and management cannot rely upon coincidence to get results. Although cooperation is always helpful and the lack of it can be destructive, its mere presence is not enough to produce a coordinated effort toward a target result. The extent to which coordination produces a united effort is important for the efficiency of the organization. Poor coordination results in lack of unity, undue confusion, and chaos of directed effort. Unity of effort means that the leadership of management has so arranged the nature and timing of activities that individual and group efforts blend into a harmonious stream of productive actions. This successful leadership achieves coordination by providing the focus around tasks which are divided between individuals and groups and brought together again in a meaningful whole in a common purpose. The degree to which the organization achieves its intended purposes a partial indication of the extent which the chief executive has been able to coordinate the organization's efforts toward that goal.

The idea of control sometimes arouses opposition in societies that value freedom, individualism, and democracy; yet every organization requires it to provide for stability and predictability in the organizational system if objectives are to be accomplished and goals achieved. Many social controls, such as traffic laws, are generally accepted. Control is thus blended into our daily lives so that we seldom recognize how the need for order restricts the autonomy of the individual. An organization is also a society, a community, made up of individuals who have chosen to work together. The members of an organization, by joining the society, implicitly subject themselves to control in order to make their concerted efforts feasible to reach the organization's desired results. Control may be viewed as a process of managerial function. It is the process and system by which managers assure that intended, desired results are consistently and continuously achieved.

Problems with coordination and control arise from constant change, weak passive leadership, and organizational complexities. The source of these problems stem from three aspects: human attributes, functional differentiation, and specialization.

The greater the number of persons involved, the more complicated is coordination and control. Individuals are unique and inclined to serve their own needs before those of the organization. They have their own work habits, approaches to situations, and relationships within and without the organization. They tend to act emotionally with personal behavior that is not always predictable or understood. They also develop self-interest that makes them resistant and reluctant to have their work coordinated. Often in the name of teamwork and coordination to seek reassurance, or simply contact with or notice from superiors, routine question may be pushed to higher levels of management. The manager so plagued by needless decision may begin to feel resentment and contempt toward subordinates further impairing the coordinating effort. These difficulties are addressed by effective control of clarifying authority, responsibility, and designating proper delegation.

Controls are essential for the strength and morale of organizations. All involved, members, workers, and participants, do not like a lack of control because they are not secure about what may happen to them. They fear the caprice behavior of undisciplined managers who due to lack of controls may treat them unfairly. The morale of the organization falls when managers have no measure of discriminating between the hard-working, honest employee and the inefficient laggard.

Human attitudes toward controls greatly affect success of the effort. Some managers, hoping that members' self-correcting influence will suffice, are hesitant to exert controls due to awareness that subordinates may resent control, particularly if viewed as heavy-handed.

Functional interdependencies within the organization dictate the need for coordination, order and controls. The operations of one area, unit, or individual may depend heavily on another. Therefore coordination and control must be exercised by a manager who has a larger scope of authority than those of the participating units. This coordination is necessary to link the interdependent functions together to assure their contribution to the targeted and desired results. Problems arise not only from interdependence of technology and work-flow, but also from conflict over authority and jurisdiction. Coordination of effort becomes difficult when domains become isolated and solidified and rigid barriers grow between them with each trying to perform independent of the others. Consider the operations of sales and production departments in a manufacturing firm. The sales personnel tries to sell all it can to meet and exceed their own goals; left to their own devices, they might commit to more sales than the production department can produce.

Specialization arising out of the complexities of technology and the diversity of tasks and personnel also contributes to coordination and control problems. Specialists believe that they are best to judge the scope and nature of the work they perform, and that they alone are qualified to coordinate and judge each other by professional criteria. However, if specialists are allowed to work without constraint or confinement to restricted missions, the end result is often costly and not related to the desired goal. Control and coordination is needed to direct their efforts productively.

Administration to achieve coordination can be defined as the art of continuously resolving differences. To minimize undesirable conflicts, independent and redundant efforts, and overall disorganization, management can focus on:

1. Clear delegation of authority, responsibility, and accountability

2. Decisions that establish or restore coordinated efforts and communications

3. Establishing coordinating units or individuals to oversee the total effort

Coordination is required both horizontally and vertically in the organization. Clarity of delegated authority and responsibility is important to achieving both directions of involvement.

Vertical coordination harmonizes the work delegated to the various groups or individuals. It is vital to assure that each act in accord with others to achieve joint objectives.

Horizontal coordination pertains to relating the efforts of functional, divisional, or branch units to each other. If the horizontal units, each created for a special and different function, are to work in harmony, each needs to know the expected limits of its authority. Some overlapping of authority may be desirable even if it could produce difficulties of coordination without an overseeing body or person to assure coordination. A committee structure is helpful in the overall analysis and problem solving for better coordination. Ad-hoc temporary committees, which may be appointed for specific purposes, usually have narrow jurisdiction and are dissolved after the mission is completed.

Benefits of committees formed for coordination efforts are:
- The application participative supervision contribute to greater uniformity of direction
- Coordination of long and short term programs
- Flexibility in emergency situations
- Broader experience for managers and interchangeability of management personnel
- Pooling of resources for problem-solving in unclear situations with no obvious answer
- Coordination of related functions, responsibility, and jurisdictions

- Greater acceptance and better execution of decisions due to active participation by those affected

Staff meetings or other group conferences also provide opportunities for coordination and improved understanding of desired objectives if management encourages open discussions for the interchange of ideas, proposals, and solutions.

Delegation alone cannot prevent all failures of coordination control procedures are also required. Management must ongoing observe activities and address lack of harmony problems and duplication of effort as they arise. This will involve continuous, judicious, personal contact with subordinates including observing and checking progress making changes when warranted, and dealing with conflicts to find the reasons for a lack of coordination and cooperation.

Effective control of coordinated efforts is achieved through two interrelated approaches: Overcoming human limitations through education, training, and supervision, and appropriate administration in the form of attention to the control cycle.

This is illustrated by safety problems in a manufacturing plant where accidents cannot be eliminated solely by mechanical means. Although safety devices are important, employees who believe that the devices interfere with their earnings will often ignore them hoping not to be discovered. Some workers like to live dangerously and out of sheer bravado and stupidity will flout safety rules. To improve the attitudes and behavior of workers, managers and supervisors should be trained to be safety minded in order to train subordinates to value accident prevention. Continuous safety education campaigns will use films, posters, meetings, contests, all to increase awareness for a safe work place.

Education and training are valuable ways to improve the human factor for better control and coordination. Employees often like to behave as though control efforts do not apply to them, believing that such measures are good for others but not necessary for them. Management control procedures must be mindful of this employee desire for autonomy while rejecting employees' notion that rules are met to be broken. Coercion or power is not effective in meeting this human problem. The best approach is one that recognizes the dignity and worth of employees, allow their self-expression and participation in decisions that affect them, and enlisting their cooperation by persuasive and educational means.

Controls are most effective when they are least obvious. Management should therefore plan the control effort at the minimum needed. Control methods should be chosen that minimize objectionable features and maximize positive aspects. It becomes more acceptable if part of a general atmosphere of competent, successful work that managers have clearly outlined the reasons for such controls. For example, the order for an additional weekly report; subordinates may object to extra effort, but when explained that the reports would help justify a larger budget which contributes to the overall objective, it is more easily accepted.

Control is best directed at achieving results and should not be aimed at dominating or regimenting employees. The purpose of time clocks, for example, is to establish the habit of punctuality and to be able to plan with confidence work schedules, not to trap employees who may be cheating the company. The focus is not on the workers, but rather on the need for accurate time measurements to assure completion of assigned work responsibilities. Positive control and coordination decisions are preferable, although many situations require the use of censure, reprimand, discharge, and other disciplinary actions.

Coordination and control have similar roots in an organization and pose similar problems. If deficient, the accomplishments of the organizations will suffer. Although a certain degree of coordination and control can be designed into the managerial process, or engineered into the technological system, the executives and managers personal involvement, activity, and attitude are critical to the overall success and acceptance of coordination and control procedures.

The traditional control process includes:

- Establishing goals, standards, or target benchmarks, projection of what you expect to accomplish
- Monitoring those results by observations and budgets to compare actual performance to the desired standards
- Taking corrective action when necessary if the actual performance is not meeting expectations and/or revising projections if it becomes apparent that such objectives are not feasible.

Effective managers and leaders of employees are required to have contradictory skills. They must be a team member and leader yet hard-driven and assertive, both nurturing and coaching yet competitive, assertive, and determined. They must be flexible, cooperative, and creative while also being controlled, stable, and rational. Therefore to be an effective manager, they must master various management skills which support one another, one of which that compliments all others is communication skills—oral, written, and listening.

Managers cannot be successful without being good leaders, and leaders cannot be successful without being good managers. Effective management and leadership are inseparable. Effective managers and leaders do exactly the same things.

The Entrepreneur Process

During an earlier banking career a former customer and business-owner advised that he did not know how to spell entrepreneur, nor did he know what it meant, but everyone said that he was one. He was without formal education but he was a master at his business. An expert in the petrochemical industry with much hands-on technical skill, a dynamic motivator of employees with excellent pragmatic communication skills, and a true leader who was always able to clearly enumerated the objectives before his company and to have others share in the vision of achieving the ultimate goal.

From the conception of the business idea, he and other entrepreneurs followed the entrepreneurial process to become a successful owner-manager by starting, growing, and managing a profitable business. They all had a strong passion for the business with targeted focus on their customers and products/services; demonstrating unfailing persistence and tenacity in pursuit of their vision.

That entrepreneurial process through which a new venture is created and an existing venture is sustained is as follows:

- The decision to become an entrepreneur; to be their own boss and work for themselves, to pursue their own ideas, and to realize the financial rewards
- The development of a successful business idea, to recognize and seize the opportunity, to generate feasibility ideas from

       industry and competitor analysis, and to develop an effective business model

- Taking the steps to move from an idea to an entrepreneurial firm, taking the calculated risks and building a new venture team; writing, rewriting, and revisiting the Business Plan (Appendix A-5), assessing the new ventures financial strengths, viability and sources of funding; overcoming adversity
- Managing and growing the entrepreneurial firm to maturity while maintaining the entrepreneur spirit, innovation, and culture with constant emphasis on the five "Ps" of marketing success (People, Product, Price, Promotion, and Place).

There is no one or simple definition of what an entrepreneur is; most would agree that it is someone who recognizes a marketing opportunity, assembles the resources to seize the opportunity with a willingness to accept the risk in pursuing the vision to create something of value and reap the reward for the effort and sacrifices. Someone with the ability and talent to convince others to join in the effort either with their energy, time, talent, and capital to share in making the dream a reality; the entrepreneur is an innovative visionary with effective communication skills to motivate others to share the vision and endure the sacrifices to reap the ultimate harvest of personal and financial satisfaction.

Surprisingly there are many that answer this call; many seeking opportunity for financial independence, monetary rewards, the recognition and accolades of others, and personal satisfaction. Some with well-planned efforts, carefully thought-out and researched, others, rather carelessly, with little thought toward the feasibility of the vision or to the capital requirements to reach fulfillment of the venture and with what to do, how to manage, if success is realized. Those that start a business with little regard with managing and growing that business, with dangerous inconsideration for all who may follow, join, or do business with the venture is not an entrepreneur but an opportunist. A few do so quite deliberately to seize a momentary personal reward no matter whom else may be hurt, but most are well-intentioned and simply not aware of the difficulties and pitfalls ahead, nor the management and people skills needed to succeed. Failure, often perplexing failure, is the usual result. Quickly the entrepreneur must realize that if this vision is to become a reality, if the venture is to grow profitably with the ability to sustain itself, management skills and a talented team must be acquired.

As a rule entrepreneurs normally do not have the resources to launch an enterprise. They must convince others to participate with money, time, effort, talent, and commitment. To solicit others to join in and to believe in their vision requires some of the management skills and traits necessary to grow and operate the venture. Most notably are communication skills and traits of trust, honesty, and integrity.

All of the boring skills that by the entrepreneur's very nature are contrary to his reason for going into business, to his personality and thinking, are required. He must obtain a working knowledge of them and must surround himself with those who can compliment him with these abilities. Besides the technical skill of the industry entered, which usually all entrepreneurs possess, are the following:

- Writing and Oral Communication
- Business Management
- Time Management
- Listening
- Ability to Organize
- Network Building
- Coaching
- Planning and Goal Setting
- Economic Awareness
- Decision-Making
- Marketing
- Finance
- Accounting
- Negotiation
- Cash-Flow Management
- Business Ethics
- Growth Management
- Leadership
- Persistence
- Innovation
- Flexibility
- Self-Discipline, Awareness, and Control

Michael E. Gerber has written *The E-Myth: Why Most Businesses Don't Work and What to Do About It.* He delineates the differences among the types of persons involved with small businesses:

- The entrepreneur creates a business that is able to work without him. He is a visionary who makes the business unique by imbuing it with a special and exciting sense of purpose, direction, and vision. The entrepreneur's far-reaching perspective enables him to anticipate changes and needs in the market and to initiate action to capitalize on them.
- The manager produces results through employees by developing and implementing effective systems and, by interacting with and supporting employees, enhances their self-esteem and abilities to produce the desired results. The manager actualizes the entrepreneur's vision through planning, motivation, implementation, and analysis.
- The technician performs specific tasks according to systems and standards management developed. The technician not only gets the work done but also provides input to supervisors for improvement of those procedures.

Gerber contends that most small business "don't work, their owners do." He believes that today's small business owner works too hard at a job that he has created for himself rather than working to create a business. Thus, most small businesses fail because the owner is more of a "technician" than an "entrepreneur" working in the business rather than on the business.

The E-Myth is that today's business owners are not true entrepreneurs who create businesses but merely technicians who now have created a job for themselves. The solution to the myth lies in the owner's willingness to begin thinking and acting like a true entrepreneur: to imagine how the business would work without him. In addition to working in the business, the owner must begin to work on the business.

The entrepreneur launching a new venture and growing an existing business must be achievement oriented and customer driven, enjoys taking control of his/her own destiny and assumes responsibility for their decisions. They usually dislike repetitive routine tasks but do enjoy a challenge. They are persistent in their pursuit with much energy and imagination to see what others cannot. They are willing and comfort with moderate calculated risk which they can perceive as being transform into the dream they aspire to create no matter how intangible it may appear to others. Most importantly, through learned skills or natural charisma, they know how to inspire and lead others to join in their quest.

An example of eight **non-**entrepreneurial profiles, those that have great difficulty in starting, growing, and managing a business and generally never understanding why they have failed are detailed in *Success*—March 1986- *Eight Demons of Entrepreneurship.*

Shotgun Sam: An entrepreneurial type who quickly identifies new promising business opportunities but rarely, if ever, follows through on the opportunity to create a successful venture.

Simplicity Sue: An entrepreneurial type who always thinks everything is a lot simpler and feels one can create a successful business through one or two easy solutions. She is usually a great salesperson. This type can make the most improbable deal seem possible.

Prima Donna Paul: He is so in love with his idea that he feels everyone is out to take his idea and take advantage of him. This paranoia does not allow any trust to be given or help to be given.

Ralph the Rookie: An entrepreneur who is well grounded in theory but lacks real-world experience.

Meticulous Mary: A perfectionist who is so used to having things under control that she cannot manage during a catastrophe and cannot handle periods of ambiguity and chaos.

Underdog Ed: He is not comfortable with actually transforming the idea into a tangible business success. He likes to attend seminars and discuss problems but does not like putting things into action and is often "paralysis by analysis." He would need a strong managerial team which he probably cannot afford at this time.

Hidden Agenda Harry: He does not have the right motives and objectives for starting a new venture.

Inventor Irving: An inventor more than an entrepreneur, who is more concerned with the invention itself rather than creating and sustaining a business.

Entrepreneur Traits vs. Bureaucratic Traits

Entrepreneur	Bureaucrat
Controls own fate	others control fate
Looks for opportunities	Looks for risk
Profit Center focus	Cost Center focus
Action—self-oriented	Action—forced upon them
Customer driven	Product driven
Can always make a living	Career is #1
Attitude against constraints	Builds constrains
Looks for reward	Fears punishment
Creates value	Manages resources
Let's do it	let's talk about it
Overcomes weakness	Maximizes strengths
Keeps it simple	makes it complex
Realistic	Unrealistic
Creates a winning environment	No winning syndrome
Loves the journey	waiting for retirement

Innovative suggestions to generate a new venture idea:

1. Borrow, improve, and expand upon existing products or services. Perhaps specialize on one or two features of other market offerings. To quote Salvador Dali **"Good artist borrow; great artist steal."** It was good enough for Steve Jobs of Apple Computer who built on unused Xerox technology.

2. Combine two related business ideas into one to create a new market opening. e.g. dinner and a movie, dry cleaning and tailoring, car wash and lube change, haircut, makeup, and manicure, work-out and gym apparel and equipment, etc.

3. Begin with a problem. Good business ideas usually address unresolved problems you and other people have with existing businesses.

4. Recognize a new trend (fad) and go with it. Such may be a short-lived opportunity but could be very lucrative. e.g. The pet rock, hula-hoops, teenage jewelry, etc.

5. Analyze a product to see how you can inexpensively make it "green." Currently a great deal of effort is dedicated to protecting the environment.

6. Keep abreast of new technology.

These are only a few options but if you are alert to whatever circumstances and situations you encounter, other opportunities may present themselves.

Steps in the Entrepreneurial Process

Decision to become an Entrepreneur

> To be their own boss
>
> To pursue their own ideas
>
> To realize financial rewards

Developing Successful Business Ideas

> Opportunity recognition and generation of ideas
>
> Feasibility analysis
>
> Industry and competitor analysis
>
> Developing an effective business model

Moving from an Idea to an Entrepreneurial Firm

> Building a new venture team
>
> Assessing a new venture's financial strength and viability
>
> Preparing a proper ethical and legal foundation, and appropriate form of Business ownership

Writing a Business Plan

Getting financing or funding

Managing and Growing an Entrepreneurial Firm

Marketing Issues, the 5 "P's"-

(Product, Price, Promotion. Place, People)

Importance of Intellectual Property

Preparing for and evaluating the Challenges of Growth

Strategies for Growth—Franchising

The four main characteristics of successful entrepreneur managers are:

1. Passion for the Business
2. Customer and Product focus
3. Tenacity and Persistence despite failure
4. Execution Intelligence

Eight Tips for Entrepreneurs

1. Work for Self
2. Get Organized and Communicate
3. Take risk
4. Innovate
5. Seize Opportunity
6. Overcome Adversity and don't take No for an Answer
7. Sell; ABC (Always Be Closing)
8. Business Can Be War

CHAPTER TWELVE

MANAGEMENT

The Management Process

"If everything seems under control, you're just not going fast enough."
Mario Andretti

The pursuit of entrepreneurial management within and without a corporate structure has arisen from several growing problems:

- Increased global competition
- Economic changes
- Seeking greater efficiency through downsizing
- Innovations and improvements in the market
- Weakness and stagnation of traditional methods of management
- Lost on innovative-minded and talented employees due to the constraints of bureaucratic organizations
- Ethics considerations

These problems must not simply be faced and endured, but must actively be attacked as a new revolutionary mindset. Gary Hamel enumerates in *Leading the Revolution,* 1991, "I am no longer a captive to history. Whatever I can imagine, I can accomplish. I am no longer a vassal in a faceless bureaucracy. I am an activist, not a drone. I am no longer a foot soldier in the march of progress. I am a Revolutionary."

Any business enterprise is simply a collection of people working together to achieve a common purpose. They are directed, supervised, coordinated and motivated by a manager who may be the founding entrepreneur, owner or one of the owners, or someone delegated by them. An effective and good manager supports and is responsible for the work of those supervised. The manager accomplished the desired common goals through the efforts of others. The good manager will utilize a team leader, coach, approach supplying critical support and assistance to help others achieve success in their work effort which enables him/her to achieve assigned objectives.

Therefore to the process of management are the planning, organizing, leading, and controlling the efforts of others and the resources available to accomplish performance goals. **Planning** is setting the objectives and determining how to accomplish them; **Organizing** is arranging the work effort, assignments, people, and resources to achieve the objectives; **Leading** is motivating and inspiring people to apply their best efforts in accomplishing the goals; and **Controlling** is monitoring and measuring results and taking corrective actions if necessary to achieve desired objectives.

To accomplish excellence in the overall performance of the organization, it behooves the entrepreneur to create a corporate culture and ethical values that enables the success of those goals.

Corporate Culture:

Culture is generally defined as the way of doing things in a particular society. When organizations have a unique way of doing things, they have their own corporate culture. This culture is developed, fostered, and evolved over time. Today, organizations try to create a corporate culture with a distinct identity or to mould the behavior of their members into a predetermined corporate culture identity. The common notion is that only giant, global organizations can afford to have a corporate culture. This view is not totally correct. One can find cultures in relatively small organizations as well as the large organizations.

Most agreed that the field of management must be viewed in a broad perspective because of the environmental influence on management practices. The cross-cultural study of management involves the study of management cultural variables, which tend to have an impact on management practices in different cultures. Managing and organizing are culturally dependent because they do not consist of making or moving tangible objectives, but of manipulating symbols which have meaning to the people who are managed.

Observations seem to indicate that the success of many organizations is related to having a strong corporate culture within the organization. Such a culture provides a foundation for the policies and practices of the organization.

William Ouchi, *1982,* identifies the following as the features of Z type, a hybrid between American and Japanese type of organizations.

- A place for criticism and honesty
- Trust, friendship, and working together
- Teamwork
- Management by walking around
- Valuing people as resources.

Any management strategy, in order to be successfully implemented, must fit the culture of the organization. The seven "S" variables most listed in the management framework are:

- Strategy
- Structure
- Systems
- Style
- Staff
- Shared Values
- Skills (Waterman, 1982).

The Seven-S framework views corporate culture as a function of the seven variables. If a strategy of an organization fails or runs into a problem, it is because the strategy doesn't fit one or more of the seven variables. All are interrelated. While the staff variable refers to people in the organization, the skills variable refers to their capabilities. The style variable is the way management acts and behaves. Shared values are the beliefs commonly shared by many people in the organization. The structure variable provides authority-responsibility relationships, systems variable indicates the processes, procedures, and flows involved in getting the desired results done. Strategy relates to the way to shape the corporate culture.

A better understanding of the mechanics and dynamics of an organization can be achieved through the culture that prevails in the organization.

Meaning of Corporate Culture:

The term culture has been borrowed from anthropology where there is no consensus on its meaning. Just as societies have their own culture, business organizations as entities also have their own culture. Culture is the collection of common views, expectations, values, and beliefs of the members of the organization. The values, beliefs, and norms usually involve the following aspects:

- The basic goals of the organization
- The preferred means by which those goals should be attained
- The role and responsibilities assigned to each member in the organization
- The behavior pattern required to perform those roles and fulfill those responsibilities
- A set of rules or principles which relates to the preserving of the organizational identity and integrity

These values and norms which constitute the corporate culture are not in writing but are understood by all members of the organization. Even the new members get to know them either through formal training programs and orientations or from their peers. When members of an organization share the same values, they will become more cohesive and committed to the shared goals of the organization. Such commitment is essential for better performance and productivity improvement. Although it may not be visible, corporate culture exists and influences people and activities in organizations.

Corporate culture can be summed up as a way of doing things in an organization, which is developed and fostered over a period of time through various socialization processes, some of which are formal while others are informal.

Formation of Corporate Culture:

In the process of forming a corporate culture, the role of the entrepreneur/ founder or the chief executive is important. It has been believed that the founder and/or the chief executive officer are not only a creator of the tangible aspects of the organization but also of the cultural aspect of the corporation.

Most successful organizations use a systematic approach in bringing new members into the corporate culture. Pascle, 1985, after examining a number of companies with a strong culture, suggests that the following steps in socializing new members into the corporate culture:

- Exercising care in selecting entry-level candidates; specific traits that are tied to the success of the company are sought by looking deeper into the candidates
- Subjecting the new member to humility-inducing experiences in the initial period which will provide an opportunity to question prior beliefs
- Practical training leading to mastery of one of the core disciplines of the business using promotions as incentives
- Focus on measuring results and rewarding individual performance
- Adapting to corporate values which will build trust between the individual and the organization
- In order to validate corporate culture, folklore is reinforced and events in the history of the company are interpreted
- Those who move up fast are used as models to be emulated

Many companies succeed in creating a sound corporate culture through the training program which communicates the culture by a variety of devices. First there is the context, which includes a careful blend of the organization's philosophy, vision and mission statement, and established personnel policy and procedures. A second element is the participation of senior officers in the training program designed to formulate and reinforce the culture.

The managing, adapting, and, if necessary, the changing of a culture is not simple. It requires constant assessments and monitoring by examining the external and internal environment. Such examination reveals the nature of changes that are anticipated or are taking place in the environment which may force the organization to adapt or modify the corporate culture accordingly. A relaxed attitude of management that believes that they have a strong culture built over the years that will cope with any and all situations is risky. A static culture may very well indicate a continuation of old, inflexible, inefficient ways.

Changing culture is a very critical matter as one does not want "to fix what is not broken." However if change is needed and called for it must be undertook with a great deal of thought and planning. Unfounded assumptions, carelessness, and taking things for granted in changing corporate culture may have disastrous consequences ranging from subtle protests to open revolt within the organization. Such poorly planned and casual cultural changes will impact an organization by a possible loss of their best people to competitors, a decline in productivity and profits, and a loss of reputation and image in the market place threatening its very survival.

However effective culture changes when warranted can achieve excellence within the organization. When management has the skills to know how to monitor the environment both within and without the organization and become aware when a changes is necessary an ailing corporate culture can be turnaround to achieve corporate success.

Basically managing corporate culture involves identifying the existing norms, values and beliefs, comparing them to the desired norms, values and beliefs, and planning and implementing the socialization process systematically.

Senior management must bear the responsibility for managing and changing corporate culture. Too often this important responsibility is delegated to a human resources department which accepts it as a routine procedure. Senior managers need to cultivate and oversee the cultural values of the organization by their devoted attention and behavior. Employee's behavior will consequently follow. Corporate culture emanates from the top. The way senior management behaves, the way they lead, and the way they think, sets the climate and ultimate culture for the organization.

Maintaining a strong corporate culture results in a number of benefits to the organization as well as to its members; it provides a solid foundation and a positive climate for productivity improvements. The culture determines both the efficiency and effectiveness of the organization. Culture by itself does not directly increase profit or decrease cost, but it influences the behavior and work habits of the people in the organization which can impact profits and cost.

Milton Moskowitz, 1985, identifies the following as characteristics of the working place in good, successful companies not found in underperforming companies:

- Make people feel that they are part of a team
- Encourage open communication
- Stress on quality
- Profit sharing
- Reduce rank distinctions.

Management Skills

"Until someone has a small business, they have no comprehension of how hard it is. People, who start businesses from scratch, if they survive, are the toughest people on the face of the earth.
Sue Szymczak, Safeway Sling

A skill is the ability to translate knowledge and information into action that achieves a desired objective.

Three different kinds of managerial skills have been enumerated: technical, human, and conceptual. The requisite degree of each varies depending on the level in the management hierarchy.

- Technical skill is the ability to use the techniques, procedures, and tools of a specific field. This skill is particularly important at the first line of the organization where the manager needs to know how the work is done.
- Human skill is the ability to communicate, motivate, and lead individuals and groups. An understanding of human relations and organizational behavior is essential to managers in the middle ranks of management. These managers are concerned with directing lower-level supervisors and other

> middle managers therefore their jobs are more human than technical in nature. The ability to persuade, negotiate with, and coordinate the activities of others is the key to success.
> - Conceptual skill is the ability to plan, coordinate, and integrate all of the organization's activities and interest. It is most important at the upper levels of the organization where long-range forecasting and planning are the principal activities.

Management is both an art and a science. As an art, management requires the use of behavioral and judgmental skills that cannot be quantified the way scientific information can.

Management is a science as well. It requires the use of logic and analysis. The manager arrives at a solution by observing, classifying, and studying facts. This scientific aspect of management has been enhanced by use of the computer and mathematical software.

<u>When dealing with people, management is approach as an art; when dealing with things, it is approach as a science.</u>

Successful managers will demonstrate the following skills:

- Communication—Good communication is the ability to deliver and share goals, ideas, and results clearly and concisely in both oral and written formats; and to receive information and feedback.
- Teamwork—Ability to be effective as a team leader and team member, able to participate in consensus building, conflict resolution, and negotiation.
- Self-Management—Ability to evaluate oneself, to modify behavior when necessary, and accomplish responsibilities and job obligations
- Leadership—Ability to motivate and support workers to achieved desired organizational goals

The manager's job is dynamic and ever changing. In *The Practice of Management*, Peter Drucker has articulated that "I'm not comfortable with the word *manager* anymore, because it implies subordinates." The rationale is that the manager today is a team leader, coordinator, coach, and facilitator more often than commander and a control person.

Decision-Making:

Decision making is every manager's primary responsibility and perhaps main challenge. The manager's decision are based upon and determined by his personal skills and abilities, and also by the resources and constraints provide by the organization and its environment. Collectively, the manager's decision gives form and direction to the work of the organization.

It is in decision-making that is management best illustrated as both an art and a science. On the side of art lie the intuitive judgment, personalities, and abilities of the decision-maker; as a science the decision's concepts and techniques are often based upon computers, research, and behavioral science.

The simplest view of making decisions is that of choosing one of several alternatives. Sometimes the result is intangible, but most often it produces tangible results, such as changes in plans, policies or procedures. Upon reviewing and analyzing all availability information even a decision not to decide is still a decision made when the status-quo is preferable to the uncertainty of changes.

Viewing decision making solely as a choice among alternatives is too simplistic as complex decision are not unique, isolated, repetitive events. Focusing only on the moment of choice among alternatives leads to a false concept of decision, and "ignores the whole lengthy complex process of exploring and analyzing that precedes the final moment" (Simon, 1960).

Major decisions involve a series of related and increasing detailed decision as time unfolds and consequences appear. The influence of time reveals that the problem develop in the past, information is accumulate and the need for a decision is perceived; alternatives are found in the present and a choice is made; the decision is carried out in the future, reviewed, evaluated, and, if necessary, changed.

Alternatives are analyzed under one of three sets of conditions: Certainty, Risk, and Uncertainty. Under certainty, the decision maker knows in advance the outcome of the decision. Under risk, a decision maker uses personal experience or secondary information to estimate the likelihood of outcomes. Under conditions of risk, expected values are used to analyze the positive or negative outcomes possible from the feasible alternative selected. If there is not enough information to ascertain clear alternatives or to estimate risk, decisions must be made under the condition of uncertainty; in doing so they rely on intuition and creativity. Intuition is derived from previous experience, accumulated judgment, and a "gut-feeling."

Management has identified the "Seven Ds" in decision making:

1. Define the problem

2. Describe and collect needed information

3. Develop alternatives

4. Develop agreement among those involved

5. Decide which alternative is best

6. Do what is indicated (implementation)

7. Determined whether the decision was a good one and follow up

Critical decisions require months of planning, fact gathering, and analysis. But even when immediately responding to an urgent situation, background conditions have influenced the mental process. The urgency has merely altered the timing.

Decisions, once made, require a degree of permanence described as commitment to realize success. Commitment is necessary for the time required to carry out a decision and to observe its consequences. Once made, a decision provides an element of stability for the organization and its members. Capital is often invested adding to the commitment. Decisions are frequently interrelated, so that a change in one area will affect other areas, e.g., a credit decision may affect sales, which in turn affect production, purchasing, warehousing, and insurance. Such a decision, once cleared with the affected areas, requires a general acceptance that reinforces commitment, for all but the most routine decisions are hard to change or reverse.

Management functions decisions are as follows:

Planning—What are our long term goals?

What are the best strategies to achieve those goals?

What are our short term objectives to achieve long term goals?

Organizing—How many employees should report directly to me and/or be delegated to others?

How much centralization and decentralization should we have?

Is our organization structure and chain-of-command appropriate or should it be changed, and when?

Leading—How do we motivate employees?

What is the best leadership style, should it changed given different situations?

When is it right and productive to stimulate inner conflict?

Controlling—What should be controlled?

How should it be controlled?

What type of information system should we have and how and what information should be disseminated?

Commitment is not equivalent to support. Support may exist while a decision is tried, but it may fade while commitment continues. Commitment can develop without support through the general expectation of the authority system. The manager's role as a leader often calls for persuading subordinates to follow and carry out decisions that are unpopular. He must try to gain their support if not their commitment. Sometimes the commitment is inevitable and irreversible, as in the merger of two businesses which do not work and, perhaps, is a senior management mistake in judgment.

Eventually release from commitment may follow from a decline in support, or the recognition of new factors that reduce the impact of that commitment. Ultimately, commitment rests on the judgment of managers and on the impact of forces that reveal the wisdom or error of a decision so that pressures for change arise. As the need for change increase, the constraint of commitment fades.

It is helpful to distinguish between organizational and personal decision, and basic and routine decisions.

Organizational and Personal Decisions:

In their official formal roles, managers make organizational decisions which are frequently delegated to others. They usually call for supporting decisions by others and start chains of behaviors to complete the work of the organization. Although decisions are largely intended to further the interests of the organization, the decision maker's personal interests and those of the organization are often intertwined. Agency theory has indicated that throughout their careers managers will make decisions which pertain to their individual interest. Most such decision will also affect the organization sometimes negatively.

Many managers view their personal and their organizational decisions separately, not allowing personal beliefs to intervene in carrying out organizational objectives. By classifying the decision as organizationally required, "just business," they are consciously free to make decisions that they would not on personal ethics; e.g. tolerating racist hiring as a company's policy while personally espousing racial equality.

Basic and Routine Decisions:

Basic decisions are unique, one-time decisions, involving long-range relatively permanent commitments and large capital investments—decisions in which a mistake could hurt the organization. They are difficult to decide in view of environment uncertainties. An example is a decision concerning a branch or plant location. To select a site involves the investigation and analysis of many complex social and economic factors: market, population, transportation, suppliers, power availability, employees, capital and return on investment, and others. The investment will be large and relatively permanent, an error would be costly.

Most policy decisions at senior levels are basic decisions, as are decisions on the organization structure, selection of key executives, and capital expenditures. Such basic decisions provide the context in which routine decisions are made.

Routine decisions, which require relatively little deliberation or are made repetitively tend to have minor impact on the welfare of the organization if in error. They are also relatively easily corrected. Standard procedures can be established for making a large number of such decisions which require little forethought, investigation, and analysis. Many, perhaps most, decisions are routine and repetitive.

Problem Solving:

*"The formulation of a problem is often
more essential than its solution."*
Albert Einstein

To a large degree, decision making is directed toward solving problems. Problem solving is an important generator of decision making behavior, but one must not exaggerate its importance. Emphasis on problem solving stresses the need for answers, whereas it may be more important to find the right question, or to prevent problems from ever occurring. Moreover, the problem solving decision tends to be the unimportant, routine, short-range, tactical decision rather than the important, strategic, long-range decision. Therefore, problem solving should be broadly conceived as more than mere arriving at an answer.

If undue rewards go to problem solvers, there is a danger that some will create or find problems solely to win such rewards wasting efforts and resources to solve false or unnecessary problems. Never-the-less, appropriate problem solving should be recognized and rewarded.

Four steps to solving problems:

1. Define the problem—Differentiate fact from opinion, specify underlying causes, involved everyone for information, state the problem explicitly, determine whose problem it is and what does it affect

2. Generate solutions—specify alternative solutions, involve all in generating alternatives and build on their ideas if feasible, outline both short and long-term alternatives

3. Evaluate alternatives and select one—Evaluate systematically relative to goals, evaluate the main effect and side effect of consequences, state the selected alternative clearly and concisely

4. Implement the selected solution and follow up—Provide opportunities for feedback from all involved, establish an

ongoing monitoring system, evaluate results on the solution and eradication of the problem.

Perception and definition of a problem are essential but alone are not sufficient for effective decisions. Positive and corrective action can only follow when there is sufficient consensus that a problem exists that warrants action. It is imperative to define a problem in terms that makes action possible. Suppose that sales are lagging and profits are declining as expenses remain fixed. To say that the company is losing money is a description of the situation, a symptom, and not the cause; it is not an analytical statement of the problem. To correct the situation, the cause must be describe and analyze. The problem can then be put into the form of a logical, solvable hypothesis.

The hypothesis gives direction to information gathering that leads to testing it. Information is gathered by observation, interviewing, questionnaires, special investigative reports, and meetings of affected and interested parties close to the problem, industry and trade studies, and any other pertinent sources. Fact findings from those close to the problem are particularly desirable, although it must be perceived objectively for those people may have bias opinions. Even when a problem is well defined, there may be difficulty in ascertaining which facts are relevant and as to how they may apply. However, it is important to get as much significant data as economical and timely efforts permit.

The effectiveness of a decision cannot be known with certainty in advance, nor are there concrete measures of the quality of the decision. Bad or wrong decision become evident through their undesirable consequences and brilliant, outstanding decisions are recognized by the desirable consequences. Between these extremes lies a wide range of routine decision making that sustains an organization's day-to-day operations. Mintzberg (1973) describes four key decision making roles of business managers for effective decision making:

1. The Entrepreneur

2. The Disturbance Handler

3. The Resource Allocator

4. The Negotiator

In the role of entrepreneur, the manager is the initiator and designer of the controlled change in the organization. Decisions emerging from this role involved exploiting opportunities, evolving strategies, and solving broad, long-range problems. The entrepreneurial decisions lead to the improvement of some aspects of organizational activities. It is made at the discretion of the manager on his team.

The role of disturbance handler is needed to deal with events that demand the attention of managers. A crisis occurs or a problem becomes acute. The manager must deal with an involuntary situation, which in part may be beyond his control. Forces beyond the manager have initiated the situation. For example, a conflict may have arisen between two subordinates which must be resolved to prevent the difficulty from getting worse affecting the organization's work.

The resource allocator's role involves important choices that reflect basic strategies. Resources such as, capital, people, time, materials, and equipment, are scarce and are demanded by competing interest. The decisions of the resource allocator include time scheduling, work programming, and the authorization of actions, projects, and programs.

The fourth role of negotiator represents a bargaining function. The manager must deal with other managers, with special groups, and with representatives of other organization. Bargaining with employee association or labor union, and settling customer's complaints are such examples. The manager must have the authority to resolve the issues under negotiation, committing resources if necessary. The negotiator role may often be performed in conjunction with the other roles. It may accompany that of disturbance handler and the entrepreneurial role with that of resource allocator.

The following factors affect the quality of decision making:
- The environment of the decisions
- The personalities of the decision makers
- The timing and communication of decisions
- The participation of those affected by the decisions

Environment of the Decisions:

"Success isn't permanent, and failure isn't fatal."
Mike Ditka, football coach

Decision making behavior has a contagious quality that arises from the way decisions relate to each other, and from the tendency of managers to emulate their superiors and other managers. Often an atmosphere of indecisiveness engulfs an organization, paralyzing the actions of managers fearful of failure. This can be prevented by vigorous leadership of senior management. A prevailing case would be a large corporation forced into reorganization due to years of losses. A turnaround new president moved quickly to supplant decision making lethargy with vitality. By exercising strong personal leadership and example, he demanded timely and appropriate decisions from the managers. Clearly a key factor in the decision environment is the expectations by senior management that expeditious and pragmatic decisions will be made at the right time and place by the right people. Decisiveness on the part of senior management will help create decisiveness throughout the ranks of the organization.

Authority is a strong and pervasive influence in the decision making environment. It is important to note that authority is also one of the limitations in making decisions. If the nature and the amount of authority is unclear, the managers decisions tend to be uncertain, erratic, or nonexistent. Rather than endure negative consequences, criticism, or challenge, the manager becomes too cautious and slow to decide. Valuable time will be wasted or the time for the decision opportunity will pass as the manager looks for ratification from above or to assure the favorable reaction of others.

The environment for decisions is both internal and external. Internally, managers work in a socio-psychological environment, interacting with others. The internal environment includes not only physical elements, but also the intangibles of human interaction among executives and employees, and the network of both formal and informal authority and communication.

The external environment consist of the social, political, and the economics locally, nationally, and internationally, as well as the actions and decisions of competitors, the evolution of science and technology, the financial community, and governmental regulations and controls.

Personalities of Decision Makers:

The personal and psychological factors that influence decisions include status, prestige, feelings of security or insecurity, and personality elements such as temperament, intelligence, energy, and emotions.

Managers vary with respect to temperament. Some are disturbed when they cannot reach a decision quickly, and others debate with themselves and analysis endlessly over possible actions to take. Some are very conservative, patient, and slow to decide; others are brash, reckless, and vigorous in making up their minds. Both impulsive eagerness and unnecessary delay are disastrous to effective action. The manager's personal profile of competence, confidence, skills, attitudes, aspirations, and career objectives are all contributing factors.

Timing and Communication of Decisions:

Timing of a decision and its communication is important not only for the manager but also to their subordinates and associates. Decisions are the mechanics of strategy and its revelation, when and how, reveals that strategy to participants and competitors alike therefore the timing of announcements should be done with care and skill. If the announcement of a decision is too long delayed to participant, they may have difficulty adjusting to it. In the meantime, the informal "grapevine" will begin to function and may distort the information causing undue concerns. Decisions altering actions and strategy affect the spirit and morale of participants. Those involved like knowing of it in a timely manner to better carry out their part. Tactical managers should learn of decisions from senior management prior to their subordinates and for the most effective implementation should be the primary communication of the decision downwards.

Central to timing and communication is a sensitivity of the degree of urgency involved and to the proper fit into other events of the organization; and an awareness of how the probable consequences of the decisions' actions will be incorporated into the overall timing plans and strategy of the organization. Public announcement should also be timed as to not give competitors a heads-up advantage as well as allowing all internal participants prior knowledge of any change in strategy.

However some decisions carry complex political, organizational or personal, connotations for those involved including the decision-maker. For example in the area of internal promotions; If an executive is being promoting bypassing other executives, the announcement may be delayed until a way has been found to deal with the bypassed executives who may be disappointed and angry. The essential dilemma is whether to risk the disadvantage of an information leak and subsequent rumors, or to face openly that a promotion decision is imminent.

Equally important is deciding how to communicate the decisions that do not arouse antagonism. Often those affected may question the source and authenticity and immediately wonder what ulterior reasons prompted the action. Announcements, particularly structural changes in management, should be clearly stated, carefully distributed, and include rationale that shows sensitivity to the consequences. Such methods should contribute to the important participation of all concerned as their cooperation and influence will be an essential contribution to the success of the decision.

Participation can exist in degrees ranging from little or none to extreme commitment and involvement in the decisions. The extent in which participation exist usually depends upon the willingness of managers to listen and be aware of subordinate concerns, management skills and style, company philosophy, and the prevailing company culture. Organizations with high participation acceptance are considered democratic in their leadership, while those with minimum acceptance are usually authoritarian.

In an authoritarian company, direction and control are firmly lodged at the top of the organization. Decisions are made primarily unilaterally by one or a few top executives, and when communicated, unquestioned obedience is expected. Democratic organization gives a voice and responsibility to lower echelons in tactical decision making. The idea of democratic participation does not allow managers to abdicate authority or avoid accountability and responsibility, nor does it mean subjecting decisions to a vote or the dilution of supervision. But the management of decisions to encourage subordinate growth, development, innovation and self-expression will contribute to their commitment and participation.

COMMUNICATION

*"To understand is hard. Once one
understands, action is easy."*

Sun Yat-sen

The key to a healthy work relationship within an organization is based on managing its communications. It has been concluded that management's number one problem is a lack of effective communications. Communication is a two way process. An employee cannot work with all of his competence, ability, intelligence, and enthusiasm if the real purpose of the job is not known to him. Equally important is the opportunity for the employee to communicate and contribute to ideas and opinion relating to job performance before the manager makes the decision to assign it.

Communication is the process of trusting employees and advising them about the job, the business, and the future plans for them, the vision and mission of the organization. Effective communication requires a competent sender and an understanding receiver. There is no communication if the receiver does not understand the message. Feedback, both positive and negative, completes the communication cycle.

Committees, conferences, meetings, group discussions, and distribution of written memorandums are methods by which good horizontal communication can be fostered. Communications among teams are also effective and are usually centralized or decentralized. Centralized team members all consult and communicate through one individual to solve problems or perform task. In decentralized teams, all communicate with each other and upon reaching consensus move to the project at hand. The centralized approach is generally much faster and more efficient.

There are several barriers to good communication within an organization which must be identified in order to overcome them.

- Distance: The physical difference between management and the employees decreases the chance of face-to-face communication. This lack of face-to-face interchange leads towards misunderstandings of the project, job, mission, and vision of goals and objectives to be accomplished. Distance will also make it difficult to clarify and correct these misunderstandings.

215

- Differences: A major barrier to effective communication is the tendency to make value judgments on the statement of others. Managers and employees tend to interpret information and message in light of their own views, values, opinions, and backgrounds rather than objectively.

- Semantics: The structure of the language and words used can lead to misrepresentations of the true meaning and nature of the intended communication. Words with multiple meanings or confusing context can lead to misinterpretation of the intended message.

- Lack of Trust: Based on past experience, if a subordinate is reluctant to report bad news due to the possible unfavorable reflection on him, then such information will be withheld.

- Inaccessibility: If management is not available, too busy, for discussion or consultation then a communication breakdown will result. Subordinate motivation will be affected and rather than seeking management direction will relied on a trial and error approach to situations.

- Lack of Clear Responsibilities: Lack of duties, responsibilities, and authority results in status and role ambiguities.

- Personal Incompatibility: A communication block can result if managers and subordinates personalities clash.

- Refusal to Listen: Due to careless attitudes or arrogant nature refusal to listen by both or either managers or subordinates will block effective communication.

- Failure to use Proper Media for message delivery: Several type of communication delivery system are available within an organization, written memorandums, e-mails, and formal letters, verbal face-to-face, meetings, and group discussions, electronic, fax, phone, group e-mail; the effectiveness will depend on choosing the proper media for the situation.

- Communication Gap: The formal communication networks are built along the authority-responsibility lines of the organization. As the organization grows, the network tends to become larger and more complex with little planning resulting in gaps in the communication delivery system. An over-reliance only on indirect formal communication methods rather than using other methods when the situation warrants with create defects.

- Over-Loading: When people are overloaded with information, they tend to perform poorly even lower than those with insufficient information.

Effective business communication within an organization faces many pitfalls. Most often the problem lies with the sender's failure to pinpoint the purpose of the message and with the lack of knowing how the receivers will perceive and understand the information and even if they are willing listeners. To avoid such pitfalls the communicator can do the following:

- Define the problem in understandable simple language for the listeners in terms of circumstances that have led to the purpose and urgency of the message to inform, persuade, and stimulate thought into action.
- Formulate and tailor the basic message by assembling relevant information to the interest of the recipients, developing the concept, and determining which is the best medium to use and often it would be wise to use several channels of communication.
- Get feedback and measure the results to determine if the message was truly understood. Remember that effective communication is a two-way process between senders and receivers with appropriate feedback to assure complete understanding.
- To build trust through communication often converse with everyone informally, evaluating the workplace culture and motivation, and learning employee's opinions and suggestion about recent organizational actions and decisions.

To be effective in any business environment or individually, the communicator, the sender of the message, must know the audience receiving the message and communicate in the language or manner that is readily understood. The message, the information, is only received and accepted when it is understood and invokes desired actions or new thoughts. Effective communication will manifest itself in several benefits for the organization:

- Increased productivity
- Improved and consistent work flow
- Stronger business, culture, and employee feedback
- Better decision making
- Better problem solving

- Improved professional image and employee/employer rapport

Good communication is a dynamic process consisting of six stages:

1. The sender has an idea to be communicated and wants to share it.

2. The sender decides on the best method to encode the idea to be effectively communicated. Depending on the audience, this consists of the actual words, method (oral or written), format (formal or informal), gestures, visual-aids, tone, and location.

3. The sender communicates the message. To transmit the information the sender must decide on the proper channel such as face-to-face, telephone, letter, memorandum, e-mail, or fax depending on the audience, speed required, and formality.

4. The audience receives the message. But at this stage the sender does not know if it has been accepted and understood, or even received.

5. The audience does receive the message and decodes it to extract the idea in a form that is understood and has meaning. At this stage the sender can only hope that the message is correctly accepted as intended.

6. The audience replies with requested feedback enabling the sender to ascertain the effectiveness of the communication.

Managers have three basic responsibilities, according to Henry Mintzberg's *The Nature of Managerial Work*, to collect and disseminate information, to make decisions based on information, and to promote teamwork. Each is accomplished through effective communications. Besides memorandums, e-mails, reports, and phone calls, they often convey such information through meetings.

MEETINGS

"No man is an island. No man stands alone."
John Donne

Meetings are the necessary bane of business organizations. Whereas they are a potentially useful tool in communicating direction, information, results, and motivation to participants; they are too often a colossal waste of time. There was a Chairman of the Board of a large local bank, who perhaps was more inclined to more direct and quick action, had a plaque on his desk that read; "God so loved the world that he did not send a committee."; Indicating his displeasure at time-consumption of meetings and committees in decision-making. Such may be the case, but in most organization to elicit complete cooperation and effective results, meetings serve a vital part in disseminate information and objectives to all concern; done correctly, they can assist in sharing the vision of the company by the inclusion of those charged with the fulfillment of that vision.

In today's business, meetings are the primary means of communications whether they are formally or informally held even if virtually conducted on the internet. Well-run meetings can help to keep everyone on the same page in the organization's effort, and help to solve problems, conflicts, develop ideas, identify opportunities, and provide a forum of employee feedback. Preparation for the meeting and the manager's communication and listening skill are paramount for successful outcomes. Poorly run meetings waste value management and employee time costing thousands of dollars.

Meetings usually come in three kinds: the "ritual meeting", the "planning ahead" meeting, and the "things-are-gone-to-hell" meeting.

Ritual meetings exist because they have always existed. The Monday morning or Friday afternoon meeting usually with the same agenda and issues in which nothing is ever resolved. But people do come together and discuss their weekend, drink coffee, but other than so comradeship, nothing is accomplished for the organization. It is a shame, for these times are wasted opportunities or simply a costly waste of time.

Planning Ahead meetings are usually better prepared and not as regular.

There is an agenda which is distributed beforehand, and although there is time allocated for new ideas, they usually start on time and end on time.

Things-are-going-to-Hell meetings are usually conducted to ask why things are going to hell and what can we do about it. They are difficult to conduct with everyone wanting to talk at once to give excuses or their point of view.

Unfortunately, many meetings are unproductive, accomplishing nothing, and a waste of time. Senior management may spend half of its time in meetings with middle manager averaging a third of their work hours. Despite the current technology of conference calls, e-mail, fax, cell phones, internet meetings, most organizations are still ran by inefficient, unnecessary meetings accounting for anywhere from 10% to 20% of personnel cost.

So how can managers make meetings more effective and productive? They should utilize the **four "P's" of effective meeting preparation: Purpose, Planning, Participants, and Process.**

> **Purpose:** Should this meeting be held? Why hold it? Can the objective be communicated some other way? If the information can be communicated by e-mail, phone, and memo, other than a pep-talk gathering, the cost of the meeting exceeds the potential rewards, and then the meeting should not be held. The objective of the meeting should be defined and the agenda disseminated in advance. To have a productive and effective meeting will required a thought out action oriented agenda in the planning step.

> **Planning:** refers to the preparation of the agenda. Items to be covered should be put in order of importance, or some other structure such as announcements, committee reports, old and new business. The time to be allocated for each should be indicated and followed. This will help to keep on schedule and to end on time. The meeting's agenda should be plan in every detail, who (will attend), what (will be discussed), where (where will it be held), when (at with time and day), and why (purpose).

> **Participants:** attendance should be limited to those people concerned with the topics on the agenda. The more people at the meeting, especially those with no purpose for being there, the

longer the discussions destroying time management and creating the potential for unrelated bull and a longer unproductive meeting. Some participants should only be invited to that part of the meeting that they have an interest and can contribute.

Process: refers to the actual conducting of the meeting to assure that it is effective. The appropriate time and place must be choosing; lighting, size, tables and chairs, audio-visual aids, and refreshments are all important. Distribute the minutes of the last meeting, and the present agenda and other material ahead of time sufficient for them to read in advance. This prevents the waste of time of reading during the meeting. Bring extra copies to the meeting for those who may forget theirs. A day or two prior to the meeting have reminders sent out as to the time and place. Close the meeting by summarizing the decisions reached, tasks assigned, progress accomplished, and key points discussed. Review action plans that will be reported upon at the next meeting.

During the Meeting

Keeping control, providing leadership and direction during the meeting can prove to be more difficult than preparing for the meeting. Good preparation will certainly assist in an effective meeting, and the following six ways will also:

1. Start on time. Give advance warning when the meeting will began and stick to it. People will arrive on time if the meeting starts on time. Discourage tardiness by having the minutes of the last meeting reflect those present, absent, or late.

2. Start with the predistributed agenda and stick with it. Put and enforce a time limit of appropriate importance on each topic.

3. An introduction before handing out related materials can save time of participants scanning prior to directing their attention to the items.

4. Try to involve everyone in attendance. If the meeting was

properly planned they all belong there and should have something to contribute.

5.   Review all results, decisions, accomplishments, and actions for the next meeting. This is a good time to set the time and place for that meeting if required.

6.   End on time.

Everyone in a meeting, leader and participants share the responsibility for successful meetings. However if you have called the meeting and are the leader, you have an extra degree of responsibility and accountability for a productive meeting. A good meeting leader will strive to stay on track as per the agenda. The leader may stimulate the participants by guiding, probing, and mediating them with occasional summarize what is being discussed and the ongoing conclusions. The leader will know when to push forward or step back to let others talk; after all they are there to participate. There will also be times to stop discussion when time is being wasted in order to stay on schedule.

To assure staying on track, it will be helpful to follow previous agreed upon rules and agenda. Formal meetings always use parliamentary procedure which can be found in *Roberts Rules of Order*. But even informal meetings are best served by following a clear set of rules that all are familiar with.

To gather new ideas and information derived from the experience and knowledge of participants, they must be encouraged to participate. As the meeting progresses, some will remain too quite while others will be too talkative dominating the allotted time. Draw out the reticent members who may simply not be paying attention, are shy, or actually expressing disagreement by their silence by asking direct questions of them. For the overly talkative, advise that time is limited and we all want to hear from others.

If you are a participant, then do participate by trying to contribute to the topic being discussed to help achieve the meeting's purpose goals. Speak up if you have something constructive to say, but don't monopolize the discussion.

As a participant, you may cringe at attending. What could be more boring or a waste of your time, as well as that of your organizations, then being forced to listen to a wind-bag in authority. Yet, meetings could very well be helpful in advancing your career for you will have the attention of senior management and this could be an opportunity to shine. It can just as easily break your career advancement hopes by demonstrating your lack of knowledge, understanding, or communication skills.

Ten things **never** to do in a meeting:

1. Be Late—Walking into a meeting already in progress indicates how disorganized, undisciplined, and disrespectful you are of your boss's and coworker's time.

2. Be Unprepared—Your time to shine. If you have been given an agenda and material beforehand, read them. Prepare any questions, comments, or contributions you may make.

3. Monopolize the Conversation—It is always wise to let more senior people contribute first. Once they have finished, concisely and succinctly make your points. Don't feel compel to speak at all if you don't have anything material or purposeful to say. It has been said, "Better to be thought a fool, than speak and remove all doubt."

4. Make Your Statements Sound Like Questions—Phrasing your statements like questions invites others to say "no", "argue" or "take credit" for your ideas.

5. Misread Signals—Try to gauge the needs and mood of the meeting. Listen carefully to what is being said to ascertain how receptive your ideas and comments will be in accordance with the meeting's purpose.

6. Get Intimidated—Some regard meetings as war fighting to get the boss's attention. If you are put-down, calmly defend yourself and your ideas.

7. Chew Gum—Nothing is more annoying than the smacking, popping, and cracking of chewing gum. It's rude and unprofessional.

8. Keep Your Cell Phone On—Hopefully, you turn it off in church, restaurants, and the movies. Turn it off in the meeting.

A ringing phone interrupts the presenter and distracts the audience. And never take a call or make a call while in a meeting. This too, is rude and unprofessional.

9. Wander Off Topic—Don't abandon the agenda to discuss something else which may be of more interest to you.

10. Skip It—If the meeting was called, especially by senior management, attend. Sure you might rationalize that you will get more done by not wasting the meeting time. But you may miss some pertinent information. Remember, it could be your time to shine. Meetings aren't always about productivity, most are actually a waste of time, and therefore, for you it may be about projecting a positive image and forming the relationships that will be essential to your career success.

After the Meeting

Meeting minutes should be prepared and distributed within 24 hours. Prepare all progress reports and insure that all action decisions are carried out. Review the progress of various established committees, and abolish those committees which have accomplished their purpose and are no longer necessary.

LISTENING

To be a truly good communicator, you must do more than improve your oral and written sending skills; you must also improve your receiving (listening) skills. To succeed in business and the ability to motivate and lead others, you must be an effective listening. Nothing will enhance the trust an employee has with management then management willingness to listen effectively to their viewpoint and ideas. Organizations with good up and down communications, requiring true listening from both, usually reach their objective and goals. All stay informed, aware, interested, current, and move toward common achievements. Conversely, poor listening skills on the part of managers and employees can substantially increase cost, create mistakes, and impede accomplishments.

The listening process involves five steps: receiving, interpreting, remembering, evaluating, and responding.

1. Receiving: Physically hearing the message and acknowledging it

2. Interpreting: Assign meaning to what is heard

3. Remembering: Store the information for future use

4. Evaluating: Evaluate the information

5. Responding: React based on what you have heard and understood

The evaluation step is crucial. You must listen actively with focus attention in order to comprehend and structure what is being conveyed. Realize that your mind can process information faster than the speaker can send it; therefore you must focus on what is being said less you become distracted.

Also strive to avoid prejudgment. We all have experience, values, and beliefs which may influence our acceptance of what is being said. Selective perceptions can distort the information to fit what we already believe about the subject. Try to listen with an open mind in order to digest any new information or another viewpoint.

Ask yourself:
- What am I being asked to do?
- What are they leading up to?
- Why am I being asked to do it?
- What is my motive, what are the speaker's motives?
- When am I supposed to do this and on what schedule?
- Why am I listening to this?
- Who is it important to?

The remembering step can prove difficult and is easily dismissed during a meeting. If the information is to be retained, do not rely on your memory. Record it in some fashion even if simply taking casual written notes.

NONVERBAL BUSINESS COMMUNICATION

In managing and leading others, it is not often what is being said but what is perceived that has an impact on performance. In this regard nonverbal communications play a huge part, too often for the negative for it is usually done without forethought and instinctively. In a positive connotation, nonverbal communication should be used to reinforce the spoken message. Nonverbal communication is the process of sending and receiving information, both intentionally and unintentionally, without using written or spoken language. Nonverbal gestures and facial expressions can strengthen a verbal message when they match and compliment the words. They can undermine and weaken the verbal message when they don't match the words or, in some cases, actually replace the unspoken word.

Nonverbal communication may often convey more than the sender intended than the words spoken. Nonverbal signals include facial expressions, gestures and posture, vocal characteristics, personal appearance, touch, time and personal space. Posture and body movements can signal your energy level, and your openness and receptiveness to an idea, or your closeness and resistance to it. Open body position is revealed in leaning forward with uncrossed arms and legs. Closed or defense body position include leaning back, sometimes with both arms and legs crossed or close together, or even hands in pockets. Notice your own body the next time you are speaking to a friend. You will naturally assume an open body position. Notice your next business meeting, you may observe that many adopt a closed posture indicated that they may be slightly uncomfortable.

- Facial Expressions—The face is the primary tool we all use to express emotion most often instinctively unless practiced (which is usually recognized and ineffective). Your eyes, called the windows of the soul, are especially effective in indicating your mood, attention, interest, influencing and motivating others, and true feelings.
- Gestures and Posture—The art and ability to use gesture can be most effective in reinforcing a point. By movement you can express both specific and general messages, some intentionally some not. Slouching, leaning forward, fidgeting, wandering around, and walking briskly are all usually unconscious actions but may indicate whether you feel confident or nervous, friendly or hostile, in agreement or not, assertive or passive, powerful or powerless.
- Vocal Characteristics—The tone of your voice, like your

face, carries intentional and unintentional messages of your true feelings. Your voice can reveal things which you may be unaware. Your volume, the inflection, speaking pace, and the little annoying "ums" and "ahs" that creep into your message, all indicate your confidence level, sincerity, your relationship with the listeners, knowledge, background, and emotions.

- Personal Appearance—People will judge you and your professionalism by your appearance, fairly or unfairly. Few of us can control our physical appearance and such is usually not suspect; but we are able to control our grooming, clothing, and accessories. We should know our audience and dress appropriately to impress, influence and be accepted favorably.
- Touch—Touch is valuable in conveying warmth, comfort, and reassurance. Touch is powerful and best left for personal relationships. Touch is a complex tool and usual not best use in a professional setting. When in doubt, don't touch.
- Time and Space—Like touch, time and especially space can be used to assert authority, imply intimacy, and send other nonverbal messages. You show respect by being on time; disrespect and disregard for others by making people wait (often a tactic to assert one's own importance). As with touch, standing too close, invading someone's private space, can be a violation or a sign of sincere emotion.

When attending a meeting as a listener, look for and pay attention to the speaker's nonverbal clues to receive the whole message. Do they enhance and reinforce the spoken words or do they contradict them? Be observant but don't assume that your observations are infallible. If you feel that there is a contradictory message being sent from the words and the gesture, respectfully ask for clarification or explore further.

When presenting at a meeting be attentive of some of the following to determine if you are holding or losing the audience:

- Scratching the head indicating confusion or disbelief
- Biting the lips indicating anxiety
- Rubbing the back of the head and neck suggesting frustration, impatience
- Avoiding eye contact indicating a lack of interest

- Crossing of arms indicating resistance, defensiveness, defiance, or a close mind
- Sighing and yawning, a sign of boredom

WRITTEN BUSINESS COMMUNICATION

Whether writing a simple memorandum, e-mail, or a more complex report or presentation, you must be aware of the recipient and their understanding of the message to initiate the desired action. To communicate effectively, you must create a message that is concise, succinct, with a clear understandable purpose. There is a three step writing process to create effective business messages in any form that is chosen as most appropriate.

It is **planning**, **writing**, and **completing** the business message.

> **Planning**—as with analyzing any situation, you must define your purpose and the intended audience. Make sure that the information being communicated is understandable by the audience for if not understood, it won't be communicated. Select the proper medium to transmit the message—written (e-mail, memorandum, letter), or oral. Organize the information, limiting your scope to the main idea to be accomplished; an outline may help in organization.

> **Writing**—after planning and organizing the message, make sure that it will fit the audience, their language skills, sensitivities, and style. Compose the message using direct, clear language with familiar words and short concise paragraphs. This is an opportunity to build further rapport with your audience, and enhance credibility, trust, and loyalty. Be mindful of their values and polite and respectful in your tone.

> **Completing**—review and revise the message (if necessary) prior to sending. Make sure that it has a professional appearance, is readable, clear, concise, and correct, and that it is being distributed to all interested parties. Produce and proofread the message for sloppy typos, misspellings, grammar, and other errors; all which will destroy your credibility and purpose.

More than likely your short messages will be by electronic means rather than hard-copy paper memorandums. Today businesses are using instant messages, texting, and blogging, as well as e-mail. However most will be by e-mail which to a great extent has replaced the printed memo and letter. No doubt you have much experience with e-mail but always be mindful that e-mail correspondence at work is considerably different than your personal e-mail communications. They are more formal than those you send to family and friends. Be sure to handle it as a professional business communication, follow your established company policy and culture. For clarity of purpose, always use a concise relative subject line and use proper language in the body of the message. Avoid slang and of course obscenities. When replying to a group e-mail, be sure to reply only to the sender and not to all (if that is the intent).

E-mail etiquette in accordance with company policy and norms is essential. Before composing and sending make sure that the e-mail is necessary and that it does not contribute to the overabundance of e-mails received every day. To not do so with relegate your e-mails to the superfluous and considered a waste-of-time damaging your professionalism and credibility.

Some tips for effective e-mails:

When requesting information or action, make it clear what you are asking for, why it's important, and when you need it. Try not to make your reader write back for these details. People will be tempted to ignore your messages if they are not clear about what you want or when you want it.

When replying to an e-mail, paraphrase the request to remind the reader what you are replying to.

If possible, avoid sending long, complex e-mails. A long complex message is better communicated as a printed memorandum or report.

Know your audience and adjust the formality of the language. Overly formal messages to peers and colleagues are perceived as stuffy and distant; too informal language to superiors and customers are perceived as disrespectful.

NEVER TYPE THE E-MAIL IN CAPS. All caps are perceived as shouting and screaming.

Don't annoy your reader with cutesy formatting, colors, or unusual fonts.

Don't compose and send an e-mail when angry. E-mails can be forwarded anywhere and saved forever. Don't let poor judgment ruin your career and reputation.

Many consider the "return receipt request" feature an annoyance and an invasion of privacy. Only use it for the most critical messages.

Don't infect anyone with a computer virus. Make sure you have a current virus protection on your computer.

Always pay attention to grammar, spelling, and capitalization. Just because it is an e-mail, do not abandon the etiquette of proper professional communication. Do not succumb to the computer language of adolescents. As your personal appearance and dress says something about you, so does the appearance of your e-mail.

Whether in an e-mail message, a written memorandum, or a more formal business report, you may encounter two commonly used abbreviations which we have all seen but often confuse or simply do not know what they mean.

They are *i.e.* and *e.g.*

The abbreviation *i.e.* stands for the Latin *id est*, meaning "that is" (The parcel exceeds the weight limit, *i.e.* three pounds).

The abbreviation *e.g.* stands for the Latin *exempli gratia*, meaning "for the sake of example" or "for example" (The management may provide an incentive, *e.g.*, a cash bonus or time off).

Staffing, Training, and Motivating

"If everyone is thinking alike, then somebody isn't thinking."
General George S. Patton, Jr.

Selection and Hiring Process:

The most important asset of a business is its employees. Therefore you should invest the time to determine the needed number (too many will be too costly and counterproductive, and too few will not be able to achieve desired objectives), and the skills each employee should possess. This process should begin with a clearly thought out job description and job specifications.

A job description will list the duties, responsibilities, and expectations of a given job. Job specifications are a well thought out, detailed written statement of work assignments and the qualifications and skills needed to perform the job satisfactory.

The selection process of an organization is not a one-shot approach in choosing the suitable candidate for the job. It involves a series of steps. Each step is important because at each stage, information may be revealed which will disqualify the candidate. Most organizations use the following steps in choosing a suitable candidate:

- Preliminary interview or screening
- Application
- Testing
- Interviewing
- Reference checks
- Meeting and interview with department head
- Physical examination
- Induction

The candidates looking for jobs respond to advertisement by sending a brief description of their resumes. The college students who are about to graduate may have had a preliminary interview or screening from a visit to the campus from a representative of the organization. Sometimes the candidate may contact the human resources department or executive of the company to request a preliminary interview. The primary purpose of these preliminary screenings is to determine the candidate meets the minimum requirements for the job and the fit of the candidate to the company and vice-versa.

This investigation centers upon an analysis of the general background, education, and experience of the candidate. The screening process is a filtering mechanism to avoid wasting time and resources of both the candidate and the company. These preliminary interviews are usually short. If they find a fit of the candidate's qualification and the job requirements, the candidate is given an application form. The application form is where the candidate supplies all of his/her particulars including appropriate personal information, education, and experience and formally applies for the position.

The next step in a formal selection process is administering psychological tests. These tests are designed to assess information about an applicant's abilities, aptitude, interests, creativity, attitude, and personality. Such insight would reveal who has the potential for successful job performance and growth.

If testing produces positive information, the interview process will follow. The interview is probably the most important step in the entire selection procedure. At this stage the interviewers match information obtained from various sources with that obtained through their own observations during the interviews. Clarification and elaboration of brief responses given on the application and the interviews are sought. This selection stage is an interaction and exchange between the interviews and the candidates. Often the final decision to hire or reject is made during this exercise.

After the interview, prior to advise the candidate of the outcome, references are checked. Reference may refer to character, ability, and experience from those familiar with the candidates academic achievements, previous employers, and sometimes from family, friends, and fellow workers.

After all the information has been gathered and the background checked with recommendations from interviewers, the manager for whom the candidate will work must decide whether to accept or reject him or her. The manager must exercise great care in making this decision both from the standpoint of will the candidate fit in the department with other workers, and because a lot of time, resources, and money has been invested to bring the applicant to this final stage.

The manager and or the supervisor will check the candidate by asking some practical questions about the job. If specific skills are required then the candidate will be given a practical job test to determine whether theoretical knowledge can be put into practice.

The candidate might meet all requirements so far but if physical qualifications fail to meet job requirements then the job will not be offered. Prior to this stage this determination may be able to be ascertained sooner. Many physical limitations would not be prohibitive to job performance and often does with such limitations prove to be outstanding workers. However, if the physically limitation is one that would restrict the specific job performance as described in the job requirements and description, then the disability would create a potential liability for the company.

In order to comply, there must be established and written job specifications outlining the human capabilities and qualifications in terms of traits, skills, and experience required to accomplish the job. A job description should also be in place identifying the specific job with the particular responsibilities, duties, and expectations of the job.

Induction completes the selection process. Neglect at this final stage could produce expensive turnover due to a new employee having difficulty adjusting to job conditions and coworkers. To avoid this problem steps must be taken to acquaint the new hire with coworkers, immediate supervisors, rules and regulations, and the facilities. Efforts should include job-orientation, lectures, film and slide demonstration, and conferences with supervisors and meetings with coworkers.

A business must conform to federal and state laws in dealing with current and prospective employees. The equal employment opportunity (EEO) provisions of the Civil rights Act and the requirements of the Americans with Disabilities Act are especially important.

"Smart Staffing" by Wayne Outlaw emphasizes the importance that new hires fit the organization. To assure that fit matches the business mission and culture as well as working well with existing employees, a thorough interview and screening is beneficial. The following are seven reasons why it is essential to hire wisely:

1. Choosing the wrong person cost money

2. Low turnover assures less cost and better customer service

3. Every employee makes an impact on profits

4. Management is legally accountable for employee's actions

5. Bad employees run away good customers

6. Good employees make managing easier

7. Hiring right is good for the long-run survival of your business.

Training:

Training is the organized procedure by which people acquire knowledge and skills for a definite purpose. For a new employee it is the means of transition and adaption from a theoretical to a practical situation to meet the requirements of the job. For an experienced worker, training is a process of reorientation to meet additional or new job requirements. The purpose of training is to increase productivity, job performance and to assure standards and quality.

Sometimes companies set up expensive training programs simply because competitors have such programs. The need for training programs should be determined to meet the purposes of the organization in accomplishing desired results and goals. There is usually an organizational analysis to determine where within the organization training emphasis should be placed; operational analysis to determine what should be the content of training in terms of what an employee must do to perform a task, job, or assignment in an effective and efficient way; Employee analysis to determine what skills, knowledge, and attitudes an employee must develop to perform the tasks which constitutes his/her job.

Training methods are usually determined by considerations of cost, nature of job, amount of knowledge and skill required background of the trainee, time available, and the policies of the organization. The following training methods are most frequently used:

- Job instruction training
- Conference or discussion
- Apprenticeship training
- Job rotation
- Coaching (ability) and counseling (attitude)
- Lecture

And for supervisory personnel:

- On-the-job training
- Off-the-job training

On-the-job training, job instruction, is most commonly used by placing the individual into a regular job and teaching the skills necessary to perform the job. The trainee learns under the supervision and guidance of a qualified employee or instructor. Apprenticeship, job-rotation, and coaching are some examples of this type of training.

Off-the-job training gives the individual training materials to study and provides lectures and seminars appropriate to the future job. Simulating actual work conditions in a class-room, role- playing, lecture, conference and discussion, and programmed instructions are some examples of this training method.

The basic training for all jobs remain to simply show an employee how to perform the job during a period of observation, allow the employee to perform the job under observation and guidance, have the employee perform the job alone, and, after monitoring that performance, have the employee teach another the job.

Frederick W. Taylor in his *The Principles of Scientific Management* (1911), stressed the need to properly select, train, and support workers for their individual tasks. He believe that if workers were left to perform their jobs on their own without clear directions and training there would be a significant loss of efficiency and the workers would not reach their full capacity. He believed that if taught and train with the support of capable supervisors the jobs would achieve desired objectives. Taylor's four principles of scientific management are:

1. Develop for every job a science that includes rules of motion, standardized work implements, and proper working conditions.

2. Carefully select workers with the right abilities for the job.

3. Carefully train workers to do the job and give them the proper incentives to cooperate with the job science.

4. Support workers by carefully planning their work and by smoothing the way as they go about their jobs.

Motivation

Motivation is a topic of much interest in management. How can managers induce employees to perform their best toward accomplishing organizational objectives and goals? The answer is simply by motivating them.

Motivation means different things to different individuals. For some it may be an incentive to perform and for others it is a psychological backing or the setting of a good example. Motivation remains abstract and difficulties arise when trying to explain its meaning and application. It can be defined as a process which governs choices made among alternative forms of voluntary activity. Motivation is actually the act of inducing an individual to follow a desired course of action which is good for the individual or the person doing the inducing or both (parallel interest). Motivation has been described as the immediate influence on an individual's direction, vigor, and persistence of behavior. It is steering one's action towards goals and committing one's energies to reaching them, an urge or tension to achieve a certain goal.

An employee's ability and job training is essential for even a highly motivated person will not do well if there is no ability or talent to perform the job. Likewise, the most able and talented employee will not perform well if not motivated.

Performance = Ability X Motivation

Motivation is the skill and ability to influence others. The ability to motivate others is one of the most essential skills of a good manager and leader. It is the quality of a self-motivated leader that he is able to communicate his vision and convince others to believe in it enough to motivate them with the desire and ambition to accomplish the shared goals of that vision.

The basic components of motivation are need, drive, incentives, and goal directed behavior. Need is the prerequisite for any motivated behavior. There are basic needs such as food, drink, sleep, air to breath; and secondary psychological needs such as to be secure, to be in groups, to achieve and be successful.

Incentives are the instruments used in inducing people to willingly perform their best for a desired course of action. Incentives may be financial or non-financial.

Examples of financial incentives are wages, salaries, bonuses, and fringe benefits. It is believe that such incentives help to attract the most qualified employees, decrease turnover, and maintain high morale and effective job performance.

Non-financial personal incentives such as opportunities for advancement and recognition, challenging work, delegated responsibility and authority, good working conditions and supervision, and recreational programs and socialization events all have an impact on personal initiative, morale, and job performance.

Maslow's Hierarchy Theory classified human needs into five groups:

1. Psychological needs—earnings for basic food, clothing, shelter, and medical care

2. Security needs—safe and pleasant working conditions, earnings to afford a good standard of living, having health insurance and a pension plan, being treated fairly and understanding the reasons for management's actions

3. Social needs—having friends and working with people you like, conforming to group norms, feeling needed, being loyal

4. Self-esteem needs—publicly recognized for achievement, being promoted, having status symbols, having a good personal and professional reputation

5. Self-actualization needs—using your talents and abilities, finding solutions to problems, serving mankind, self-respect and pride, being the best you can be

Accordingly when one need is fulfilled, the next order of needs become important. This suggests that the importance of monetary incentives decline as an individual progress through the need hierarchy.

Herzberg's Two Factor Theory deals with the satisfaction and dissatisfaction of an employee. The factors which produce satisfaction are known as satisfiers or motivators, and the factors causing dissatisfaction are known as dissatisfiers or hygienic factors. Eliminating dissatisfiers may not necessarily cause satisfaction.

Achievement, recognition, responsibility and advancement, the work itself are satisfiers. Dissatisfiers are most often company policies and administration, supervision, salary, relationships with co-workers, and working conditions. Satisfiers are associated with the job itself, and dissatisfiers with the context in which the job is performed.

The level of job satisfaction is important for peak performance. The design of individual jobs, the structuring of positions and organizations, and the choice of technologies has major implications for job satisfaction. It hardly seems wise to make choices likely to invoke negative feelings. Creating an environment in tune with the expectations, goals, and requirements of the organizations, managers, and workers is more productive and profitable.

<u>Expectancy Theory of Motivation</u> presented by Dr. Victor Vroom describes that motivation is dependent upon our desire to achieve something and our expectation to achieve it. The theory is based upon three factors:

- Expectancy—it is the expectation of a person to achieve something
- Instrumentality—it is the expectation that performance will lead to the desired result
- Valence—it is the perceived value of an outcome expected by the individual

Dr. Vroom concludes that desirability to achieve is the real motivator. He calculates motivation in his expectancy model as:

Motivation = Expectancy * Instrumentality * Valence

If any one of these factors is missing in the equation them motivation is not achieved.

Trust and Loyalty

Trust plays a very important role in employee-organization relations which leads to company loyalty. Trust is built by including internal communication in the performance management system. Imagine a system in which employees can evaluate management and ownership as well as being evaluated themselves. Such an exercise strengthens the organization, built morale and motivated workers, determines the strengths of management and how to best utilize them for improved productivity of the organization.

Consider the following surveys and studies:

An Opinion Research survey of approximately 30,000 workers revealed that 47% were either not satisfied at work or that they did not like the company they worked for.

A recent Louis Harris poll of 230 physicians indicated that 93% agreed that better communication between their hospital staff and management could help avoid serious medical problems. (Medical Practice Communicator)

A University of North Carolina School of Business survey revealed that the rudeness of management hurts employee commitment, productivity, morale, and subsequently the very business itself by decreased work effort due to the behavior of management. Almost 505 revealed that they were seriously thinking about quitting and 12% had actually quit.

A nationwide survey by the San Francisco Examiner showed that many executives contend that 14% of each 40 hour workweek is wasted by poor communications between employees and managers, which is equal to almost seven weeks out of the year; And that most managers spend 15% of their time dealing personally with employees due to ineffective primary communication.

The Denver Business Journal study showed that a higher percentage of absenteeism, tardiness, turnover, and decreased productivity are directly linked to poor managerial skills and miscommunication.

Levering and Moskowitz said in their book, *The 100 Best Companies to Work for in America,* that open communication between management and employees is the key aspect of the corporate culture of the highest ranked companies.

Business success will depend greatly upon the loyalty and trust of employees. Employees who feel a sense of belonging to the organization will help the company to increase profits, improve productivity, and achieve objectives and goals. The ability to trust and be trusted is a basic difference between an entrepreneur and a bureaucrat. Both attempt to minimize risk and loss but while the entrepreneur will do so with calculated risk, delegation, and faith in employees, the bureaucrat does so through micro-management and little faith in employees.

The success of a business and even the prosperity of a nation depend upon the values which support trusting relationships. Francis Fukuyama said in his book, *Trust,* "The degree to which people value work over leisure, their respect for education, attitude toward the family, and the degree of trust they show toward their fellows all have a direct impact on economic life and yet cannot adequately explain in terms of the economist's basic model of man…for example, certain societies can save substantially on transaction costs because economic agents trust one another in their interactions and therefore can be more efficient than low trust societies, which require detailed contracts and enforcement mechanisms."

It has been observed that in the absence of trust between management and employees efficiency and performance is corrupted. In such organizations management rules by fear and negative reinforcement and employees do just enough to avoid repercussions with little value to the work effort. With the disappearance of trust, employees put their interest ahead of company interest. They believe that they can only trust themselves, their own competence and ability, to produce results that are more beneficial to them rather than to the company. There is no company loyalty.

Excessive wages, company picnics, and great working conditions will not alone build trust within an organization. To build and improve trust and loyalty management must be fair and honest in all dealings with employees, the personnel policy must be fairly practiced, and informal communication should be used frequently. Fairness is often regarded by employees as fairness in pay as compared with other employees doing similar work and in job security. Distribution of rewards, bonuses, and wages depicts what is valued and desired by an organization and such recognition is a motivation for employees to excel.

Employee's trust in management is just as important as pay, job security, and rewards. To earn employees trust, management must have trust in employees. Mutual trust will foster company loyalty and better performance, e.g., employees will not care for customers or customer service if they believe that the company does not care for them.

This trust is best employed by empowering employees by giving them the authority, tools, and information needed for their jobs. Empowering is a strong motivational approach. It gives the employees greater autonomy and self-confidence to perform effectively. It enables employees to fully use their potential satisfying the need for achievement, recognition, and self-actualization.

As outlined in *10 Steps to Empowerment* by Diane Tracey (William Morrow & Co., New York), the following are ten principles for empowering people:

1. Tell people what their responsibilities are.

2. Give them authority equal to the responsibilities assigned to them.

3. Set standards of excellence.

4. Provide them with training that will enable them to meet the standards.

5. Give them knowledge and information.

6. Provide them with feedback on their performance.

7. Recognize them for their achievements.

8. Trust them.

9. Give them permission to fail.

10. Treat them with dignity and respect.

Such empowerment enhances employees' attitude toward their jobs by self-efficacy (personal competence), self-determination (personal choice), personal control (having impact), meaning (personal value in the activity), and trust (a sense of security).

Employee Attitude

A person's attitude will and can affect job performance. A well-trained person with the necessary ability but perhaps with a bad attitude toward the job or management will interfere with the motivation to perform effectively. To quote Stan Salathe, Chairman and President of Salathe Oil, "an employee with a '<u>can do</u>' attitude is good; one with a '<u>will do</u>' attitude is better."

An attitude is a predisposition to react and respond to a job, people, or events in either a positive or negative manner; Expressions of "I like my job, boss, working conditions." Or "I don't like my job, supervision, or management." Indicate attitude which can impact job performance. Therefore it is helpful to be aware of the level of job satisfaction among workers. Job satisfaction usually includes: Compensation—How much and is it equitable?, Job and Tasks—Are they interesting and challenging, are there opportunities for training, learning, and autonomy of responsibility?, Advancement and Promotion—Are such opportunities available and fair?, Supervision—Does the supervisor and manager exhibit interest and concern for the welfare and satisfaction of employees?, Co-workers—Are associates friendly, cooperative, competent, supportive and perceived to carry their share of the work load?

Employee Management

The difficulty of the entrepreneur transition to manager is never more evident than in managing and supervising employees. Seldom in a small business are employee manuals written and often job descriptions and specification are scarce. The employees, like the entrepreneur, are generally expected to wear many hats. Further the entrepreneur may be lacking in communication skills and assumed that all knows and sees what he/she does and shares the vision for the business.

As the company grows and employees increase, the manager will not be able to be involved in every aspect of the daily business activity and must move from the direct supervision of a few employees to that of indirect management of several and their activities. For the employees too this growth will alter their work routine, whereas before they did wear many hats and were perhaps comfortable with that variety, but now with growth, some of that autonomy may change.

At conception the entrepreneur may have tended to micromanage the business. But now such oversight will inhibit the business growth and take the entrepreneur manager away from those tasks that only he or she can do by being involved in activities that are best delegated to others freeing him to do the job of managing. Many managers finding that they are more comfortable doing these tasks, or fearful that others will not perform properly, remain in such micromanagement status which not only limits the success and growth of the business but also stymies the development of competent employees.

It has been <u>wrongly</u> commented that the problem with human resource management is the humans. It is the humans, the employees that are the most valuable resource of any business for they multiply the efforts of management and create larger possibilities of profits. It has been observed that "the plant of the future will have only two employees: a man and a dog. The man will be there to feed the dog and the dog will be there to see that the man doesn't touch the equipment." Fear not; such will never occur, particularly with small business which continues to remain the largest creator of jobs and opportunities in the country.

Conflict and Stress Management

The term organization has been viewed in different ways by different people. For some, it may be a physical structure while for others; it is a group of people trying to achieve something. During one's lifetime, an individual belongs to and passes through a number of organizations such as family, school, club, association, company, union, religious group, and so on.

Some organizational theorists interpret organization in terms of principles while others view organization as a system in which people act and interact in accomplishing certain goals. Based on these and other views, several theories have been formulated which explain the structure and functioning of several types of organizations such as: formal and informal; profit and non-profit; service and manufacturing; public and private.

Most agree that the field of management particularly in the start-up of a new business venture must be viewed in a broad perspective because of the environmental influence on management practices and the isolation of the entrepreneur. The cross-cultural study of management involves the study of management cultural variables, which tend to have an impact on management practices in different cultures. Managing and organizing are culturally dependent because they do not consist of making or moving tangible objectives, but of manipulating symbols which have meaning to the people who are managed.

There are a number of issues which comprise the behavior of individuals in an organization. As there are different people working in an organization, there is a great probability that there will be different conflicts between them. It is the responsibility of management to avoid conflict and to resolve conflict to assure productivity. The functions of management: planning, organizing, leading, and controlling cannot be accomplished in the presence of unresolved negative conflict.

What is a Conflict?

A conflict is a mental struggle or a competitive encounter between two individuals or groups resulting from opposing actions or views causing disagreement on mutual actions.

Conflict can also exist within a person. Internal conflict occurs when one must decide between two opposing choices e.g. the ethical right choice or the acceptable norm right choice. It has been said that there is always two reasons for doing something; the good reason and the real reason. Therefore conflict can be seen as a clash of wants or needs within ourselves or with others.

In order to resolve conflict the source of the conflict must be understood. The potential source of conflict is often different within or between people. It could be triggered by job requirements or a communication breakdown.

Conflicting values within a person is most often the cause of internal conflict. Value is the worth, utility, or importance that people assign to ideas, things, or other people. The most obvious expression of value is the price one is willing to pay for an item. If it is regarded as too expensive, the price is believed to be higher than the value assigned to the item. As a young Ben Franklin had said upon saving for a considerable time and purchasing a whistle which produced somewhat diminishing pleasure, "I have paid too much for the whistle."

People also assign value to ideas and concepts that influence their lives such as friendship, honesty, character, integrity, freedom, and self-respect.

Conflicting values with others with differing perceptions is a common source of conflict. Difference in perception occurs when two or more people understand the same event or idea differently. For example, someone is content in their present job or position. But a good friend, perhaps a spouse, urges him to apply for another position as, in their opinion, a competent, ambitious person would seek advancement. This difference in the perceived values of the two persons might result into a conflict between them.

Conflicting job requirements may arise from expectations of the job. A new business owner and manager is expected to enforce performance standards and evaluates subordinates' performance; yet may be reluctant to enforce rules because the subornates are friends and former colleagues. The subornates may test the manager's new role to see how the demands of friendship and supervisor are balanced. The opposing expectations could lead to conflict for the manager.

Another example is that of banks that expect tellers to process transactions quickly and accurately while also cross-selling other services. The employee may find it difficult to juggle these two responsibilities, especially if long lines are developing. They experience a conflict in their job requirements.

Even when job requirements do not conflict, they can be communicated incompletely which promotes conflict. Whenever people have inadequate, insufficient, or inaccurate information regarding the job to be performed, they will not be able to do the job well. Rumors and gossip are a source of inaccurate information which may generate upset feelings and needless conflict. Therefore the first step in resolving conflict is to find its source and remedy it.

Other causes of conflict are: scarce resources, jurisdiction ambiguities, power and status differences, and goal differences.

Scarce resources within an organization can sometimes become a cause of conflict. Organizational resources are its capital, supplies, equipment, information, time, and even the employees. Whenever individuals or teams must compete for scarce or declining resources to achieve their goals, conflict is almost always inevitable.

Jurisdiction ambiguities arise when the job responsibilities are not clear to employees. People know what is expected of them with clear responsibilities; without, people may disagree about who is responsible for specific tasks or who has a claim on necessary resources to accomplish tasks.

Power and status differences are caused by undesirable influence of one party over another. Low-prestige individuals or even whole departments may resend and resist their low status in resource allocations. Conflict may arise as they strive to increase their power and influence to accomplish goals.

Goal differences are often imbedded within an organization as different individuals, teams, and departments have competing goals to achieve, e.g., salespeople may have individual targets which pit them against each other, the sales department, or the manufacturing department.

Effects of Conflict:

When conflict situations are unresolved, the problems behind them also remain unresolved. Ignoring conflicts and their underlining cause may result in interference with job and project accomplishment. Employees, people in general, tend to stay angry and dissatisfied when their needs and wants are not addressed. They become closed to others, employers and managers, point-of-view resulting in poor communication and decision-making abilities. They divert energy from accomplishing goals to coping with the stress of the conflict. Suspicion and distrust increase, cooperation decrease, and morale declines. Groups may become polarized in different camps or postures. Frustration and tension grow and job satisfaction and performance diminishes.

Conflict brings stress to everyone involved; those directly involved and those indirectly witnessing the conflict or working with those in conflict. This stress can cause a multitude of physical and emotional symptoms that interfere with job productivity, and employees' health and well-being.

However, when the conflict and its causes are address directly and skillfully, problems are recognized and defined. A broader understanding of the problem becomes possible. Individuals are able to communicate their ideas for handling the situation and the conflict. This process can promote healthy interaction and involvement from the conflicting parties who develop greater commitment to finding mutually agreeable solutions. When their feelings and viewpoints are acknowledged and they are participants in the process of finding the solutions to meeting their needs, they are happier and more effective employees able to benefit and contribute to the business.

Conflict Resolution:

Conflict is inevitable. The challenge for management is to reap the benefits and reduce the risks. There are several helpful techniques for confronting and resolving conflicts.

- Subordinate Goals: subordinated goals are those that cannot be achieved by any one individual, team, or group. A subordinated goal requires the cooperation of the conflicting parties for achievement. To the extent that all must focus on the organizational goals, the conflict will decrease because they will see the big picture and realize that only by working together will they achieve it.

- Bargaining and Negotiation: the process of reaching a common solution through communication and mutual understanding. Conflicting parties apply logical problem solving efforts to identify and correct the conflict. This approach works well if the individuals involved can set aside personal animosities and deal with the problem in a professional businesslike manner.
- Mediation: the use of a third party to solve the conflict. The mediator can discuss the conflict with each party and work toward a mutually agreeable solution. If a satisfactory solution cannot be reached, the parties must be willing to turn the conflict over to the mediator and abide by his solution.
- Well-Defined Tasks: when the conflict results from ambiguity, it can be reduced by clarifying responsibilities and tasks. Conflicts can be resolved when all involved know the task for which they are responsible and the limits of their authority.
- Facilitating Communication: good communications to, from, and among all involved ensure that there is accurate and clear perceptions of the tasks to be achieved and the areas of responsibility and accountability. Providing opportunities for conflicting parties to come together and exchange information and viewpoints reduces conflicts. Misinformation, suspicion, and distrust diminish and improved teamwork becomes possible.

Conflict Response Options:

There are five most common key responses to conflict as follows:

1. Withdrawal: withdrawal is sometimes used for avoiding conflicts. It is most often used on a short-term basis but has some inherent weakness. For example if the matter is important and long-term, then this approach is not useful as it may only work on unimportant short-term problems. In important and long-term pressing issues, withdrawal will only further augment and increase the problem.

2. Suppression: this option is used when the situation is important to conflicting parties but not so to others in the organization. Both the withdrawal and the suppression response tend to have the potential for the negative feelings of the conflicting parties erupting from an isolated minor conflict into a more serious organizational wide major conflict.

3. Dominance: dominance is the approach that one party's needs are fulfilled and satisfied over those of another often adopted by authoritative managers. This style of leadership is built on power with the subordinate motivated by fear. There is very little if any delegation of authority and the manager gives no explanations for the decisions or actions. Sometimes in a crises situation when quick action is required, dominance is useful and effective. But this type of response is capable of often creating negative feelings in subordinates.

4. Compromise: compromise provides satisfactory solutions to the conflict that are appropriate and desirable for all conflicting parties. It is actually all the conflicting parties bargaining in good faith to gain some results while sacrificing others.

5. Collaboration: is the option used to find the best solution for all parties. The conflicting parties themselves find a satisfactory solution that is appropriate to achieve all their goals. This is the best response option providing all the parties are honest in their negotiation and have faith and trust in each other. It requires very good communication, mutual respect, and a desire to make the collaboration successful.

A good conflict resolution strategy helps to create a more cohesive organization and a more ethical working climate. The following suggestions for managers may be helpful in resolving conflicts between employees:

- Use good listening skills and strive to behave as open and non-judgmental as possible
- Never mix feelings with facts and be clear and specific in all communications
- Share the thoughts, feelings, and needs of all involved
- Recognize and show respect to the personality difference of the participants

- Deal with one issue at a time
- Put agreements between the conflicting parties in writing
- Review the performance and results after action to resolve the conflict

Stress:

Dr. Hans Seyle, a Canadian physician and researcher is considered the father of stress management because of his pioneering research in the field. He defines stress as "the body's nonspecific response to any demand placed on it, whether or not that demand is pleasant." He discovered that people's bodies exhibit a specific series of biological reactions in response to some demand or threat. The surprise is that the body goes through the same reaction in positive as well as negative situations. The same physical reaction occurs if one is cut off in traffic, or given a surprise party by friends. The body does not know the difference between positive or negative events; only the mind does.

Stress takes a toll on individuals and business. Both business and the healthcare industry spend billions of dollars per year helping people cope with and overcome the negative health and poor work performance effects of stress. "All of corporate America worries about stress. United States industry spends about $150 billion a year on stress, a figure that now exceeds the after-tax profits of the Fortune 500 companies combined." *American Banker Publication, 1987*

It has been estimated that nearly 75% of all doctor visits are stress related. They are usually diagnosed in the short term as temporary negative effects. However, if stress is frequent or prolonged, several very real physical problems can be experienced. Among the medical difficulties are back pains, headaches, digestive, and coronary problems. Psychological effects include irritability, depression, and anxiety. Negative job performance effects are increased absenteeism, higher turnover, job dissatisfaction and low morale, accidents, ineffective communication, poor quality of work, and increased conflicts.

Sources of Stress:

Factors such as workload, erratic schedules, poor planning, job instability, and competition influence stress levels. Managers and supervisors also feel stress in coping with promotions, added responsibilities, changes in senior management and company policies, as well as the overall transition from one career stage to the next. Turbulence and uncertainty associated with the establishment and career stages can be overwhelming, especially if the career is perceived as not going well or if there is a lack of mentor relationship.

A key source of stress can be external conditions such as the threat of termination due to recessionary slow-downs, cutbacks, and mergers and acquisitions. The fear and uncertainty surrounding possible job loss often creates stress as great as that from actual job loss.

Despite the negative consequences of severe stress, not all stress is bad. Dr. Seyle observed that the only people who have no stress are dead. A moderate amount of stress can have a positive effect on performance, but extreme high stress contributes to performance decline. Extended periods of high stress can lead to burnout, which is emotional exhaustion arising from overexposure to stress. Moderate job stress is a natural part of managerial work. Although executives may complain of stress, many thrive on it and few would want lower pressure jobs. Most have learned to cope with stress by learning to relax through mediation or regular exercise. They built resistance by effective behavior such as regular sleep, good eating and health habits, and discussing the stressful situation with coworkers, family, and friends. Managers can learn to say no to unacceptable work overloads and to delegate responsibility to subordinates, and requesting the necessary resources to remove the cause of the stress.

Areas under managerial control such as performance feedback and clear job expectations, job decision latitude, and social support are essential in helping subordinates cope effectively with job stress. However each person must find his or her own strategies for coping with internal stress. Techniques like having other interests and hobbies, maintain a sense of humor, keeping in shape, deciding not to let things bother them, not taking matters too seriously, and keeping a balance in their lives, will all help in stress coping efforts.

Stress for the entrepreneur manager can be especially chronic and painful. Besides constantly striving for money, perhaps stemming from little discipline and launching the venture undercapitalized, causes for such stress once immersed in the business are usually related to (1) loneliness, (2) immersion in the business, (3) people problems, (4) the need to achieve.

1. Loneliness—Although surrounded by many—employees, customers, vendors, bankers, lawyers, and others- they are isolated from those with whom they can confide. Family can and should fill this void but often are not acclimated to the business and heaven to forbid may even be an investor in the enterprise. Long hours and weekends at work may prohibit seeking out friends, mentors, and family that may be helpful. Social activities and events are not an escape as there is no time for such unless a business benefit is perceived.

2. Immersion in the Business—Most start their own business for the independence and wealth opportunity, but due to the demands of the business there is little time to enjoy the rewards with vacation, trips, or other leisure luxuries because the business will not let them go. A personal experience to relate is my purchase of a large sailboat and the declaration that every Wednesday I would be sailing. Well, the Wednesdays off never came and the sailboat sailed seldom.

3. People Problems—The business owner and manager out of necessity must work and depend upon a large number of people, employees, customers, lawyers, bankers, investors, vendors, and other professionals. It is with great disappointment how frustrating and aggravating such dealings can be, especially when they do not live up to commitments or obligations. Part of this problem lies with the managers themselves for they tend to be constantly striving for perfection in their dealings and have little tolerance for anything less.

4. Need to Achieve—Achievement is how an entrepreneur manager equates success. More often than not, they attempt too much always falling short and creating self-imposed stress.

It should be noted that not all stress is bad. If kept contained and controlled could contribute to efficiency, improve performance, and achievement of high expectations.

CHAPTER THIRTEEN

MARKETING

*"Genius is one per cent inspiration and
ninety-nine per cent perspiration."*
Thomas Alva Edison

Marketing is everything you do to promote your product and everything that interacts with your customers. Marketing is the delivery of customer satisfaction at a profit. It is the process of developing, pricing, promoting, and distributing goods, services, and ideas to satisfy the needs and wants of customers. The entrepreneur must look at all aspects of the business from a marketing point of view and not just from an operational or product standpoint. This is often very difficult for an entrepreneur starting a business as he/she did not go into business to be a salesperson and may be more comfortable with the operational and product aspects of the venture. They will quickly realize that marketing the company is a continuous effort. To be most effective and productive, it should be done daily and be involved in all areas of the business.

The marketing part (Appendix A-5) of your Business Plan describes how you will attempt to create and maintain customers for a profit. You need to describe your industry, your market, your competition, your prospective customers, your marketing mix, your method of distribution, and what you plan to be your competitive advantage.

Our free-enterprise system encourages competition. This means it is a buyer's market rather than a seller's. You must be customer oriented rather than simply product oriented. If you do not offer what the market desires and you are no better than your competition, then you will fail. People do business with people they know, like, and trust. It is your task to ensure that everything you do and say will cause customers and potential customers to know you better, like and trust you more.

It is common for the entrepreneur to focus on the product rather than the customer. Remember, you must be customer oriented and not product oriented. Get to know the customer and provide the customer value that they want. To measure customer satisfaction, you must constantly strive to get feedback from the customer. Be mindful that –

> You will never hear from 95% of unhappy customers,

> 85% of those unhappy customers will not buy from you again,

> For every complaint you receive, on average there will be another 25 you have not heard,

> If you resolve the complaint, 75% of them will do business with you again,

> The average unhappy customer tells ten people about the problem with you,

> The majority of customers that leave a business do so due to indifference- something you can control.

To succeed, your business must offer what your competitors don't offer at all and/or provide better customer service. You must provide potential customers a good reason to bypass your competition and come to you. You must offer customer value that includes quality, price, convenience, and before and after the sale service. You need to offer what people want to buy, not what you want to sell them. Customers do not buy what you like, they buy what they want. Instead of trying to start a business in search of customers, listen to the market and find customers in search of a business.

The marketing part of the business plan begins with the identification of customers' wants that are not being met at all or well enough. You will need to research the market and the specific geographic area you have selected. You need to know about the population, the level and rate of business activity growth, what are the major employees and are they doing well.

In general, what are the business conditions of your market area? You are trying to identify the number of potential customers, who they are, how often they buy, who they are currently buying from, how much they spend, and if they are brand or store loyal. Getting customers is half of the battle. Keeping them is the other half. Do not be product oriented and only sell products or service; but be customer oriented and sell satisfaction. You have not obtained customers unless they come back for more products and that they talk favorable about you and your business to others. Always be aware that the average business losses one third of its customer base each year either due to their death, moving away, or switching to a competitor.

Now that you have analyzed the market, determined the strengths and weaknesses of the existing businesses, and identified your target customers, you are in a position to develop your marketing mix. The marketing mix represents your way of creating and maintaining customers for a profit. It reflects what you plan to do for a competitive advantage and how you will be able to offer greater satisfaction and value to your customers than your competition.

The marketing mix consists of four components, the four P's., these are Product and service strategy, Price strategy, Promotional strategy, and Physical distribution strategy. The four C's of the marketing mix are Customer Solution and Satisfaction, Customer Cost, Convenience, and Communication.

The marketing mix represents your way of creating and maintaining customers for a profit.

One of the basic principles for business success is, "To succeed, you must be better than your competition, "To be better, you must be different." Your marketing mix must be better than your competition in areas your target market values.

Being different does not automatically mean you will be better. Your market offering is better only if your target market considers it to be better. Better means your market values it and is willing to pay for it. This is why you must be in tune with your potential customers and that you try to see the world through their eyes.

A business must be tailored to the needs, desires, interests, preferences, and behaviors of their target market. Your target market is the judge and jury when your business goes on trial in the marketplace. You may believe you have the lowest prices in town, but if your target market is price-sensitive and believes (their perception) you are not the lowest, then they will go elsewhere. The same applies to your location, delivery system and other components of your market mix offering.

The target market will most likely be the primary market that will purchase your products and services. Your secondary market will consists of those purchasers outside the target market and will require a different market strategy.

Product/Service Strategy

Each component of the marketing mix plays an integral role in your effort to create and maintain customers. Product/service strategy may play the most significant role. Businesses are usually described in terms of the kind of products and service they offer. Pricing, advertising, and physical distribution are also important. But, if the product you offer is not what people want, then it will not matter how low your prices are, how catchy your advertising, or if you are convenient located.

Pricing Strategy

There are two ways of marketing: (1) Saturate the market with your message- may be effective but very expensive; and (2) Innovative marketing in a dollar conscious manner.

The second choice is often the only option available to small business owners on a limited budget. However it can be very effective but cost conscious without being innovative is just being cheap and will often not be very effective. Many businesses have adopted a percentage of sales approach to spending on marketing. This may be a good benchmark for cost but all spending most mindful to contribute towards the goal. It has been said that half of all money spent on advertisement is wasted; the problem is the business does not know what half. The objective, particularly for a new small business, is not to waste any.

Your pricing strategy will depend on numerous factors. Prices will need to reflect the target market you select, the nature and extent of competition, the strength of your location, your cost structure, and the type of product you will offer. There may be as many approaches to pricing as there are factors that affect a business's pricing strategy.

The Standard Markup Approach or "cost-based approach" is used by many businesses. The standard markup means that a business will base its selling price on what the product cost the business plus a percentage of that cost. The percentage added to the cost is known as the markup.

Selling price = cost + markup

The percentage of markup may be suggested by your suppliers or it could be based on other cost-related factors. Recognize that it must be competitive or your product will not sell without some other perception of added value that is better than competition (premium product). If you cannot be competitive and do not have a premium product that customers want and are willing to pay for then you do not have a business.

The Match-the- Market Approach resembles the standard markup approach. Businesses that compete against one another may offer similar products, perhaps even the same product from the same suppliers, at comparable prices. If so, what will clearly make the difference is in superior service and delivery. A primary drawback is that if you have a competitive advantage valued by your market, then you should be able to charge higher prices. The match-the-market approach is a "play it safe approach" that fails to consider your unique strengths.

Promotional Strategy and Physical Distribution Strategy

Promotional strategy can be viewed as how you communicate with your customers. Physical distribution refers to how you get your product to them.

Promotional strategy includes advertising, publicity, sales promotion, personal selling, and public relations. Your promotional strategy must address the: who, what, when, where, and how much money to spend. The most common media used to advertise are: Newspapers, Television, Radio, Magazines, The Internet, Direct Mail, and Outdoor Billboards.

Physical distribution represents the way you provide products to your customers. If the customers are to come to you, then your location and facility is important. The location decision is like going fishing- You should find out where the fish are and fish there. Many business fail because the location was convenient for the owners but not for the potential customers.

Offering your goods or services to charities is an excellent way to gain exposure, and give back to the community at the same time.

In addition to the Marketing Section in your Business Plan (appendix A-1); the following should be considered:

RESEARCH PHASE

1. Define your concept

What business are you really in?

List your products or services

Define you market position

Define your target market and how will you reach it.

Define your desired image

2. Your business image

What business do your customers think you are in?

What are they buying?

What compliments or complaints do you get?

What sells you?

3. Understand your market

Market size

Trends

Economic Environment

Technological changes

Political/Legal changes

Social/Culture environment

Demographic changes

Resources

Skills

Substitute markets

4. Know your competition

Who are they?

Identify strengths/weakness

Market share

5. Know your customer

Identify needs, wants, and desires

Customer profile

Demographics

STRATEGIC PHASE

1. Product/Service

2. Distribution

3. Location

4. Pricing

5. Promotional Mix

6. Customer Relations

7. Image Review

The internet is an excellent source for gathering market research data. In addition to the U.S. government web-site, the following web-sites will be helpful:

Better business Bureau—www.bbb.org

Census Bureau—www.census.gov

General Printing Office—www.gpo.gov

Federal Trade Commission—www.ftc.gov

U. S. Department of commerce—www.doc.gov

SEC's Edgar Database—www.sec.gov/edgarhp.htm

Free EDGAR—www.freeedgar.com

Edgar Online—www.edgar-online.com

Robert Morris & Associates—www.rma.org

CHAPTER FOURTEEN

EXIT STRATEGY

"All that we do is done with an eye to something else."
Aristotle

We have worked hard, we have built and managed a business to some modicum of success, we have treated others well—employees, customers, suppliers, and creditors, now is the time to harvest the fruits of our labor. Did we plan for this eventually, perhaps, perhaps not? Over the years the company has grown with a competitive advantage being sustained, primarily through persistent attention to customer-service, quality products with an efficient delivery system, and well-cared for dutiful, conscientious, loyal employees. By plan or out of necessity, your daily involvement and input has been diminished. No doubt, it is simply good management which you have nurtured and installed, so well that the business appears to managed itself. You know that is not true, but it may very well true that you are not as essential in the successful operation as you once were. That is good. You have wanted it to be so, and perhaps have always plan for it to happen—somewhat, after all, have you not been travelling more and remotely maintaining contact with the office.

Now is the time for serious consideration of your formal exit and the realization of the years of success and hard work that is due you. But how; how are you going to get your money out of the business? How are you going to determine what is due you and how to recapture it and leave the business a viable entity (if that is your desire)? Or, is total liquidation what you envision, if so what of the employees and other stakeholders?

Few would realize, and even less have actually so planned, but the time to first formulate this exit strategy was best considered at the business conception and the original business plan. Not that it had to be revealed at that time to bankers, suppliers, and employees, but with the awareness that the business plan is first written for your eyes, some though to an exit plan would assist in realizing the ultimate personal goal for the business venture. To have done so might have answered some of the questions and helped steered the business to a successful future which would meet your personal aspirations.

As Stephen Covey stresses in his book *The Seven Habits of Successful Living,* the entrepreneur manager should "begin with the end in mind." You have built a successful business, one that has provided for your needs, perhaps paid for your house, maintained your lifestyle, and even sent your children to school. You know it did not happen by osmosis but by hard work, long hours, planning, organizing, controlling, leading, and a little luck. If not already done so, now may be the time to plan an exit strategy for leaving the business.

Unfortunately few plan for leaving or ending the business and most end disappointedly especially when the entity is a partnership. Just as planning is important to start, grow, and manage a successful business, so is harvesting the end results. To be successful in your exit strategy, you must plan for what has been described as the contingent four "D's" of business endings—Death, Disability, Divorce, and Departure.

Death: In order to provide for family, loved ones, and possible continuation of the business, the possibility of an early an unexpected death should be part of the start-up planning of any venture. Proprietorship in particular ceases with the death of the proprietor, and so will partnerships without specific provisions in a partnership agreement. It is always surprising that otherwise savvy business men only consider the protection and comfort of insurance like key-man policies at the suggestion of an insurance agent.

Disability: When the success and prospect of a business depends on one or more important contributions from key individuals, their inability to perform with greatly impact the business and may very well destroy it. Additionally, if the business is able to continue the financial strain of continued support to the disable member and the affected family can be devastating. Again, a form of insurance will accommodate this need and, if appropriate, also a buy/sell agreement.

Divorce: Often business are starting by married couples, rather a proprietorship, formal partnership or not, or even if incorporated; much like disability or death, such a rift can destroy the business—both operationally and financially. Insurance cannot solve this problem only sound planning may, such as a properly prepared buy/sell agreement, marriage contract, and an in-depth management team.

Departure: This is especially damaging with partnerships. What may have started out as a mutual interested endeavor, with all parties having the same vision, goals, and dreams, may suddenly and unexpectedly change. Divorce and disability could contribute to this as well as simply a life-style change of priorities by one or another. Who will be left to carry on the business? Is someone officially leaving or has he or she simply quit working? What is due, if anything, the departing partner, and where would such payment come from? Insurance and a buy/sell agreement may be helpful and should be part of the formal planning of the business.

As reference, a formal buy/sell agreement will prove most helpful in handling these four "D's" in handling the requirements of family, income, taxes, and transfer of assets. Particularly as concerns death and disability, family concerns and their income can conflict with the financial soundness of an ongoing business. It may appear harsh, but the agreement should call for the business to exist as a separate entity from the individuals and a fair agreement should be in place prior to the necessity for it. In this regard any sound planning for the business development and as part of an exit strategy calls for the entity of choice to be a corporation.

Exit Strategies

There basically are five exit strategies available to a small business. They are: total liquidation, keep and sell the business in the family, sell to employees, sell to another in the open market, or sell to another business. A sixth exit strategy which is generally not available to a small business is to launch an IPO (initial public offering) and take the company public by selling shares of stock.

Liquidation: This is the end of the business, it will no longer be operationally as an enterprises. As such there is no value in the business other than tangible assets, minus any debt upon them, such as tools, equipment, vehicles, building, and land. No added value for years of operations and future potential cash flow. Hopefully, the market place will be inclined to buying the assets at a fair market value and not as a quick sale going-out-of-business liquidation. This is not a good option but it is often the only one when the business was essentially a one-man shop totally depending on the output of that individual. There is nothing else to sell but those saleable assets which may have been accumulated over the years. Best would postpone liquidation and attempt to restructure the business to be of value for someone else to buy it. Then not only will the assets add to resale value but also the potential for future income.

Bankruptcy is often an option under a liquidation plan. No honest entrepreneur starts a business with bankruptcy in mind, but too often the business is unable to meet its obligations and this is the only exit option available. Bankruptcy is normally a voluntary event; however a company can be forced into bankruptcy by its creditors.

There are two bankruptcy chapters relevant to entrepreneurs:

Chapter 11—under the bankruptcy code is really not a bankruptcy as we normally refer to bankruptcy in liquidation. It is simply a reorganization of the company's finances so it can continue operations and establish a repayment plan for debts.

Chapter 7—of the bankruptcy code is essentially the liquidation of the assets of the business and the discharging of debts. This is used when the business does not have the resources to continue operations and establish a repayment plan for creditors.

Family Business: We all know of small business in our areas which are in the third and fourth generation of ownership. How have they managed it, was it easy or hard, what were the difficulties?

The hope of many a business founder is that the business will succeed, ensures your legacy, and continues to provide for the family. Often family members, children and their siblings, work in the business providing an opportunity for the founder to select and groom the successor. However developing a family succession plan, transferring assets and control, can prove most difficult because of the financials and emotions involved; the larger the family the larger the problem. Besides family members are never comfortable discussing aging, death, and their personal financial affairs.

If it is truly a family business, succession planning should be a priority, not just for the founder, but as the business progresses to subsequent generations planning should not be abandoned. Eventually, we all want to retire, but if yours is a family run business, it is not simply a decision not to work anymore. To ensure that the business continues and you have enough money to retire, the future of the business without you is important. Who is going to manage the business? Who will be responsible for what? Who is going to control the finances? Who will do these things when you are no longer in the business? How will control and ownership be transferred to remain viable or will you have to liquidate; and if so what of the family and other employees then? Taxes must also be considered both capital taxes and inheritance & gift taxes. All call for a formal family business succession plan.

The business owner who wants to pass the business to family should consider forming a family limited partnership in which he/she is the only general partner. Using this exit strategy, the business can be transferred without sacrificing control and management of it until deemed more appropriate. The general partner can retain as little as one percent of the business with the partnership agreement giving the general partner complete control of the business. The family owns 99 percent of the business but has no control or little say as to how to run the business until the founder decides that it is time to turn over management. Not only will this make the transition more palatable but will also provide significant tax savings avoiding taking cash up front with the heavy capital gains tax burden.

There are three main issues to consider; management, ownership, and taxes.

Be mindful that management and ownership are not synonymous. You may deem it wisest to transfer management and control to one child and ownership equally, or not, to all others whether involved in the business or not.

The tax questions related to succession planning are best address by professionals. There are tax strategies to minimize taxes upon death and asset transfer strategies to children and loved ones.

Sell to Employees: If there are no family members to sell to or to whom it would be appropriate to transfer ownership, often a business owner, out of appreciation for excellent years of service or as good business, elects to sell to current managers and employees if there is an interest. Such a sale is often a win-win situation for all involved. The employees will get an established business that they are thoroughly familiar with and you will see your business continue while receiving fair compensation. Advance planning for such a transfer could involved establishing an ESOP (Employee Stock Option Plan also call an Employee Share Ownership Plan).

An ESOP is a form of employee benefit plan in which a trust created for employees purchases the employer's stock. The company transfers shares of its stock to the ESOP trust, and the trust uses the stock as collateral to borrow enough money to purchase the shares from the company. The company guarantees payment of the loan, principal and interest, and makes tax-deductible contributions to the trust to repay the loan. The company then distributes the stock to employee's accounts on the basis of a predetermined formula. In addition to the tax benefit an ESOP offers the owner to transfer all or part of the company as gradually or as quickly as preferred.

Sell to Others: Often when an owner has built a growing self-sustaining business with a good team of managers and employees and the time for retirement has arrived, he or she may put the business on the market at an asking price that fairly compensates for the business. Planning and time should be spent on making the business as attractive as possible for sale. To maximize the potential sales price know the worth of your business and its potential based upon a proven track record and trends.

To prepare and enhance your business for sale whether to others or to family, you must identify which assets to include or exclude from the transfer. You must be prepared to accept that the business may not be worth as much as you would like, particularly if it is to operate without you. Therefore be realistic in your pricing and consider staying on for a period to assist with the transition and provide the overlooked but valuable nuances of operations and customer knowledge. Clean the business of worthless assets such as old inventory or uncollectible accounts receivable. Make sure your financial records are and accounts payable are current in order to enable an interested buyer to ascertain the financial facts of the business. Be able to assure any buyer that the business is in compliance with any regulations, license, or contracts the business may have.

Finding a buyer, if not family or employees may take some time, therefore advance planning and preparation will ease the stress of the search. When a sale is consummated be sure to sever any legal obligations affording you further personal liability. Prepare your final financial statements and tax returns to establish the tax implications for assets, gains, losses conveyed to the owners. File articles of dissolution with the State licensing departments which will require formal filings to terminate and change the legal and tax status of the business. Receive a tax clearance notice from the appropriate agencies and retain it and all other business records for at least seven years. Close your bank accounts, the new owners will reestablish their own.

Exiting a business, while may be easier than starting a business, can be very stressful. To do so properly and profitably will require the same attention to advance planning as did starting and running the business.

A simplistic, realistic, and convenient way to evaluate the business for seller and buyer alike is BIGMOP—Evaluation of a Business (appendix A-10)—based upon the Balance Sheet, Income Statement, Growth, Management, Operations, and Planning.

PART THREE

ETHICS

CHAPTER FIFTEEN

ETHICS

*"A business that makes nothing but money
is a poor kind of business."*
Henry Ford

Ethics is not an easy term to define. In a general sense, ethics is the code of moral principles and values that govern the behavior of a person or group with respect to what is right or wrong. These principles are based cultural, religious, and philosophical beliefs held by us all. They come from our family, friends, school, religion, work, and the media we view and read. These derived ethics values sets standards as to what is good or bad in our conduct and decision making. They define how we think and act toward others and how we expect them to think and act toward us. We don't deliberately think of these values, but rather instinctively act based on them. It's only when faced with a compromising situation that raises a moral or ethical dilemma that we may reflect on what is right or wrong. Entrepreneurs and managers of small business particularly have difficulty in maintaining ethical behavior within their organizations. Invariably their operations are more informal and lacking the resources to have sophisticated controls to assure ethical behavior while striving to keep the business alive. In addition to working the business and attempting to make all the daily decisions necessary to achieve a profitable operation, the entrepreneur manager faces regular ethical decision on (1) individual values, such as integrity and honesty, (2) company values concerning employees well-being, (3) customer well-being and satisfaction, as reflected in the value provided to the customer, and (4) external responsibilities as to how the business relates to the community and the environment.

Ethics can be more clearly understood when compared with behaviors governed by laws and by free choices. Human behaviors fall into three categories: codified law, free choice, and ethical behavior.

The first is codified law, in which values and standards are written into the legal system and enforceable in the courts. In this area lawmakers have ruled that people and corporations must behave in a certain way, such as obtaining licenses for cars or paying corporate taxes.

The domain of free choice is at the opposite end of the scale and pertains to behavior about which law has no say and for which an individual or organization enjoys complete freedom. An individual's choice of a marriage partner or religion or a corporation's choice of the number of items to produce is examples of free choice.

Between these domains lies the area of ethics. This area has no specific laws, yet it does have standards of conduct based on shared principles and values about moral conduct that guide an individual or organization. In the domain of free choice, obedience is strictly to oneself. In the domain of codified law, obedience is to laws prescribed by the legal system.

In the ethical behavior domain, obedience is to unenforceable norms and standards about which the individual or organization is aware.

Many individuals and organizations get into trouble with the simplified view that choices are governed by either law or free choice. It leads people to mistakenly assume that if it is not illegal, it must be ethical, as if there were no third domain. A better view is to recognize the domain of ethics and accept moral values as a power for good that can regulate behavior both inside and outside an organization. As the principle of ethics and social responsibility is more widely recognized, companies can use code of ethics and their corporate culture to govern behavior, thereby eliminating the need for additional laws and avoiding the problems of unfettered choice.

Because ethical standards are not codified, disagreements and dilemmas about proper behavior often occur. An ethical dilemma arises in situations when alternative choice or behavior is undesirable because of potentially negative ethical consequences. Right or wrong cannot always be clearly identified. Values conflict arise in situations like: Lying is wrong—but what if you lie to protect a loved one? Stealing is wrong—but what if you stole to feed a starving person? Killing is wrong—but what if you killed in self-defense, defending a family member, or in a war?

An action may be legal but is it right, is it ethical? Charging an uninformed customer an exorbitant price may be legal but is it ethical?

We are all familiar and strive to follow the Golden Rule—"Do unto others as you would have them do unto you." But what of the lender who practices a different Golden Rule—"He who has the gold makes the rule." Most of us believe ourselves to be more ethical than others. But are we, or is such a belief distorted? Is it possible that others may be more ethical if not more so or could we be mistaken about what is ethical and what is not?

How are these conflicts resolved, particularly for the business manager whose goal for success and survival should be to always do what is right for the company and add value for the owners? Many employees hold that unethical behavior and decisions are acceptable if their managers are aware of them. Managers often lead others to unethical behavior by instructing employees to do whatever is necessary to succeed no matter the consequences, that the ends justify the means.

Managers and supervisors faced with ethical choices may benefit from a normative approach, one based on norms and values, to guide their decision making. Normative ethics uses several approaches for guiding ethical decision making. The following four are relevant:

1. Utilitarian Approach—The utilitarian approach holds that moral behavior produces the greatest good for the greatest number. By this method, a decision-maker is expected to consider the effect of decision alternatives on all parties and select the one that optimizes satisfaction for the greatest number of people. Because optimization to satisfy all can be very complex, simplifying the effort is considered appropriate. Such as a decision that only considers those directly affected and not those that are indirectly affected.

2. Individualism Approach—The individualism approach, also called egoism, contends that acts are moral when they promote

the individual's best long-term interests. Individuals calculate the best long-term advantage to themselves as a measure of a decision's goodness. The action that is reached to produce a greater ratio of good to bad for the individual compared to other alternatives is the right one to perform. With everyone pursuing self-interest, the greatest good is ultimately served because people learn to accommodate each other in their own long-term interest. From the viewpoint of Adam Smith, an 18th century economist, in his *Wealth of Nations,* "an individual pursuing his own interests tends to promote the good of his community."

Individualism is believed to lead to honesty and integrity because that works best in the long run. Lying and cheating for immediate self-interest just causes others to lie and cheat in return. Thus pragmatic individualism ultimately leads to behavior towards others that fits standards of behavior people want towards themselves. Because individualism is easily misinterpreted to support immediate self-gain, it is not popular in highly organized and group-oriented societies. However individualism is the closest domain to free choice.

3. Moral-Rights Approach—The moral-rights approach asserts that individuals have fundamental rights and liberties that cannot be taken away by another's decision. Therefore an ethically correct decision is one that best maintains the rights of those affected by it. Such rights are: free consent, privacy, freedom of conscience to refrain from any decision that violates their moral or religious norms, free speech, due process, and the right to life and safety. A decision to eavesdrop on employees would violate the right to privacy, sexual harassment would violate the right to freedom of conscience, and the right of free speech would support whistle-blowers who call attention to illegal or inappropriate actions within an organization.

4. Justice Approach—The justice approach holds that moral decisions must be based on standards of equity, fairness, and impartiality. Distributive justice requires that different treatment of people not be based on arbitrary characteristics. Individuals that are similar in respect to a decision should be

treated similarly. Thus men and women should not receive different salaries if they are performing the same job. However, people who differ in a substantive way, such as job skills, experience, or responsibility, can be treated differently in proportion to that difference. This differential should have a clear relationship to organizational tasks and goals.

The justice approach is closest to the thinking underlying the domain of law because it assumes that justice is applied through rules and regulations. This application does not require complex calculations such as demanded by the utilitarian approach, nor does it justify self-interest as does the individualism approach. Management is expected to define attributes on which different treatment of employees is acceptable. This approach justify as ethical behavior efforts to correct past wrongs, playing fair under the rules and insisting on job-relevant differences as the basis for different levels of pay or promotion opportunities. Most present day human resource management is based on the justice approach.

Ethics in Management:

"Ethics is about how we meet the challenge of doing the right thing when that will cost more than we want to pay."
The Josephson Institute of Ethics

When managers are accused of lying, cheating, and stealing, the blame is usually placed on the individual or on the company situation. Most people believe that managers make ethical choices because of individual integrity and honesty, which for the most part is true, but it is not the whole story. The values and culture held in the infrastructure of the organization also shape ethical behavior.

Managers bring specific personality and behavioral traits to the job. Personal needs, family influence, and religious background all shape a manager's value system. Specific personality characteristics such as ego, self-confidence, and a strong sense of independence and internal-locus-of-control may enable managers to make ethical or unethical decisions. It has been suggested that every manager prior to making a decision which may have ethical consequences ask himself: How would I feel if my family learned of this decision? How would I feel if this decision was on the front page of the newspaper?

An important personal trait is the three stages of moral development: Preconventional, Conventional, and Principled.

At the preconventional level a manager is concerned with the external rewards and punishment and the concrete personal consequences. At conventional level, while still respecting external rewards and punishments, people learn to conform to the expectations of good behavior as defined by colleagues, friends, family, and society. At the principled level, individuals develop an internal set of standards and values. They will even disobey laws that violate their principles. Internal values and beliefs are more important to them than the expectations of others.

The great majority of managers operate at the conventional level. A few have not advanced beyond pre-conventional and only about 20 percent of American adults reach the principled level of moral development. Individuals at the principled level are able to act in an independent, ethical manner regardless of expectations from others inside or outside the organization. These managers will make ethical decisions whatever the organizational consequences for them.

The values adopted within an organization are important, especially when it is understood that most people operate at the conventional level of moral development believing that their duty is to fulfill obligations and expectations of others. Corporate culture can exert a powerful influence on internal behavior of the organization. Often incidences of theft and kickbacks in a business are found to stem from the historical acceptance of such practices within the organization. Employees were socialized into those values and adopted them as appropriate. In most cases, employees believe that if they do not go along with the ethical values expressed, they will not fit in and their jobs will be at risk.

Corporate culture can be examined to see the kind of ethical signals that are being given to employees. Culture is not the only aspect of an organization that influences ethics, there are others like job satisfaction, trust and loyalty, leadership and decision processes, motivation, promotion and selection processes, but the culture within the organization is the major force because it generates all others and defines company values.

Management methods to improve the ethical work climate and to help the organization to be more responsive to ethical problems include: leading by example, developing a code of ethics, supporting an ethical organizational structure and whistle-blowers, encouraging team cohesiveness and standards of behavior, improving job satisfaction and effective motivation, providing stress and conflict management, and assuring an overall excellence in corporate culture.

Ten Ethical Issues That Most Businesses Face

Ethical dilemmas occur either from internal activities and operations or external operations; and sometimes it is imposed through forces outside the company's control. The following is ten common dilemmas:

1. Cutting Costs versus Maintaining Quality and Safety

How to strike a balance between costs, quality, and safety may be the quintessential question in any business. Even when the economy is robust and sales are high, businesses works hard to keep their cost under control in order to budget for profit and positive cash-flow. When the economy slows, sales may slack, and the temptation to cut costs even more arises.

A business should always take the long-term view even at the expense of short-term goals. Maintaining quality and safety standards during difficult times may temporarily damage the bottom line, but sacrificing quality and safety can lead to bankruptcy.

2. Overpromising and Under Delivering

"Actions speak louder than words" may be trite, but it is true. People remember what you do long after they forget what you say. And if you say you'll do something and you don't, people remember that forever.

Overpromising can be tempting especially with start-ups promising impressive returns to investors. Yet, too often, the company doesn't deliver, falling short of meeting customers' needs and investors expectations. Businesses offering goods and services promises to deliver at a certain time on a certain date. If the promise is broken, you have angry customers and investors.

A business should say straight out, "I don't want to make promises I can't keep." That way you engage the other party in problem solving, and together you may be able to work out a plan that meets everyone's needs.

3. Controlling the Market

Competition can be cutthroat, and business owners and managers are under tremendous pressure to improve sales, cut cost, boost profits, and get a bigger piece of the market. Sometimes businesses react to competition by using unfair practices. And sometimes competitors even conspire to control the market through price fixing.

Resorting to unethical practices most likely will come back to haunt you. Antitrust investigator will no doubt eventually look into the practice of unethical behavior. Such investigation, once made public, even if found not to be illegal will erode consumer confidence and affect sales.

4. Coping with Bad Publicity

The saying that there's no such thing as bad publicity just isn't true. In fact, in these days of social media and the 24 hour news cycle, bad publicity can quickly develop into a public relations nightmare. Recall recent events with Tylenol, Toyota, or British Petroleum.

How bad publicity is handled speaks volumes to the public. If company executives try to ignore or spin the bad news, they simply put off the inevitable and often make the situation worse. If they come across as defensive, angry, or arrogant, they add to the problem.

Transparency, honestly, and accountability are the best antidotes for bad publicity; if handle this way, the story becomes less about the bad news and more about the appropriate response.

5. Being Honest with Consumers

Consumers would rather have bad news delivered straight up than have businesses skirt the real reasons why they can't fulfill consumer needs. As a result, companies need to be truthful with their customers at all times.

Misleading customers and potential customers, beyond just annoying them, gives them a reason to tell friends and acquaintances to be wary of doing business with you. Potential customers may now avoid you due to your tarnished reputation.

6. Being Honest with Employees

The age-old joke among employees is that management treats them like mushrooms. They keep them in the dark and feed them manure. Actually, being honest with employees is the best way for a company to encourage them to be honest with the company.

Being honest isn't always easy for management. When companies have to lay off workers or restructure pay and bonus programs, many managers are tempted to either downplay the changes or react with a "hard-line-of-take-it-or-leave-it." And sometimes employees seek information that management is not ready to share, the proper response should be, "I can't answer that right now." Telling employees that certain information is confidential at this time is always better than lying to them.

7. Being Honest with Stockholders

Stockholders naturally want their investments in a company to grow in value. But contrary to what you may think, they don't want growth at any cost. When the situation is a question of doing the right thing versus making money, stockholders likely prefer doing the right thing as long as the company is as honest and transparent with them as it can be.

When communicating with stockholders, management should always:

Share Information—Knowledge is power and the more information they have, the more likely they are to understand and approve your decisions.

Be Realistically Hopeful—If going through difficult times acknowledge the challenges being faced and explain what you are doing to meet those challenges. Without overselling, give your investors a reason to look to the future with hope and confidence.

Lead by Example—If you feel like you are not up to the challenge, others can sense it, and they will lose confidence in you and the company. An air of confidence, not arrogance, coupled with honest and transparent communication, can do more to influence stockholders than any number of quarterly reports.

8. Keeping Accounting Honest

The Sarbanese-Oxley Act (SOX Act) is supposed to make executive officers, auditing firms, and board of directors more accountable for the companies' accounting practices. In real life, the pressures associated with accounting practices haven't changed very much. "Tweaking the numbers" can be tempting when you are looking for new financing, launching an IPO, or wanting to get the analysts and bankers off your back. The temptation increases when salaries, bonuses, and other incentives are tied to meeting financial goals.

9. Lobby for and against Regulation

Even if you are a proprietorship, small partnership, or LLC, as opposed to a large corporation, you have to deal with laws and regulations particularly at the local and state level as well as the federal level. Telling lawmakers and government what you think and how laws and regulations affect you is part of being a good businessperson.

To keep governmental communications appropriate;

Remember who your stakeholders are and what they need and focus on them in your contacts with government officials.

Make your case with facts, not with your personal relationships.

Grease with genuine gratitude, not with cash or gifts.

10. Contributing to Political Campaigns

Giving money to a candidate is a common way for a business to build relationships with elected officials. And nothing about contributing to political campaigns is inherently unethical. But such contributions can blur ethical boundaries when they lead to conflicts of interest.

Make sure you know the limits of campaign contributions, and never pressure employees, vendors, or other stakeholders to support a candidate or campaign.

If you set up a Political Action Committee (PAC), make sure its activities are separate from the business.

Respecting Cultural Difference

One of the toughest ethical questions for multinational businesses is whether they should follow the adage "When in Rome, do as the Romans." Different cultures have different moral norms and practices—a situation know as *cultural relativism*. When multinational companies assume that their moral values (what they ought to do) depend on the culture in which they operate, they practice *ethical relativism*. That is, these companies apply different ethical and moral standards according to the physical locations of their operations.

Companies that do business in the Middle East, for example, have to contend with cultural norms that prohibit women from driving or appearing in public without a male escort or without the religious attire (such as head coverings) that their society requires. If your company is committed to gender equality (as it should), how do you live up to your own ethical principles in a culture that places severe restrictions on the activities of women? Do you require your female employees to conform to those cultural rules? Do you avoid hiring women in that culture or deny the women in your company the opportunity to work in your Middle East locations?

The following list three guidelines when doing business in other cultures:

1. **Adhere to universal moral standards.**

   The first obligation of any multinational company is to follow *universal moral standards*—the standards that societies develop in order to survive. Although cultures differ in many of their traditions of what constitutes right and wrong, all societies share some universal moral views. For example, murder is a universal wrong. Some society recognize extenuating factors that may lead you to kill another person, such as defending yourself against an assault, in which case the killing does not meet the definition of murder. But all societies prohibit killing another person for the sake of killing, or in the process of committing another crime. Other universal moral standards include prohibitions against stealing and assault and obligations to care for children and the elderly.

2. Recognize trust and honesty as basic business standards.

Multinational companies should adhere to the minimum business standards of trust and honesty. Trust is an essential ingredient of any business transaction. Businesses have to trust suppliers to provide the proper materials or services, and suppliers have to trust their clients to pay them fairly. Workers have to trust their employers to pay them and to protect their safety on the job, and businesses have to trust their employers to do their jobs. Customers have to trust businesses to give them fair value in exchange for the money they pay. Trust is nurture through honest dealings, so honesty is the basic moral currency of any business. Trust and honesty also preclude engaging in bribery or other forms of corruption.

3. Value human rights.

Because business depends on economic freedom, multinational businesses should respect basic human liberties. Economic freedom is an element of civil and political liberty, so ethical companies have an obligation to defend and promote human rights wherever they do business. The dilemma for multinational businesses is to walk the fine line between respecting cultural differences and conforming to universal ethical norms.

Developing countries often lack the regulatory structure to ensure that business conforms to the basic moral principles we experience in our own country. And, unfortunately, the absence of an outside monitor can make unethical behavior more tempting, especially if moral breaches would increase revenues or profits. In the information age of instant news and viral videos, a company runs a serious risk of exposure by flouting universal moral standards. Even if government regulators aren't watching, human rights groups and the news media are. And public opinion can deliver a severe blow to a company's reputation, and to its profits.

Ethics in Leadership:

*"Ethics is a code of values which guide our choices and
actions and determine the purpose and course of our lives."*
Ayn Rand

In improving organizational ethical behavior no role is more crucial than that of senior management visible commitment to ethical conduct. It must give constant leadership in renewing and enforcing the ethical values of the organization. The commitment must be actively communicated in speeches, directives, company publications, and especially in actions which set the tone of the organization.

In resolving ethical problems as in solving all problems managers should: analyze the consequences, analyze the actions, and make a decision.

1. Analyze the consequences—Who will be helped by what you do? Who will be harmed? What kind of help and harm is involved? What will be the result in the long run as well as the short run?

2. Analyze the action—consider the options from a different viewpoint. What are the different consequences? How do they measure against moral principles like fairness, equality, honesty, integrity, and respect for others? What is the common good?

3. Make a decision—View all perspectives and make a decision and evaluate the results. Alter your actions if called for.

   *"An action without thought is nothing and a
   thought without action is nothing at all."*

Code of Ethics

A code of ethics is a formal statement of the company's values concerning ethics and social issues; it communicates to employees what the company stands for and how it should behavior. When a code of ethics is written, employees tend to take it more seriously and accept that management also considers it very important. Having such a written system in place is the best well to stop ethical problems before they start.

Codes of ethics tend to exist in two types: Principle-Based statements and Policy-Based statements.

Principle-Based statements are designed to affect corporate culture, define fundamental values, and contain general language about company responsibilities, quality of products and service, and treatment of employees. These general statements of principle are often call corporate credos.

Policy-Based statements generally outline the procedure to be used in specific ethical situations such as: marketing practice, conflict of interest, observance of laws, proprietary information, political gifts, and equal opportunities.

Codes of ethics state the values and behaviors that are expected and those that will not be tolerated within the organization. They must have full management support to assure that the code will be meaningful and followed.

A well-written code of ethics should establish several things. It can state what the company expects and understands what is and is not ethical behavior, a values statement. It can establish a clear and detailed guide to acceptable behavior. It can articulate exact policies of behavior for specific situations. And, it can outline what punishments and reprimands will be forthcoming for violations.

Before a company can create a code of ethics that everyone can respect and adhere to, it needs to be relevant to the organization and industry and have a foundation on what a code of ethics is. The best ethics codes have the following:

Apply to everyone:

From the newest hire to the board of directors, every person in the company is expected to adhere to the code. And just as important, everyone is subject to the same disciplinary measures for violating the code, regardless of position in the company.

Are consistent, even when the market isn't:

When economic pressures increase, compliance with the company's ethical code can easily decrease. However, the company that compromises its ethics to survive a slump risks both its reputation and its future. A dynamic, living code of ethics is relevant in boom and bust times.

Promote transparency and accountability:

"Sunlight is said to be the best of disinfectants; electric light the most efficient policeman." The less secretive the procedures and policies are, the less opportunity employees have for skirting or ignoring the rules. Less opportunity for unethical conduct means less temptation to indulge in questionable behavior.

Keep up with the times:

This means applying core values to new developments in technology, regulation, and any other conditions that affect the employee's on-the-job conduct.

Ethical Structure:

Ethical structure represents the various systems, positions, and programs a company can undertake to implement ethical behavior.

An ethics committee is a group of executives appointed to oversee company ethics. The committee provides ruling on questionable ethical issues. The committee assumes responsibility for disciplining violators of the code, which is essential in order to directly influence employee behavior. The ethics committee will generally report directly to the Board-of-Directors.

A senior executive, reporting to the CEO, may serve as an ethical ombudsman given the responsibility of corporate conscience that hears and investigates ethical complaints and indicates potential ethical failure to top management prior to the necessity of full committee action.

Other effective structures are formal ethics training programs and "hot" lines availability.

Ethics training seeks to help people understand the ethical aspects of decisions and to incorporate high ethical standards into their daily activities. Ethics training programs require all employees to attend an orientation session and on-going seminars at which they read and sign-off on the corporate code of ethics. Executives are providing training in ethical decision-making.

A "hot" line is a toll-free number to which employees can confidentially report questionable behavior as well as possible fraud, waste, or abuse. No reprisals will be taken against anyone using it.

Ethics and Technology

> *"Big Brother is watching you."*
> George Orwell

Advances in technology have greatly enhanced the efficiency, effectiveness, and productivity of business. The computer, internet, e-mail, instant messaging, fax, cell-phones all have made communication of information and product delivery more assessable to employees and customers alike. With such ease of use and available has also produced perhaps a loss of privacy. As a customer and even a medical patient, your records are easily obtained by others, often by the very companies you are doing business with to lower their cost. As an employee, your e-mail and web-site visited are no doubt being monitored as is your business phone to assure your work productivity.

Google and other search engines keep records of our individual searches, why?

Many internet based business acquire personal information which their privacy policy declares that they won't sell to third parties but only used to assist you. Purchase a book on the web and more than likely, the book sellers will advise you of previous purchases and recommend similar material.

As an employee of a business, your productivity during work hours represents your work obligation for pay you owe the company. Therefore your actions during that time are at the discretion of the company. Other than lunch or other breaks, all your activity should be work related, and any monitoring should not be regarded as an infringement of your privacy. If you want to do something in private don't do it at work.

Many employees take the position that whereas the time at work does represent the fulfillment of an obligation for which compensation is received, however this obligation should not intrude on individual civil rights. I am an employee not a servant and as such should be notified of any surveillance and monitoring. Why should all suffer for the violations of a few? Such monitoring implies that I cannot be trusted; if not then why was I hired.

Ethical Accounting Issues in Business

> *"Earnings can be as pliable as putty when a charlatan heads the company reporting them."*
> Warren Buffet

An ethical issue in business is a problem, situation, or opportunity that requires an individual decision maker, group of people, or organization to choose among alternative actions that must be evaluated as (the better) right or (the lesser) wrong, ethical or unethical.

It has been said that there is no such thing as "business" ethics. That a single standard of ethics applies to both our business and to our personal lives. Remember, that it is individuals that manage businesses and it is individuals that make decisions for those businesses.

While most recognize that business must earn a profit to survive; it is the steps taken by those individuals running the business to make a profit that concerns ethicists. The "ends do not justify the means". If it did, business could rationalize not taking the necessary steps to protect the environment based on excessive costs to comply with the EPA laws. If a company via the decisions of its managers takes such a position, it would be placing its own self-interests, perhaps in the guise of maximizing shareholder wealth, ahead of the interest of society.

Five major ethical issues have been identified: honesty and fairness, conflicts of interest, fraud, discrimination, and information technology.

With an emphasis on business transactions in accounting producing accurate and reliable financial statements and transparency of events, focused is placed on the first three.

Honesty and Fairness

Abraham Lincoln once said, "No man has a good enough memory to be a successful liar." A person who lies about a matter then has to remember what was said and be sure to provide a consistent response when questioned; otherwise the story will come apart.

You have an obligation to be honest and trustworthy in your business dealings as well as your personal life. What kind of example do you set for your family; sons and daughters, if you do improper things in business while touting ethical behavior at home in your personal life.

Fairness, of course, is the treatment of others equally in ethical decision making. Fairness is not often regarding in accounting or financial reporting but it too requires objective disclosures with the interests of its stakeholders. These include the stockholders, creditors, employees, suppliers, customers, and government agencies that regulate business. Accounting professionals should approach their roles as preparers of financial statements without bias of how transactions should be reported and disclosed. The statements should be transparent: accurate, reliable, and reflect full disclosure; and, of course, should be prepared in accordance with GAAP and not be misleading.

Conflict of Interests

A conflict of interest is a situation in which private interest or personal considerations could affect or be perceived to affect an employee's judgment to act in the best interests of the business. Examples include using an employee's position, confidential information, or personal relationship for private gain or advancement.

Objectivity and integrity are essential qualities for employees of any organization. It is the perception that a person may be influenced by matters or relationships not relevant to a decision that creates many of the conflicts of interest problems in business. When such occurs creating a conflict of interest, one should step aside or recuse himself from the matter and avoid the appearance of bias. (A member of the Supreme Court should have done so in regard to the ObamaCare debate as she was instrumental in its development prior to her appointment to the Supreme Court.)

Honest people not only avoid lying but also have as a goal the disclosure of all information that another party has a right to know (lying by omission).

FRAUD

Fraud can be defined as a deliberate misrepresentation to gain an advantage over another party.

The Association of Certified Fraud Examiners (ACFE) defines occupational fraud as "the use of one's occupation for personal enrichment through the deliberate misuse or misapplication of the employing organization's resources or assets."

ACFE identifies four key elements of fraud schemes: the activity is clandestine; the activity violates the perpetrator's fiduciary responsibilities; the act is committed for the purpose of direct or indirect personal financial benefit; and it costs the business assets or revenue. These schemes occur because of a lack of internal controls and ineffective corporate governance.

Fraud occurs as a result of a failure in organizational ethics because financial statement fraud cannot occur without the involvement of top management and either a breakdown or override of internal controls. In these organizations, the tone set by top management does not promote ethical behavior, and the result is increased pressure on accountants and auditors to detect and report the fraud.

Whistle-Blowers

> *"The word whistle-blower suggests that you're a tattletale or that you're somehow disloyal... But I wasn't disloyal in the least bit. People were dying. I was loyal to a higher order of ethical responsibility."*
> Dr. Jeffrey Wigand

Employees' disclosure of illegal, immoral, or illegitimate practices on the employer's part is called whistle-blowing. A whistleblower exposes the misdeeds of others in the organization. Anyone in the organization can blow the whistle if he or she detects such organizational activity. Whistle-blowers often report wrongdoing to outsiders, such as regulatory agencies, law enforcement, newspapers, and senators or representatives. In enlightened companies that strive for ethical behavior, whistle-blowers are able to report internally to an ethic ombudsman or ethics committee.

Whistle-blowers must be protected if this is to be an effective safeguard, otherwise, they will suffer and the organization may continue its unethical or illegal activity. Federal and state laws offer whistleblowers defense against potential retaliatory action from organizations accused. However legal protection can still be inadequate. Laws vary from state to state, and federal laws mainly protect government workers in their efforts to report misdeeds in government agencies. Within the organization, whistleblowers may still encounter difficulties by a strict chain of command that makes it hard to bypass the boss; a strong work group identity that encourages loyalty; and ambiguous priorities that make it hard to distinguish right from wrong. It has been observed that the top reasons for not reporting wrongdoings are; the belief that no corrective action would be taken, and the fear of retaliation by the revelation not being kept confidential.

Cohesiveness

Cohesiveness is another important aspect of creating and managing an ethical work climate and corporate culture. Employee team cohesiveness is the extent to which members are attracted to the team and its effort, and motivated to remain in it and contribute. Members of highly cohesive teams are committed to team activities and projects, attend and participate in meetings, and are happy and satisfied when the team succeeds. Members of less cohesive teams are less concerned about the team's accomplishments and welfare.

The characteristics of an organization's structure, context, and corporate culture influence team cohesiveness.

First is the interaction between the employees of the organization. The greater the amount of contact among employees and the more time spend together, the more cohesive the organization. Through frequent and productive interaction employees get to know one another fostering better cooperation and become more devoted to the objectives and goals of the organization.

Second is the concept of shared goals. If the employees agreed on the goals of the organization and its vision, they will more cohesive in a team effort. Agreeing on the purpose and direction of the organization binds them together.

Third is the personal attraction each has to the organization. They desire to be with others who share in similar attitudes and values to accomplish common goals and enjoy being together in achieving that task. Competition with another organization is also a factor in increasing cohesiveness of an organization as, with a team effort, it strives to win. When the success and favorable evaluation of the winning effort is recognized by senior management and outsiders greatly adds to the pride, job satisfaction, commitment, and cohesiveness of the organization as the team members feel good with their accomplishment.

The outcome of the cohesiveness of an organization can fall into two categories: morale and productivity.

As a general rule, morale is higher in cohesive companies because of increased communication, a friendly climate, commitment and loyalty to the organization, and employees' participation in organization decisions, activities, and objectives.

Cohesiveness may have several effects; first, employee's productivity tends to be more uniform. Productivity difference among employees is small because the team exerts pressure on each other towards conformity.

In addition cohesive organizations have the potential and tendency to be more productive with the degree of productivity efficiency related to the relationship between management and the working team.

Behavior Norms

Norms of the organization is a standard of conduct that is shared by the employees and guides their behavior. Norms are informal and often part of the corporate culture. They are not written down as are rules, regulations, and procedures. They are valuable to an organization as they define the boundaries of acceptable behavior. Norms make work performance easier for employees as they provide a frame of reference of what is right or wrong and expected behavior for key values and company survival. They began to develop in the very first interaction among employees.

Ethical Principles for Entrepreneurs:

(*Ethical Obligations and Opportunities in Business Ethical Decision Making*, Josphenson Institute of Ethics.Los Angeles, CA)

The following list of principles incorporates the characteristics and values associated with ethical behavior.

1. HONESTY: Ethical entrepreneur managers are honest and truthful in all their dealings and they do not deliberately mislead or deceive others by misrepresentations, overstatements, partial truths, selective omissions, or any other means.

2. INTERGRITY: Ethical entrepreneurs demonstrate personal integrity and the courage of their convictions by doing what they think is right even when there is great pressure to do otherwise; they are principled, honorable, and upright; they will fight for their beliefs. They will not sacrifice principle for expediency or be hypocritical or unscrupulous.

3. PROMISE-KEEPING AND TRUSTWORTHINESS: Ethical entrepreneurs are worthy of trust, they are candid and forthcoming in supplying relevant information and correcting misapprehensions of fact, and they make every reasonable effort to fulfill the letter and spirit of their promises and commitments. They do not interpret agreements in an unreasonably technical or legalistic manner in order to rationalize noncompliance or create justification for escaping their commitments.

4. LOYALTY: They are worthy of trust, demonstrate fidelity and loyalty to persons and institutions by friendship in adversity, and display support and devotion to duty; they do not use or disclose information learned in confidence for personal advantage. They safeguard the ability to make independent professional judgments by scrupulously avoiding undue influences and conflicts of interest. They are loyalty to their employees and colleagues. They respect the proprietary information of former employers, and refuse to engage in any activities that take undue advantage of their previous positions.

5. FAIRNESS: Ethical entrepreneurs are fair and just in all dealings; they do not exercise power arbitrarily, and do not use overreaching nor indecent means to gain or maintain any advantage nor take undue advantage of another's mistake or difficulties. Fair persons manifest a commitment to justice, the equal treatment of individuals, and tolerance for and

acceptance of diversity and are open-mined, they are willing to admit they are wrong and, when appropriate, change their positions and beliefs.

6. CONCERN FOR OTHERS: They are caring, compassionate, benevolent, and kind; they live the Golden Rule, help those-in-need, and seek to accomplish their business objectives in a manner that causes the least harm and the greatest positive good.

7. RESPECT FOR OTHERS: Ethical entrepreneur managers demonstrate respect for the human dignity, autonomy, privacy, rights, and interests of all those who have a stake in their decisions; they are courteous and treat all people with equal respect and dignity regardless of sex, race, or national origin.

8. LAW ABIDING: They abide by laws, rules, and regulations relating to their business.

9. COMMITMENT TO EXCELLENCE: Ethical entrepreneurs pursue excellence in performing their duties, are well informed and prepared, and constantly endeavor to increase their proficiency in all areas of responsibility.

10. LEADERSHIP: Ethical entrepreneurs are conscious of the responsibilities and opportunities of their position of leadership and seek to be positive ethical role model by their own conduct and by helping to create an environment in which principled reasoning and ethical decision making are highly prized.

11. REPUTATION AND MORALE: They seek to protect and build the company's good reputation and the morale of its employees by engaging in no conduct that might undermine respect and by taking whatever actions are necessary to correct or prevent inappropriate conduct of others.

12. ACCOUNTABILITY: Ethical entrepreneur managers acknowledge and accept personal accountability for the ethical quality of their decisions and omissions to themselves, their employees, their colleagues, their companies, and their communities.

COMMON OBSTACLES TO ETHICAL ENTREPRENEUR BEHAVIOR

"If ethics are poor at the top, that behavior is copied down through the organization."
Robert Noyce

GREED

Greed is defined as "a selfish and excessive desire for more of something than is needed." "Personal Greed" appears as the main factor in the ethics scandals of the early 2000s. Even though most business executives are basically ethical, there is tremendous pressure to create profits which could lead to "ethically vulnerability" encouraging questionable activity.

Greed isn't always about money. Sometimes people are greedy for power, status, influence, or anything else they desire in excess.

So for a business to attempt to keep greed in check, the following should be exercised:

Establish an ethical culture that puts principle ahead of profits

Set up a system of checks and balances that promote accountability and transparency

Set up a reward system that combines financial and other incentives to do good, not just to do well.

GROUP-THINKING

Group-thinking is the failure to invite, recognize, or listen to different points of view. It is tough to overcome because group thinkers can intimidate the people who might present different viewpoints in a number-of-ways. i.e. If managers display a don't-tell-me-anything-I-don't-want-to hear attitude, or if they react with anger when someone expresses an opinion that's different from theirs, chances are they'll seldom get any valuable input from the people around them.

TUNNEL VISION

Tunnel vision is closely related to group-thinking in that both conditions involve not paying attention to differing viewpoints and ignoring relevant details. While group-thinking typically occurs when contemplating a specific action, tunnel vision can make you stay committed to a course of action even when you should abandon it.

Tunnel vision is most common when the corporate culture doesn't make allowance for failure. Business is risky by nature, and expecting unbroken success is unrealistic. Nevertheless, many managers feel enormous pressure to always be successful, and sometimes they are so focused on that goal that they don't even realize that they are crossing ethical lines to achieve it.

SELF-INTEREST

Most people tend to do what will benefit them and avoid what may harm them. But often strong motivated self-interest can tug people toward unethical behavior.

Motivated self-interest can stem from any number of needs, desires, or goals including:

- Fear of losing a job
- Desire for more pay
- Desire for status, power, or influence

ARROGANCE

Every business leader needs confidence, but, all too often, confidence develops into arrogance- the belief that you are smarter, more visionary, and more right than those around you. Arrogant people don't tolerate dissent, and they dismiss questions and alternative viewpoints as unworthy of consideration. They firmly believe that they are superior to everyone else and that, because they are better than everyone else, they can do whatever they want.

LABOR COSTS

Hiring workers is expensive, and labor is always a target item when companies have to trim the budget. The temptation to focus on costs and ignore inconvenient facts about your workers' conditions can be powerful.

PRODUCTION COSTS

Even if you can get cheap labor without violating ethical standards, the cost of materials, equipment, and space can easily be astronomical. And when production costs encroach on profits, the pressure to reduce those costs can be overwhelming. The temptation to shave these costs often results in less quality, employee morale, and customer satisfaction which will impact profits even more.

LACK OF TRANSPARENCY

Transparency is simply making information available to both employees and customers. The more open a company is about its operations, the less likely it is to suffer from ethical nearsightedness.

FEAR

Fear is a double-edged sword when it comes to business ethics. On the one-hand, it can help people fight the temptation to behave unethically because they fear the consequences of getting caught: feeling embarrassed or humiliated, disappointing relatives and friends, going to jail, and so on. But, on the other hand, if this is the only reason they behave ethically, then the business has a corporate culture and management problem.

DOUBLE STANDARDS

Managers who take a "do as I say, not as I do" approach to supervising surrender the most valuable currency they have in promoting ethical behavior: their own integrity. Employees who don't respect their managers can become cynical and even retaliatory by stealing time, supplies, or money, or by otherwise sabotaging the company.

The same issues arise when management ignores ethical violations from high performers but punish the same infractions from average or low-performing employees. The message is: "You can do whatever you want as long as you make money for the company."

Ethical Guidepost

Rotary Club, a worldwide organization of business and professional leaders, has set a high standard for business conduct. It calls on its members to ask the following four questions when they prepare to make a decision about the things they think, say, or do:

1. **Is it the Truth?**

2. **Is it Fair to all concerned?**

3. **Will it build Goodwill and Better Friendships?**

4. **Will it be Beneficial to all concerned?**

In addition to these four the following ten rules should be followed:

Ten Ethical Guideposts

1. Respect All People

Regardless of differences (or similarities) in skin color, religious beliefs, or any other area of life, every individual is an autonomous agent capable of making his or her own decisions about what's right and wrong. When you respect others' autonomy, you don't view them as a means to an end and are more likely to treat them fairly.

Helpful tips to respect others:

Mind your manners. Saying "please" and "thank you" isn't just common courtesy; these words are an implicit acknowledgement of the other person's individuality.

Invite Opinions. When you ask others what they think, you place them on an equal footing as people—even if they aren't equals in your business.

Give credit where it's due. Anyone can work hard and generate good ideas, no matter what their job title. But the managers who take credit for their employees' efforts undermine the employees' standing as individuals deserving respect. Take pride in the people on your team whom you may have very well assembled, brag about them, their efforts and ideas. You will be surprised how much your own reputation will shine.

2. Don't Lie

Telling the truth is a universal ethical standard because societies can't function if lying is okay. Commerce would grind to a halt because consumers wouldn't be able to trust businesses.

On the other hand, sometimes telling the whole truth goes against the company's best interest. You don't have to lie to avoid telling the whole truth. Be honest with information you can release, and, for information you can't share, say, "I'm not at liberty to discuss this particular issue."

3. Avoid Bribes

Every country in the world officially outlaws bribery for one simple reason: Bribery creates an unequal playing field that disproportionately penalizes small companies and poor people. Bribery basically is offering to exchange something-usually money-in return for an unfair advantage in some aspect of business, such as bidding on contracts.

Giving one bribe cam make your company vulnerable to repeated demands for "gifts" to receive the permits you need to do business. Staunch refusal to bribery demands keeps your company's reputation clean and lowers the pressure to "play the game" in areas where bribery is commonplace.

4. Don't Make a Mess

For decades, companies spewed pollutants into the air, water, and soil without a second thought. But these days, companies have an ethical obligation, and sound business reasons, to ensure that their activities are eco-friendly.

From an ethical viewpoint, protecting the environment is good business because good corporate citizens strive to improve the communities they operate in, generating benefits for everyone. If your operation employs people but makes the water undrinkable, you aren't helping the community nor your very employees and consumers who are essential to your operation.

Often, especially due to government mandates, cleaning up messes is more expensive (and more damaging to your reputation and future sales) than avoiding them in the first place.

5. If You Make a Mess, Clean It Up

Accidents can happen, even if you're careful about you conduct. Messes can be physical, such as oil spills or asbestos in buildings. But messes can also arise from simple human interaction- ranging from innocent misunderstandings to outright bad behavior. Whatever causes the mess and whatever kind of mess it is, you still need to clean it up.

You don't have to do the cleanup alone; asking for help is okay as long as you take responsibility for your part in making the mess. But leaving the mess for someone else to take care of is unacceptable.

6. Take Responsibility for Your Actions

Nobody likes to watch the companies play the blame game. Unfortunately, owning up to mistakes can cost a fortune in government fines and civil lawsuits, too many companies have forgotten the value of combining a sincere apology with a genuine effort to correct the problem.

Taking responsibility involves the following four steps:
- Acknowledge the problem.
- Offer a sincere apology.
- Repair the damage.
- Take steps to avoid a repeat of the problem.

7. Play by the Rules

Sometimes rules are silly and ineffective. But even if they are, most rules are intended to make sure everyone has the same opportunities. Breaking the rules violates the universal ethical standards of honesty and trust, and no business (or society) can survive for long without those acceptable standards.

The ethical way to cope with rules that don't make sense is to work to change them, not to break them.

8. Work Hard

Working hard is how you ensure that you earn your rewards. Most ethical theories and religions hold that hard work enhances your character and is morally beneficial, while laziness is typically reviled. The concept of a *meritocracy* (a society in which effort and achievement are rewarded with more money, status, or both) places its highest premium on working hard and smart.

Working hard means:

- Consistently giving your best efforts at your job every day;
- Showing up on time and putting in a full day's work;
- Using your skills and talents to advance both the company's interests and your own

This does not imply that leisure is bad; everyone needs some leisure time to take care of themselves physically, mentally, emotionally, and spiritually. However, when at work, your employer and your fellow employees deserve your full attention and commitment.

9. Be Humble in Success

Celebrate your wins, but don't get cocky. Remember, success in business is always a team effort, coupled with good fortune. If you start believing your own hype, you end up arrogant and blind to situations that can threaten your business.

You can take pride in your achievements. But don't allow pride to interfere with your vision to see both threats and opportunities, nor interfere with your dedication to doing things right and doing the right thing.

10. Be Generous

Generosity is more than just writing a check to your favorite charity. A generous spirit comes from an attitude of abundance—a focus on what you have rather on what you don't have. Generosity allows you to feel joy at other's accomplishments and good fortune, to forgive colleagues for their human fragilities and mistakes, and to empathize with those whose circumstance are less pleasant than yours.

Generosity also enables you to offer help for the sake of helping (not because you can get good publicity from it) and to motivate your employees to do their best work. Your generosity provides an example for others to cultivate a generous spirit, helping to create a company culture in which success is measured by ethical behavior as well as profits.

How to Keep the Company Ethical

Choose Ethical Leaders

Hiring ethical managers may be the single most important thing you can do to build and maintain an ethical culture. If your company's leaders aren't committed to ethical behavior, all your other attempts- establishing a code of ethics, applying ethical standards to everyone, having an independent board of directors- are likely to have limited impact. Why; because employees have no respect for a "do as I say, not as I do" manager.

So how do you choose ethical leaders? By asking probing questions during the interview process, such as:

- Describe a workplace dilemma encountered and explain how resolved.
- Pose a hypothetical ethical dilemma and ask how they would handle it.
- Ask an opinion on current business ethics in the news.

Have an Independent Board of Directors

The board of directors is responsible for ensuring the organization's future, creating the policies and objectives, and appointing the managers who actually administer the policies and implement the objectives. Also they have a responsibility to the stockholders.

In reality, boards of directors don't do enough in probing and questioning management's decisions to make sure they're ethical and in the company's best interest. Sometimes directors are more interested in what they can gain than in what's best for the company. Sometimes they have conflicts of interest that hamper their ability to make good decisions. Most boards:

Rely on management to keep them informed.

Often don't have the time and sometimes the skills or background to understand complex transactions or other details of the company's business.

Foster a "go along to get along" mind-set that discourages questioning of a company's actions or performance.

Have a Living Code of Ethics

Codes of ethics are often posted prominently for everyone to see. Unfortunately, they often spend their existence gathering dust. One of the keys in keeping your company ethical is making sure your code of ethics isn't just a forgotten piece of paper. It should be a dynamic, living document, continually reviewed for relevance and reinforced through training, managerial example, and self-policing among employees.

Explain the Reasoning behind the Code

Knowledge is power, and the easiest way to get employees to adhere to the code is to explain why the code the code is important. New hires are too often asked to sign off on the code but then never think about it again.

Apply Ethical Standards to Everyone

Nothing saps morale and commitment to ethical conduct more quickly than the perception that different rules apply to different people. Most will accept that those in positions of authority get paid more. But very few believe it is okay to hold different people to different ethical standards.

Value Ethics over Performance

Often higher-performing workers aren't held to the same ethical rules as poor performers.

Engage Stakeholders

To engage stakeholders a company has to figure how to communicate with them and how to encourage them to communicate with your company. The more communications established, the more successful will be needed input to maintain the company's ethical culture.

Support Industry-Wide Regulation

Companies that sincerely promote sensible regulation gets an image boost that can translate into new customers and higher revenues. Your stakeholders want to be proud of their association with your company, and by supporting ways to ensure and enforce ethically standards; you show stakeholders that your company is genuinely committed to doing the right thing.

Create an Environment Where People Want to Come to Work

Employees who feel valued, who are paid a fair wage, and who feel that they have a voice and an important contribution to make are far less likely to resort to ethical lapses.

Stay Alert to Ethical Threats

Creating and maintain an ethical culture is not a one-shot deal; it requires long-term commitment and integration into the overall business strategy. Regular training and review of ethical policies and procedures, combined with input from stakeholders, are essential elements of your strategy.

"...there is one and only one social responsibility of business-to use its resources and engage in activities designed to increase its profits so long as it stays within the rules of the game, which is to say, engages in open and free competition without deception or fraud."
Milton Friedman, "Capitalism and Freedom"

THE PROBLEMS WITH RULES

Rules are external
They are made by others
They present us with a puzzle to be solved and loopholes to be found.

We are ambivalent about rules
We know we need some and we want others to play by them,
But we say, "Rules are meant to be broken."

Rules are reactive
They respond to past events

Rules are both over and under inclusive
Because they are proxies, they cannot be precise.

Proliferation of rules is a tax on the system
Few people can remember them all.
We lose productivity when we stop to look them up.

Rules are typically prohibitions
They speak to *can* and *can't*.
We view them as confining and constricting.

Rules require enforcement
With laxity, they lose credibility and effectiveness.
They necessitate expensive bureaucracies of compliance.

Rules speak to boundaries and floors
But create inadvertent ceilings
We can't legislate "The sky's the limit."

The only way to honor rules is to obey them exactly
They speak to coercion and motivation.
The inspiration to excel must come from somewhere else.

Too many rules breeds overreliance
We think, "If it mattered, they would have made a rule."

FINAL THOUGHTS

"Nothing great was ever achieved without enthusiasm."
Ralph Waldo Emerson

If you have gone through all the steps of analyzing the market, identifying opportunities, and developing a business plan, then you have made substantial progress toward preparing yourself to start a business. However, if you are like most people, you probably found that for every question answered, more questions surfaced.

At this point, much like when you graduate from school; you learned a lot, but you still don't know all you need to know. There is a lot more to learn. This is why graduation is called commencement rather than completion. You still have to set up your accounting system, get your federal employer identification number, hire your people, get insurance coverage, develop your advertisements, and do numerous other activities before you open the doors.

This book has helped you address many of the major questions that will need to be answered. No class, no one, can provide all the answers or, even identify all the questions. It will be up to you. **"If it is to be, it is up to me."**

Hopefully, this book has pointed you in the right direction. And provided a basis for preparing a business plan that will give you a better than 50/50 chance for succeeding. When it comes to starting a business, there are no guarantees and there are no shortcuts. Starting a business always involves risks. All you can do is try to minimize the risk by thinking things through and preparing yourself for surprises.

Leadership is one of the central problems of entrepreneur managers and executives at all levels. Leadership is the capacities to guide, direct, motivate, and influence the behaviors of others with imagination and innovation toward given ends. The trait theory contends that leadership is uniquely inherent in the psychological makeup of individuals. The situational pattern of circumstances views leadership as rising to the situation contingent on the needs and resources of a given environment. Both have contributed ideas of value, but neither approach along is satisfactory to explain the talent, art, and skill of leadership require to move others to buy into a shared vision for the good of the organization.

The role of first line leaders is the management function of planning, organizing, controlling, and leading. The business owner supervisory entrepreneur manager's role is traditionally viewed as the man in the middle of employees and everyone else, the liaison and communicator between them. Although this is a fair portrayal of the role, in reality, the entrepreneur/manager's beliefs and goals are closer to those of other business owners than to those of non-managerial employees.

The basic duties of a leader in an organization are decision-making, planning, coordination, control, communication and motivation, staffing and training. Along with these duties, the leader is responsible for managing an ethical culture, building loyalty and trust among employees, conflict and stress management, and job satisfaction. Therefore the primary duty of a good and true entrepreneur manager is to lead and run an organization in an effective, efficient, and ethical manner.

To succeed in business requires persistence. To manage for success, to achieve financial independence, to succeed in life, one must persevere. Sooner or later the person who wins is the person who thinks he/she can, and is able manage and convince others that together they can.

"Nothing can take the place of persistence. Talent will not. Nothing is more common than unsuccessful people with talent. Genius will not. Unrewarded genius is almost a proverb. Education alone will not. The world is full of educated derelicts. Persistence and determination alone are omnipotent."
Calvin Coolidge

ABOUT THE AUTHOR

Daniel R. Hogan, Jr., Ph.D.

Dr. Hogan is a career banker, financier, consultant, and educator; He organized and obtained approval for a national bank, Louisiana Guaranty National Bank, and a state bank, State Bank of Commerce. Prior to being Chairman of the Board and President of these banks, he was Senior Vice President and Chairman of the Commercial Loan Committee of the National Bank of Commerce. Concurrently with organizing the new banks, in 1985 he incorporated, and presently operates as President, Hogan Financial Corporation, *"The Entrepreneur's Edge"*, a commercial lending and consulting company, and as of January 2003 organized and incorporated Hogan Business School, Inc., *"The Entrepreneur's Source."*

He is or has been Visiting Professor at Our Lady of Holy Cross College, Loyola University, Nunez Community College, Delgado Community College, Concordia University, and the University of New Orleans with emphasis on Entrepreneurship, Financing, Franchising, Money and Banking, Economics, and Management. He has served as a business consultant at the University of New Orleans Small Business Development Center and has conducted various Small Business Development Center's entrepreneur, business and banking seminars. He has been an instructor for the Kauffman Foundation's FastTrac Entrepreneur Program. He has taught at the American Institute of Banking. He served as a member of the Board of Directors of the University of New Orleans Alumni Association and as Chairman of the Strategic Management Committee.

He holds a Doctor of Philosophy in Business Administration/Management from Kennedy-Western University, Dissertation, *Effect of Entrepreneur Leadership on Management*, Master of Business Administration and

Bachelor of Science Business Administration Degrees from the University of New Orleans, a Graduate Commercial Lending Certificate from the University of Oklahoma and a Commercial Banking Certificate from the Louisiana State University Graduate School of Banking. He has earned a certificate designation as a CFE, Certified Franchise Executive, from the University of Texas at El Paso, and is a Dun & Bradstreet Certified Financial and Credit Analyst.

Having sat for and passed the State of Louisiana Examination requirements; he has been sworn in as a Louisiana Civil Law Notary and empowered as a Notary Public in the State of Louisiana, Orleans Parish.

Texts Written:

$$$ The Entrepreneur's Edge—Finding The Money—
ISBN 9781425989057

$$$ The Entrepreneur Manager- The Business Man's Business Plan—I
SBN 978144011352

$$$ The Entrepreneur's Guide—
To Start, Grow, and Manage a Profitable Business,
ISBN 9781456765255

Personal Motto: *"It's Always Too Soon To Give Up!"*

Contact information: Hfc9485@bellsouth.net

P.O. Box 791568

New Orleans, La. 70179

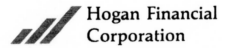 Hogan Financial
Corporation

"The Entrepreneur's Edge Since 1985"

Mission Statement for Hogan Financial Corporation:

"Organized to assist entrepreneurs with the skills, knowledge, and financial resources to start, grow, and manage a profitable business; and to assist individuals in realizing financial dreams and aspirations."

APPENDIX

A-1

FINANCIAL ANALYSIS

Financial analysis is the process of collecting and refining financial data on a firm and presenting the refined financial information in summary format suitable for effective decision making.

Financial analysis requires reliable and pertinent information on the financial performance and financial position of the firm. This means having answers to such questions as:

- Is the business generating cash flows sufficient to maintain a profitable level of operations?
- Are the operating cost adequately controlled?
- Is the rate of inventory turnover sufficient to maintain a satisfactory profit margin and avoid the unnecessary use of scarce cash by tying it up?
- Is the collection rate on account receivables sufficient to maintain satisfactory cash flow and also avoid the unnecessary use of cash tied up in slow or bad receivables?
- Are accounts payable effectively controlled?
- Is the firm generating a satisfactory return on its assets and on owner's invested capital (ROE)?

The more detailed information you have on how the business operates and how it has been doing so over the past three to five years, the easier it is to provide reliable answers to these critical questions. The needed information is provided by the basic financial statements (balance sheet and income statement) that are produced by the firm's accountants.

Simply stated, financial analysis is a problem-solving process similar to that used in working a crossword puzzle. Solving a crossword puzzle is accomplished through a combination of using the information given by printed clues; using the clues provided by adjoining words and letters; and, using the skills and judgment of the analyst. Similarly, financial analysis combines clues from various sources of financial information (balance sheet and income statement) with the skills and knowledge of the analyst to solve the firm's financial puzzle.

Financial analysis consists of two basic steps: generating the information, and evaluating the results. Manufacturing the information is a straightforward procedure of obtaining the financial data for the desired given periods and doing the number crunching with the appropriate ratios.

Evaluating the information is the critical step in the analysis process. Effective analysis requires an understanding of the financial principles, knowledge of the business, and sound management judgment, in order to interpret this numerical language of the business.

Financial statements, in the form of the balance sheet and income statement, reflect the continual changes in revenues, expenses, assets, liabilities, and owner's equity that result from the operation of the business. (Refer to our discussion and hand-outs on the balance sheet, income statement, and financial ratios.)

Financial ratios are the principal tool of financial analysis.

Financial ratios can be used to answer at least five questions:

1. How liquid is the company?
2. Are profits being generated?
3. How is the company financed?
4. Is there a good return on equity (capital)?
5. Is management creating value?

The company's ratios (benchmarks) can be tracked internally over time to compare current and past performance, and, it can be externally compared to the ratios of other firms.

Realize that a financial ratio analyst based solely on the financial statements may not be enough. We can also look to market price of the company's stock relative to its cash flow, earnings, and equity book value.

A-2

ACCOUNTING REVISITED

The Balance Sheet

The balance sheet is a snapshot of the financial condition, what a business owns and owes at a given moment in time. Its main intention is to provide all interested parties, owners, managers, bankers, and suppliers, a listing and as accurate as possible estimation of the value of all assets and liabilities with the resulting owner's equity position.

The balance sheet accounting equation is:

ASSETS = LIABILITIES + OWNER'S EQUITY,

OR

ASSETS—LIABILITIES = OWNER'S EQUITY,

OR

OWNER'S EQUITY = ASSETS—LIABILITIES

The equation is an algebraic relationship, the equality of which must be maintained;

i.e. whatever is done to the left side of the equation, the opposite must be done to the left side of the equation or do the same to the right side of the equation.

The two-sided nature of the accounting equation is the basis for double

313

entry accounting that records both sides of the company's transaction—what is received and what is given in the economic exchange.

Assets are the economic resources owned by the business (cash, accounts receivable, inventory, equipment, and buildings) that are expected to benefit future time periods.

Cash and cash equivalents, such as short-term investments maturing in less than one year, are the most liquid and enable a company to meet current obligations.

Accounts Receivable is too often a large portion of current assets. Most companies either compelled by industry and market demands must sell on credit. As such they allow their customers to pay at a later date which may not always be timely to meet current obligations. As a result accounts receivable must be monitored carefully to assure the company's liquidity. Unfortunately, resulting from poor credit judgment in allowing the purchase on time or general economic conditions, doubtful accounts can arise when the debtor will not pay the obligation greatly impairing the company's ability to meet its obligations.

Inventory is another major portion of current assets. It is easy for a company to become lackadaisical about inventory quantities. Often too large a level of inventory will accumulate as a result of bulk or bargain buyer with the thought of saving money. If rapid sales do not materialize, such purchases will result in a wasteful tie-up of essential working capital which will cost more than any purchase savings. Besides the drain on cash, there is the need to care for and protect the inventory, additional space, insurance, and the ever present danger of damage, pilfering and fire. Accounting for inventory won't help this drain rather using LIFO (last-in, first-out) method, or FIFO (first-in, first-out) method. Regretfully, with inattention to inventory levels and purchasing, the method will be FISH (first-in, still here).

Liabilities are the economic obligations of a business (debts owed to banks, finance companies, individuals, suppliers and other accounts payable) to be paid at a definite time in return for a past or current benefit.

Owner's Equity may also be called net worth or shareholder's equity is the owners' interest in the assets minus the liabilities of the business (the leftovers).

Liabilities and Owner's Equity are the two basic types of claims on a business.

In accordance with generally accepted accounting standards, assets are listed on the debit (left) side of the balance sheet in decreasing order of liquidity. Cash and cash equivalents, the most liquid, is listed first, follow by account receivable (credit sales one step from cash if collectable) and inventory (generally two steps from cash with credit sales); next would be equipment and then the least liquid asset of building and land. Current assets are those with the expectation to be turned into cash within one year, and noncurrent or fixed assets (also called capital assets) conversion rate into cash is longer than one year. Intangible assets, no liquidity at all) are items such as patents, trademarks, copyrights, licenses, and goodwill.

Liabilities are on the credit (right) side of the balance sheet in increasing order of maturity with the quickest due for payment first. Short-term liabilities are listed first, and long-term liabilities last. Current liabilities are to be paid within one year, and noncurrent liabilities are not due until after one year. Liabilities are followed by Owner's Equity, also on the credit side of the balance sheet, which does not have to be repaid because it is the owner's investment and retained earnings of the company. Owner's Equity is a residual value. It is equal to whatever is left after deducting all the liabilities from all of the assets. If total liabilities exceed total liabilities, the business is technically bankrupt.

The Income Statement

The Income Statement, also called the Profit and Loss (P&L) Statement, presents a summary of the operating and financial activity of revenue and expense that affects changes in the owner's equity. As the Balance Sheet is a snap shot of the company's activity at a given point in time, the Income Statement is a motion picture of how the company has performed for a period of time.

The Income statement equation would be:

Income = Revenues—Expenses

For most businesses net sales are the main source of revenues. Without sales revenue there is no business to monitor and manage. To achieve the contribution margin or gross profit, cost of goods sold or cost of sales (a variable expense which depends on the level of sales) are deducted, sales less cost of goods sold. Therefore the resulting gross profit is the difference between net sales and the cost of goods sold. To achieve net profit, all fixed operating expense, those cost that are constant regardless of sales activity, e.g. rent, payroll (not commission), utilities, all expense that would be considered overhead, are deducted from gross profit.

The three accounts to monitor carefully are: Net Sales, Cost of Goods Sold, and Operating Expense. They should be measured not simply by dollar amounts but as a percentage of gross sales.

Net sales are the gross sales minus cost of goods sold, allowance for return goods, and discounts.

Cost of goods sold is the cost of sales which includes all direct cost of producing and delivering the product or service including direct labor cost.

Operating expense are all expense including fixed expense and other expense not directly related to producing the product. The general and administrative expense generally referred to as the overhead expense.

The Cash Flow Statement

The Cash Flow Statement is similar to the Income Statement with the exception that it does not record accrued expenses or revenues but is the recordation of how a company has produced and used from operations, financing, and investing actual cash for a period of time. Cash flow is not the same as accrual basis profits. The bottom line profit in the income statement does not increase cash for the period and is not available to meet current obligations. Cash flow almost always differs from the amount of bottom line profit reported in the income statement. Positive cash flow is the sustaining lifeblood of the business. No matter how much cash you have flowing in, it never seems enough to cover what is flowing out.

Operating activities include net income or loss, depreciation, and changes in current assets and current liabilities.

Investing activities are the purchase, sale, or investment in fixed assets, such as real estate, buildings, and equipment.

Financing activities is the cash raised by borrowing money or selling stocks or bonds, and the cash used to pay loans, dividends, or buy back stock and redeem bonds.

A Break-Even analysis would assist a company in managing cost and revenue to cover variable and fixed expenses to plan for profit goals. The break-even analysis is described in the Business Plan appendix (A-5).

The three financial statements, the balance sheet, the income statement, and the cash flow statement may appear to be separate and stand alone, but in fact they are intertwined and interconnected and fit together like pieces of a puzzle; the puzzle that is your business.

To assist in solving the puzzle, the key financial ratios will provide a picture of the financial activity affecting your business.

BALANCE SHEET—Snap shot of what a company owns and owes at a given POINT IN TIME.

A Balance Sheet is a **snapshot** of a business financial condition at a **specific moment in time,** usually at the close of an accounting period. A balance sheet comprises assets, liabilities, and owners' or stockholders' equity. Assets and liabilities are divided into short-term and long-term including cash accounts such as checking, money market, or government securities. At any given time, assets must equal liabilities plus owners' equity (recall the accounting equation A=L+OE). An asset is anything the business owns that has a monetary value. Liabilities are the claims of creditors against the assets of the business.

What is a Balance Sheet used for?

A balance sheet helps a small business owner quickly get a handle on the financial strength and capabilities of the business. Is the business in a position to expand? Can the business easily handle the normal financial ebbs and flows of revenues and expenses? Or should the business take immediate steps to raise cash reserves?

Balance sheets can identify and analyze trends, particularly in the area of receivables and payables. Is the receivables cycle lengthening? Can receivables be collected more aggressively? Are some receivables uncollectable? Has the business been slowing down payables to forestall an inevitable cash shortage?

Balance sheets, along with income statements, are the most basic elements in providing financial reporting to lenders such as banks, commercial finance companies, investors, and vendors who are considering how much credit to grant the business.

1. ASSETS

Assets are subdivided into current and long-term assets to reflect the ease of liquidating each asset. Cash, for obvious reasons, is considered the most liquid of all assets. Long-term assets, such as real estate or machinery, are less likely to sell overnight or have the capability of being quickly converted into a current asset such as cash.

2. CURRENT ASSETS

Current assets are any asset that can be easily converted into cash within one calendar year. Examples of current assets would be checking or money market accounts, accounts receivable, and notes receivable that are due within one year's time.

CASH

Money available immediately, such as in checking accounts, is the most liquid of all short-term assets.

ACCOUNTS RECEIVABLE

This is money owed to the business for the purchases made by the customers.

INVENTORY

Consists of products that are ready for sale; There is an also Material product to be used in production and Work in Process inventory on which production has been started but not yet finished.

NOTES RECEIVABLES

Notes receivables that are due within one year are current assets. Notes that cannot be collected within one year should be considered long-term assets.

3. FIXED ASSETS

Fixed assets include land, building, machinery, and vehicles that are used in connection with the business.

LAND

Land is considered a fixed asset but, unlike other fixed assets, is not depreciated, because land is considered an asset that never wears out.

BUILDINGS

Buildings are categorized as fixed assets and are depreciated over time.

OFFICE EQUIPMENT

This includes office equipment such as copiers, fax machines, printers, and computers used in your business.

MACHINERY

This represents machines and equipment used in your business.

VEHICLES

This would include any vehicles used in your business.

TOTAL FIXED ASSETS

This is the total dollar value of all fixed assets in your business, less any accumulated depreciation.

4. TOTAL ASSETS

This represents the dollar value of both the short-term and long-term assets of your business.

5. LIABILITIES and OWNERS' EQUITY

This includes all debts and obligations owned by the business to outside creditors, vendors, or banks, plus the owners' equity.

ACCOUNTS PAYABLE

This is all short-term obligations owed by the business to creditors, suppliers, and other vendors.

NOTES PAYABLE

This represents money owed to banks, mortgage obligations, vehicles loans, and perhaps vendors' loans.

ACCRUED PAYROLL AND WITHHOLDING

This includes any earned wages or withholdings that are owed to or for employees but have not yet been paid.

TOTAL CURRENT LIABILITIES

This is the sum total of all current liabilities owed to creditors that must be paid within a one-year time frame.

LONG-TERM LIABILITIES

These are all debts or obligations owed by the business that are due more than one year out from the current date.

OWNERS' EQUITY

Also refer to as stockholders' equity, net worth, or capital. Owners' equity is made up of the initial investment in the business as well as any retained earnings that are reinvested in the business.

RETAINED EARNINGS

These are earnings (profits) reinvested in the business after any deduction for dividends distributed to shareholders as dividend payments.

6. TOTAL LIABILITIES and OWNERS' EQUITY

This comprises all debts and monies that are owed to outside creditors, vendors, or banks and the remaining monies that are owed to the owners, shareholders, including retained earnings reinvested in the business.

INCOME STATEMENT—Motion picture, how a company has performed, its income or loss, for a PERIOD OF TIME.

An Income Statement, also known as a profit and loss statement, is a summary of a business' profit or loss during any one given period of time (**a motion picture**) such as a month, three months, or a year. The income statement records all revenues for a business during the given period, as well as the operating expenses for the business.

WHAT ARE INCOME STATEMENTS USED FOR?

You use an income statement to track revenues and expenses so that you can determine the operating performance of the business over a period of time. Business owners use these statements to find out what areas of their business are over budget or under budget. Specific items that are causing unexpected expenditures can be pinpointed, such as phone, fax, mail, or supply expenses. Income statements can also track dramatic increases in product returns, cost of goods sold as a percentage of sales. They also are used to determine income tax liability.

It is very important to format an income statement so that it is appropriate to the business being conducted. All businesses will not have the same accounts but will follow GAAP (General Accepted Accounting Principles).

Income statements, along with Balance Sheets, are the most basic elements required by potential lenders, such as banks, investors, and vendors. They will used the financial reporting contained therein to determine credit limits.

1. SALES (REVENUE)

The sales figure represents the amount of revenue generated by the business. The amount recorded here is the total sales, less any product returns or sales discount.

2. COST OF GOODS SOLD

This number represents the cost (variable cost) directly associated with making or acquiring your products. Costs include materials purchased from outside suppliers used in the manufacture of your product, as well as any internal expenses directly expended in the manufacturing process.

GROSS PROFIT

Gross Profit is derived by subtracting the cost of goods sold from net sales. It is also known as the contribution margin. It does not include any operating expenses or income taxes.

3. OPERATING EXPENSES

These are the daily expenses incurred in the operation of the business; including selling, general, and administrative expenses.

SALES SALARIES

These are the salaries plus bonuses and commissions paid to the sales staff.

ADVERTISING

These represents all costs involved in creating and placing multi-media advertising.

OTHER SALES COSTS

These include any cost associated with selling the product. They may include travel, client entertainment, sales meetings, and equipment rental for presentations, copying, or miscellaneous printing costs.

OFFICE SALARIES

These are salaries of full and part-time office personnel.

RENT

The fees incurred to rent or lease office or industrial space.

UTILITIES

The costs for heating, air conditioning, electricity, phone equipment rental, and phone usage.

DEPRECIATION

Depreciation is an annual expense that takes into account the loss in value of equipment used in the business; a non-cash expense.

OTHER OVERHEAD COSTS

Expense items that do not fall into other categories or cannot be clearly associated with a particular function are considered to be other overhead costs. These may include insurance, office supplies, or cleaning services.

4. TOTAL EXPENSES

This is the total of all expenses incurred in running the business, exclusive of taxes.

5. NET INCOME BEFORE TAXES

This total represents the amount of income earned by the business prior to paying income taxes. This figure is derived by subtracting total operating expenses from gross profit.

6. TAXES

This is the amount of income taxes you owe to the federal government and, if applicable, state and local government taxes.

7. NET INCOME

This is the amount of money the business has earned after paying income taxes.

CASH FLOW STATEMENT—How a company produced and used cash for a

PERIOD OF TIME

BREAK-EVEN ANALYSIS—How a company manages cost and revenue to cover variable and fixed expenses to start to make a profit, a minimum target to plan for profit.

ACCOUNTING EQUATION

Assets = Liabilities + Owner's Equity

Assets—Liabilities = Owner's Equity

Assets—economic resources owned by a company that are expected to benefit future time periods.

Liabilities—economic obligations of a company to be paid at a definite time in return for a past or current benefit.

Owner's Equity—the owners' interest in the assets of the company; assets minus liabilities (the leftovers)

The Accounting Equation is an algebraic relationship, the equality of which must be maintained, i.e.

Whatever I do to the left side of the equation, I must do the opposite to the left side of the equation or do the same to the right side of the equation.

Liabilities and Owners' Equity are the two basic types of claims on a company.

The two-sided nature of the accounting equation is the basis for double entry accounting that records both sides of the company's transaction—what is received and what is given in the economic exchange.

ACCOUNTING BASICS

Assets are things you **own**, things that are in your possession such as cash, land, cars, buildings, etc.

Liabilities are bills, debts, obligations … anything you **owe** to others.

If you add everything you **own,** and then you subtract everything you **owe,** what's left over is what you are **worth.** In other words:

Assets—Liabilities = Net worth (other names are Equity and Capital)

The fundamental Accounting equation is:

Assets = Liabilities + Net Worth

Equity (worth, capital) is what is left over after liabilities are deducted from asset.

As evidenced on a **Balance Sheet...** so called because the two sides are equal; The Balance Sheet is a **snapshot** of the accounts on one particular day, one moment in time, and the accounts will change from day-to-day.

Everything you have is either owned by you, or you owe someone for it, or a combination of both.

i.e. You have a car which you bought for $7,500 and paid $500 down. The rest you borrowed from Hogan Financial Corporation.

You have a $7,500 car to drive which is your **Asset.**

You **owe** HFC $7,000, and therefore, what's left over is your **worth** or your claim on the car. The liability of $7,000 would be HFC's claim on your car (asset).

Your balance sheet for this transaction on this day would look like this:

ASSETS	=	LIABILITIES + EQUITY
CAR $7,500		HFC $7,000
		EQUITY $500
TOTAL $7,500		TOTAL $7,500

Notice the Assets on the **LEFT (DEBIT SIDE)** equals the **LIABILITIES** and the **EQUITY** on the **RIGHT (CREDIT SIDE).**

A transaction **(business or personal)** is a financial event that changes your resources (accounts).

Accounts are written records of your (business or personal) assets, liabilities, and equity.

What is a **T account**? A type of account resembling a T, used to analyze the effects of a transaction; Debits on the left, Credits on the right.

At this point you should know:

What an Asset is: What a Liability is: What is Equity: What is the fundamental Accounting Equation: Which side are the Assets (Debits) on: Which side are the Liabilities (Credits) on: Which side is the Equity on: What is a transaction?

RULES FOR DEBITS and CREDITS

Debit means the LEFT side; CREDIT means the RIGHT side

ASSETS are on the left and are debits; Liabilities and Owner's Equity are on the right and are credits.

ASSETS		LIABILITIES and OWNER'S EQUITY	
increase	decrease	decrease	increase
Debits	**Credits**	**Debits**	**Credits**

EXPENSES and LOSSES		REVENUE and INCOME	
increase	decrease	decrease	increase
Debits	**Credits**	**Debits**	**Credits**

Financial Effects of Revenue and Expenses

Revenue = Assets increase (debit) or Liability decrease (debit)

Expense = Asset decrease (credit) or Liability increase (credit)

A-3

KEY FINANCIAL RATIOS

Ratios are the most commonly used method for analyzing financial statements. These ratios are meaningful only when they are compared over time, or with other companies, or within particular industries.

Ratios can provide an indication of financial health to both the business owner and the financial institution. While no single ratio is all encompassing, ratios can provide a basis on which to form a judgment.

Some Definitions and Terms Used in Financial Ratios:

Cash Flow—net profit after tax plus depreciation/amortization, deferred taxes and other non-cash expenses

Current Assets—total of cash, deposits, trade receivables, inventory and other assets due within one year

Current Liabilities—total of trade accounts payable, bank operating loans and other debt due within one year

Tangible Net Worth—net worth less intangible assets, for example, Goodwill

Working Capital—Current assets less current liabilities (also called current ratio)

Liquidity Ratios:

These ratios, such as current and quick (current without inventory) ratios typically compare all or some of the company's current assets to its current liabilities. They suggest how capable the company is to meet its debt obligations in the near term.

Current Ratio:

Current Assets / Current Liabilities Current assets (or working capital) / Current liabilities (due under 1 yr) A high current ratio or a rising ratio indicates more current assets are free from debt claims of creditors. Quick Ratio: Current Assets –Inventory/ Current Inventory

Asset Management Ratios:

These ratios such as accounts receivable and inventory turnover indicates how efficiently and effectively a company is employing assets.

Age of receivables: Turnover rate—Annual credit sales / average monthly account receivable / into 360 days (commercial year) A long period may indicate the company's credit policies and collection procedures need attention.

Inventory turnover rate:

Cost of Goods annual sales / average monthly inventory /into 360 A long period indicates ineffective investment of funds; a rising trend may indicate a buildup of unsalable goods.

Debt Ratios:

These ratios such as debt-to-equity place in perspective how the company is capitalized and how much is it leveraged Debt-to-equity ratio: Total Liabilities/Net Worth Tangible net worth a low ratio indicates a cushion against loss to creditors.

Profitability Ratios:

Measures how efficiently the company is operating

Sales/revenue

Indicates company's markup: A reducing percentage may show company is not increasing prices in relation to costs

Net profit / net worth

Measures return on owner investment. An indication of the marketability of the company, a return of 10%or more is desirable. Sales growth Current yr sales—Previous yr sales x 100% Previous year's sales, a check to see if the business is keeping pace with inflation Net profit after tax growth Current year profit—Previous year profit x 100% Previous year's net profit Indicates whether profit margins are being maintained year-to-year, and whether any profits are being "siphoned off"

A-4

PATENTS, COPYRIGHTS, TRADEMARKS

The United States patent system was designed 200 years ago by Thomas Jefferson to protect the inventions of the independent inventor.

The laws of the United States as passed by Congress in its "Title" legislature arising out of the statues of the United States, specifically Title 17—Copyrights; and Title 35—Patents attempt to resolve the nagging questions of how to protect an idea, intellectual property, and essential knowledge.

Patents, copyrights, trade-secrets, and trademarks are protected under these statues but where unclear in application legal standards are juridical decided through common-law to modernize interpretation of the statues to be relative to present day usage. It is these common-law decrees that have grown the intellectual property protection of trademarks and trade secrets.

Patents are issued by the United States Patent and Trademark Office. There are three specific types of patents:

Utility Patents: for new useful and non-obvious processes, articles, machines, inventions, devices etc.; Issued for a term of **20 years** from date of application. Utility patents are always granted to an individual and then, perhaps, assigned to a corporation.

Design Patents: for new and original ornamental designs, the nonfunctional features of useful objects, for articles of manufacture; they are issued for **14 years.**

Plant Patents: for new varieties of plant life which an individual is able to produce asexually. A plant patent is issued for **20 years.**

A patent does not grant individuals exclusive rights to an invention or process. They already have that right via the creation of the invention. They may simply keep it a secret and use it exclusively. The patent does afford the protection of the "negative right" to preclude others from making or using the invention. The right is granted in exchange for placing the information in the public domain. (David A. Burge, *Patent and Trademark Tactics and Practice* –John Wiley & Sons)

Such disputes are settled in Civil Courts.

Copyright protection is given to artists and authors, giving them the sole right to print, copy, sell, and distribute the work. Books, musical and dramatic compositions, software, maps, paintings, sculptures, motion pictures, and recordings can all be copyrighted.

Copyrights are issued for a term of **50 years beyond the death of the author.**

A **Trademark** is any name symbol, or configuration used to distinguish a product from others.

There are three methods to register a trademark:

1. If the mark has already been in use, you can file a use application requesting registration and ownership of the mark. You will also have to submit three specimens showing actual use (i.e. letterhead, envelope, business card, etc.).

2. If the mark has not been in use, you can file an intent-to-use application. After the mark is in use, you must submit the three specimens.

3. Depending on international agreements with a specific country, an applicant can file based on having a trademark in another country.

A **Service Mark** is a name used to distinguish a service, rather than a tangible product.

Trademark law is not derived from the Statues of the United States Constitution, but is derived from the common law dealing with unfair competition.

In order to protect a trademark, an owner must have it in continue use to avoid it becoming a "generic". Examples of lost trademarks due to a failure to protect them by diligent usage are: Aspirin, Thermos, Zipper, and Escalator.

A-5

BUSINESS PLAN OUTLINE

COVER LETTER

The following is an example of how a letter of introduction to a lender or investor could read.

Dear Lender:

My name is _____ and I am in the _____ business. The business has been (will be) operating (opening) _____. The location is easily accessible and the population base is appropriate for _____ (type of business).

I have determined the total asset needs of the business to be $ _____. I will contribute _____% of the needed capital ($_____). We are seeking debt financing in the amount of $ _____. The loan will be repaid in monthly installments of $ _____ over a period of _____ years. The proceeds of the loan will be distributed as follows: $ _____ for land, $ _____ for building improvements, $ _____ equipment, $ _____ for inventory, and the remaining $ _____ will be held as working capital.

A current balance sheet, list of collateral, 12-month pro-forma income statement, 12-month pro-forma cash flow, two year pro-forma income statement, and break-even analysis are included in the attached business plan under the finance section. Your prompt consideration is appreciated. If additional information is needed, please contact:

Your Name

Your Address

Your City, State and Zip Code

Phone Number Including Area Code

E-mail address

Sincerely,

EXECUTIVE SUMMARY

The executive summary is the last thing written and one of the first things read. It should be clear, concise, accurate and inviting. The goal of the executive summary is to summarize each major section of the business plan. Try to limit your summary to one or two paragraphs per section. Do not introduce anything in this section that is not supported in the body of the plan. Remember, a summary just focuses on the main points that your intended reader wants or needs to know.

Company Summary

Focus on ownership, structure, history, and size. Include a brief overview of the history of your business, plus a summary of current activities.

Product or Service Summary

Focus on your products, what makes them better or different, pricing, gross profit margin of goods, and any patents or other protection you have.

Market Summary

Focus on your geographic market area, customer profile or target market, market opportunities, industry trends, and sales potential. Make sure you demonstrate that you understand your market and industry.

Management Summary

Focus on the management expertise, who will be making the decisions and who will be running the business on a daily basis. Show that you have the right people doing the right things. You will need resumes as well as a summary of experience, qualifications and credentials for all key members of your management team.

Financial Summary

Focus on owners' equity injection, time and sales volume necessary to break-even, your financial needs and your ability to service the debt. You want to summarize how the proposed loan will be used, how it will be repaid and how it will benefit your business. Include projected income and cash-flow statements for two to three years. Your assumptions should be clearly stated and realistic. The loan package must include both business and personal financial statements. Make sure that you fully understand the "story" that your financial statements tell.

THE COMPANY

This is a profile of the company and is usually one or two pages. In a start-up company this should illustrate how you envision the company. In an existing company you should explain the "before" and "after" position of the company.

- When was the company founded; by whom?

  Give company history and if a start-up, explain how and when you plan to be operational. If it is an existing business, what events happened to need a bank loan or expansion, etc.?

- Ownership Structure—Is it a sole proprietor, corporation, partnership? Who are the owners and what is their ownership position? If the business is a partnership then include a partnership agreement in the appendix.
- Mission Statement—Why are you in business? What are you trying to accomplish?
- What type of business?

  Retail

  Manufacturing

  Service

- What type of products?
- What target markets do you intend to serve?
- How large is the company? You can use the number of employees, average monthly payroll, and sales number of units per month, etc. to illustrate the size of the company.

When the reader leaves this section, he should know the company's history, ownership, product offering, target market, and size of company.

THE PRODUCT

This section is designed to educate the reader about your product or service. Discuss in detail your product's specifications, patents, unique characteristics, costs, sales price, and other similar information. Organize this section according to similar product and service categories and discuss each category separately. It is not uncommon to have several categories or departments. For example, a convenience store might have the following categories: gasoline, drinks, canned goods, alcoholic beverages, diary, and snacks. You should address the following issues for each product/service category or department.

- Detailed description of products or services

    Are your products name brand products, or a mix of name brand products and generic products? How many different types of products, colors, styles, and models do you carry? If you manufacture your product, include a drawing or sketch as an exhibit. How is the product used? Is it used in conjunction with other products?

- Patents, Copyrights, and Trade secrets
- Your product's competitive edge or strengths:

    What makes your product or service different? Are you the only distributor? Why would anyone use your product over another product?

- R & D efforts and future products:

    Are you going to have other products on the "drawing board"? If so, discuss them.

- Product sales:

    What percent do you expect each category of products and services to contribute to total sales?

- Product margins:

    Describe the price-vs.-cost relationship. This information will help develop part of the pro-forma income statement. You can use the gross margin approach (price—variable costs = gross margin), or the mark-up approach (cost divided by sales price = mark up).

- Inventory

  Does this product/service require an inventory? If so, how much inventory for each category of goods and how much will it cost? How many times in a year does it turn over? Is it perishable? What is the product's shelf-life?

- Suppliers

  Who are your suppliers and what is the lead time on orders? If one supplier goes out of business are there other sources of suppliers?

  When the reader leaves this section they should know how you will make your revenue, how much gross profit margin each category of products or services will make, what percent of total sales each product will account for, and the products competitive strengths.

MARKETING

This section should present the facts to convince the investor or banker that your product or service has a market in a growing industry and can win sales from the competition. This is one of the more difficult sections to prepare. This section represents the most risk to a business. It is best to complete this section of the business plan early since all estimates of future sales come from the market analysis. Contrary to popular belief, a business does not sell to "everyone." Therefore, it is important to accurately identify your customer base.

This section should address:

1. Market Size
    -   Describe the total geographic market area that you intend to serve.
    -   What does this total market look like in terms of demographic variables like age, sex, income, etc.?
    -   Estimate the total market size by each market segment.

2. Industry
    -   What are sales for the industry as a whole?
    -   Identify any recent trends in the industry. Is demand for this product or service increasing, decreasing; If so, why?
    -   Are the sales seasonal? If so, what are the busy months?

3. Customer Analysis
    -   Describe your specific customers using a demographic profile. For example, age, sex, income, etc.
    -   Identify where your customers are located (city, zip code, neighborhood, etc.)
    -   How many people fit your customer profile in the area you want to target? You can find this in demographic books at the library.
    -   Explain why your customers come to you instead of the competition (competitive advantage).

4. Potential Market

   - Show how you calculated your potential market. Include things like how often they will purchase, which products/services they will purchase, and average amount of each purchase. Be sure to take into account the seasonality of sales. Some products are sold only at one time of the year (Christmas) and others are sold year round (gasoline).Strengths and Weaknesses of the Competition
   - Identify and discuss each major competitor and their market share.
   - Do an S.W.O.T. analysis. That is, assess the competition's Strengths, Weaknesses, Opportunities and Threats. Knowing the competition's strengths and weaknesses can help you develop a strategy that takes advantage of their weaknesses while avoiding their strengths. Your ability to take advantage of an opportunity in the market may threaten the competition and keep them off balance.
   - You need to indicate who are the industry leaders in service, pricing, performance, cost and quality; discuss any firms that have recently entered or dropped out of the industry.

5. Advertising Plan

   - Are you going to find your customers or are they going to find you?
   - How are you going to advertise to them—Radio, TV, mail, fliers, signs, yellow pages, etc.? For example, advertising eye glasses on a youth oriented rock-n-roll radio station may not work well, but it might work on a more adult oriented radio talk show.
   - When will you advertise and how often?
   - How much will it cost to advertise? What percentage of sales will it represent?

6. Marketing Plan

   - In retail business, how will you cultivate more sales?

Will you use direct sales, direct mail, coupons, and promotions with other vendors?

- In a service company, how will you generate sales leads? Will you use seminars, trade shows, telephone sales, purchase client lists or customized mailing lists?

The reader should leave this section with a clear understanding of your geographic market, target markets, potential of each of those markets, your share of the potential market, and how you are going to communicate with those markets.

MANAGEMENT & LABOR

This section should identify owners with 20% or more ownership who could influence the business. This section should illustrate that the right people are in charge and doing the right things. The management should have experience in the industry or at the very least similar experience in a similar industry. If you do not possess the right skills then you may need to hire an employee or a consultant with those skills.

This section should address the following:

- Ownership and owner's compensation:

  Who owns what percent of the company? What are the owners' responsibilities and how much are they being paid?

- Other investors:

  Who are they and how are they going to be paid back for their investment?

- Key management and experience

  Give names, resumes and brief backgrounds on all key people; these people should know what they are doing and have experience doing it. What are their job responsibilities and how much will they be paid?

- Employees:

  Identify your labor needs. List the type and number of employees. Will they need any training, licenses or certifications? What are their duties, estimated total labor hours, and how much you will pay them?

- Professional Advisors, Accountants, Attorneys, and Consultants

  The reader should leave this section with some degree of confidence that the people in charge have assembled a team that will run the business profitably.

FACILITY

This section should discuss all issues pertaining to the facility.

- Location

    Is the location appropriate for this type of business? Are there any complementary businesses nearby? If so, discuss them.

- Zoning

    Is the location zoned for this type of commerce?

- Utilities

    Is there adequate power for your needs? If not, how much will it cost to up-grade it?

- What are the store hours?
- Lease or purchase

    Will you purchase the building? If so, how much will it cost? If you will lease, for how long and how much is the lease? Will you have to do any construction or improvements to make it ready for business?

- Parking

    Is there adequate parking for your customers?

- Inventory

    How much space do you need and can you accommodate it?

- Monthly fixed costs

    What will be the fixed costs that you expect to incur on a monthly basis? Include things like rent, utilities, telephone, insurance maintenance, salaries, etc.

- Overhead

    How much will it cost to operate the facility per department, per hour, per product? That is, how much should each department or product be charged for its share of the overhead? (Fixed monthly costs)?

FINANCIAL

The financial section consists of several pro-forma financial statements that are generated from the previous sections. In some ways, the other sections of the business plan are just supporting information for the financial section. To build the financial statements the previous sections of the business plan are combined with the following information.

- List of start up costs
- Capital equipment expenditures
- Depreciation schedule
- List of collateral
- Sources and uses of financing—a detailed statement of how you will use the loan proceeds. Don't forget to include the proceeds of the loan in your cash-flow projections and the interest expense in your projected income statement.
- Amount—Remember that you are offering the bank/investor a deal that will make them money; you are not asking for an allowance. The attitude you should have is to ask, "This is how much money I need, and how much will they lend/invest?" and not, "Will they lend/invest it?"
- Repayment Plan—You will have to make some assumptions about the terms of the loan or the investment in your proposal.

The following are the typical financial statements found in a business plan financial section.

- Balance Sheet after start-up, loan, or expansion
- 12 month projected cash flow statements on a month-by-month basis
- 12 month projected income statements on a month-by-month basis
- Annual projected balance sheets and income statements for two to three years
- Break-even analysis
- Ratio analysis
- Assumptions used in financial statements

BREAKEVEN ANALYSIS

Sales Price per Unit less Variable Costs per Unit =

Contribution Margin $ _____

     OR

Total Sales less Total Variable Cost =

Total Contribution Margin $ _____

Contribution Margin Divided by Sales Price =

Contribution Ratio   _____ %

     OR

Total Contribution Margin Divided by Total Sales =

Contribution Ratio   _____ %

Total Fixed Costs $ _____

Breakeven in Number of Units =

Total Fixed Costs divided by

Total Contribution Margin   Units _____

Breakeven in Sales =

Total Fixed Costs divided by

Contribution Ratio   Sales _____

BUSINESS PLAN APPENDIX

The appendix is where you put supporting data that does not easily fit into the business plan narrative.

- **Market research data**

- **Resumes of key owners and managers**

- **Personal financial statements of owners with 20% or more ownership**

- **Patent or product information**

- **Leases**

- **Contracts**

- **Articles of incorporation or partnership agreement**

- **Newspaper or magazine articles relating to the product or industry**

- **Other supporting data**

A-6

77 QUESTIONS EVERY BUSINESS PLAN SHOULD ANSWER

1. Why will this business succeed?
2. Why is this product or service useful?
3. What will the product do for the user?
4. What is the expected life cycle of the product?
5. How do advances in technology affect your product and business?
6. What is the product liability?
7. What makes this business and product unique?
8. Does the product meet a specific need or perceived need of the customer?
9. Does the product have brand-name recognition?
10. Are there repeat uses for the product?
11. Is this a high quality or low quality product?
12. Is the consumer the end user of the product?
13. Are there any substitutes for your product?
14. Do you lease or own the property/facilities?
15. What are the terms of your lease?
16. How much do you owe on the mortgage?

17. Are the facilities adequate for future expansion based on your business plan?

18. Will the expansion require relocation?

19. Who owns the patent?

20. What licensing arrangements have been made between you and the patent company?

21. Does anyone else have a licensing arrangement? If so, how does this impact your company?

22. Why does this business have high growth potential?

23. What makes this business situation special?

24. Does this product have mass appeal or single large buyers?

25. How large is the customer base?

26. What is the typical demographic of your customer base?

27. What are the current market trends?

28. What are the seasonal effects in your industry?

29. What advantages does your competition have over you?

30. What advantages do you have over your competition?

31. Compared to your competition, how do you compete in terms of price, performance, service and warranties?

32. What is the lag time between initial buyer contact and the actual sale?

33. How does your company and product fit into the industry?

34. What are the keys to success in your industry?

35. How did you determine total sales of the industry and its growth rate?

36. What industry changes most affect your company's profits?

37. Who is your competition?

38. Do your competitors have an advantage due to equipment?

39. What makes your business different?

40. Why will your business succeed when it must compete with larger companies?

41. How do you expect the competition to react to your company?

42. If you plan to take market share, how will you do it?

43. What are the critical elements of your marketing plan?

44. Is this primarily a retail or industrial marketing strategy?

45. How important is advertising in your marketing plan?

46. How sensitive are sales to your advertising plan?

47. How will your marketing strategy change as the product/or industry matures?

48. Is direct selling necessary?

49. What is the capacity of your facility?

50. Where do you see bottlenecks developing?

51. How important is quality control?

52. What is the current backlog?

53. Is the product assembly line based or individually customized?

54. What are the health and safety concerns in producing this product?

55. Who are your suppliers and how long have they been in business?

56. How many sources of suppliers are there?

57. Currently, are there any shortages in components?

58. How old is your company's equipment?

59. What is the yearly maintenance cost?

60. What is the current research and development?

61. What is the annual expenditure on R&D?

62. How does R&D impact future sales?

63. What type of business experience does the management team have?

64. Are the members achievers?

65. What motivates each team member?

66. Can the team accomplish the job outlined in the business plan?

67. How many employees do you have?

68. What is the anticipated need in the immediate future?

69. Where does the labor supply come from?

70. What is the employee break down, i.e. full time, part time, managerial staff, support staff, production/service?

71. What is the cost of training?

72. Is the labor force primarily skilled or unskilled workers?

73. Is there a union and what is the company's relationship?

74. What are your capital requirements over the next five years?

75. For what will the capital raised via the plan be used?

76. What is the exit strategy? (How will investors get their money out?)

77. What return on investment can the investors expect?

A-7

HOGAN'S ONE PERCENT RULE

Sales	$800,000	100%
CGS	599,500	75%
Gross	$200,500	25%
Fixed Cost	183,900	23%
Net Profit	$ 16,600	2%

1. Increase sales 1%:

   Sales 800,000

   8,000 1% increase

   New Sales 808,000

   CGS 599,500

   6,000 75% of additional 8,000 in sales

   New CGS 605,500 75%

   New Gross 202,500

   Fixed Cost 183,900 23% no significant increase on 8,000 of sales

   New Net Profit 18,600 2.3%

   Old Net Profit 16,600

   2,000 12% increase in profits

2. Increase price 1%:

New Sales 808,000

8,080 1% price increase

New, New Sales 816,080 100%

New CGS 605,500 74%

Gross 210,580 26%

Fixed Cost 183,900 23% remains same

New Net Profit 26,680 3.3%

Old Net Profit 16,600

10,080 61% increase in profits

3. Obtain 1% savings in CGS: 4. Reduce Fixed Cost by 1%:

Sales 816,080 100% 816,080 100% Sales

CGS 605,500 599,445 73% CGS

Less 1% 6,055 savings 216,635 27% Gross

New CGS 599,445 73% 183,900 old fixed cost

Gross 216,635 27% 1,839 less 1%

Fixed Cost 183,900 23% 182,061 New fixed cost

New Net Profit 32,735 4% 34,574 4.2% new net profit

Old Net Profit 16,600 16,600 old net profit

16,135 97% increase in 17,974 108% increase in profits
profits

A-8

BUSINESS LOAN CHECKLIST

_____ Three years Federal Tax Returns on Company

_____ Current Profit/Loss Statement and Balance Sheet (no older than 60 days)

_____ Accounts Receivable and Payable aging

_____ Copy of current lease on premises (if applicable)

_____ Three years Federal Tax Returns on Principals of Company

_____ Business Plan with monthly projections and assumptions

_____ Any Affiliate information

_____ Leases, Notes to be refinanced (where applicable)

_____ Purchase contract (if Business Acquisition)

_____ Asset allocation (giving a break-down in the purchase price for equipment, inventory, etc)

_____ Equity documentation (3 months' bank statements, etc)

_____ Other documents may be requested by underwriters upon receipt of the above information.

A-9 VENTURE CAPITALIST

DUE DILIGENCE CHECKLIST

In connection with a potential transaction with venture investors, please provide us with the following materials or information relating to [name of company], and any subsidiaries (together, the "Company"). Upon review, we may request additional documents. If compiling any of the requested items would be unduly burdensome, please let us know so that we may arrange a less burdensome alternative. If you have already delivered any of the information, please so indicate and you need not provide an additional copy.

(A)   Corporate Documents of the Company and Subsidiaries

(1)   Articles of Incorporation and all amendments thereto.

(2)   Bylaws and all amendments thereto.

(3)   Minutes of all Board of Directors, committee and shareholders meetings and all consents to actions without meeting.

(4)   List of states and jurisdictions in which qualified to do business and in which the Company has offices, holds property or conducts business

(5)   Material information or documents furnished to shareholders and to directors during the last two years.

(6)   Most recently obtained good standing certificates for all

states and jurisdictions where the Company is qualified to do business.

(B)   Previous Issuances of Securities

(1)   All applications and permits for issuance/transfer of securities.

(2)   Sample copy of stock certificates, warrants and options.

(3)   Stockholder information, indicating number of shares held, dates of issuance, and consideration paid.

(4)   All stock options, stock purchase and other employee benefit plans and forms of agreements.

(5)   List of any outstanding stock options and warrants.

(6)   Any voting trust agreements, buy/sell agreements, stockholder agreements, warrant agreements, proxies, or right of first refusal agreements.

(7)   Any registration rights or pre-emptive rights agreements.

(8)   Powers of attorney on any matter.

(9)   Convertible debt instruments.

(10)   Other contracts, arrangements, or public or private documents or commitments relating to the stock of the Company.

(11)   Any debt arrangements, guarantees or indemnification between officers, directors or the shareholder and the Company.

(C)   Material Contracts and Agreements

(1)   List of banks or other lenders with whom Company has a financial relationship (briefly describe nature of relationship - lines of credit, equipment lessor, etc.).

(2)   Credit agreements, debt instruments, security agreements, mortgages, financial or performance guaranties, indemnifications, liens, equipment leases or other agreements evidencing outstanding loans to which the

Company is a party or was a party within the past two years.

(3)   All material correspondence with lenders during the last three years, including all compliance reports submitted by the Company or its accountants.

(4)   List of major clients and their locations.

(5)   Any other material contracts.

(D)   Litigation

(1)   Copies of any pleadings or correspondence for pending or prior lawsuits involving the Company or the Founders.

(2)   Summary of disputes with suppliers, competitors, or customers.

(3)   Correspondence with auditor or accountant regarding threatened or pending litigation, assessment or claims.

(4)   Decrees, orders or judgments of courts or governmental agencies.

(5)   Settlement documentation.

(E)   Employees and Related Parties

(1)   A management organization chart and biographical information.

(2)   Summary of any labor disputes.

(3)   Correspondence, memoranda or notes concerning pending or threatened labor stoppage.

(4)   List of negotiations with any group seeking to become the bargaining unit for any employees.

(5)   All employment and consulting agreements, loan agreements and documents relating to other transactions with officers, directors, key employees and related parties.

(6)   Schedule of all compensation paid to officers, directors and key employees for most recent fiscal year showing separately salary, bonuses and non-cash compensation (i.e. use of cars, property, etc.).

(7)   Summary of employee benefits and copies of any pension, profit sharing, deferred compensation and retirement plans.

(8)   Summary of management incentive or bonus plans not included in (7) above, as well as other non-cash forms of compensation.

(9)   Confidentiality agreements with employees.

(8)   Description of all related party transactions which have occurred during the last three years (and any currently proposed transaction) and all agreements relating thereto.

(F)   Financial Information

(1)   Audited financial statements since inception (unaudited if audited financials are unavailable).

(2)   Quarterly income statements for the last two years and the current year (to date).

(3)   Financial or operating budgets or projections.

(4)   Business plan and other documents describing the current and/or expected business of the Company including all material marketing studies, consulting studies or reports prepared by the Company.

(5)   A description of all changes in accounting methods or principles during the last three fiscal years.

(6)   Any documents relating to material write-downs or write-offs other than in the ordinary course.

(7)   Revenue, gross margin and average selling price by product or service.

(8)   Management letters or special reports by auditors and any responses thereto for the last three fiscal years.

(9)   Letters of counsel to the Company delivered to auditors for the last three fiscal years.

(10) Aging schedules for accounts receivable for the last two years.

(11) Breakdown of G&A expenses for the last two years.

(12) Copies of any valuations of the Company's stock.

(13) Description of all contingent liabilities.

(G)   Property

(1)   List of real and material personal property owned by the Company.

(2)   Documents of title, mortgages, deeds of trust and security agreements pertaining to the properties listed in (1) above.

(3)   All outstanding leases with an original term greater than one year for real and personal property to which the Company is either a lessor or lessee.

(4)   Documents pertaining to proprietary technology developed/owned by the Company, including any copyright or patent filings. This will also include information confirming that the Company's systems, software and technology is owned solely by the Company and does not infringe on any other party's rights.

(H)   Taxation

(1)   Any notice of assessment, revenue agents' reports, etc. from federal or state authorities with respect to any currently "open" years.

(2)   Federal and state income tax returns for the last three years.

(3)   Evidence of Company being current on sales tax, unemployment, social security, and other tax payments.

(I)   **Insurance and Liability**

(1)   Schedule or copies of all material insurance policies of the Company covering property, liabilities and operations, including product liabilities.

(2)   Schedule of any other insurance policies in force such as "key man" policies or director indemnification policies.

(3)   All other relevant documents pertaining to the Company's insurance and liability exposure, including special reserve funds and accounts.

(J)   **Acquisition, Partnership or Joint Venture Agreements**

(1)   All acquisition, partnership or joint venture agreements.

(2)   Documents pertaining to potential acquisitions or alliances.

(3)   Any agreements regarding divestiture or assets.

(K)   **Governmental Regulations and Filings**

(1)   Summary of OSHA inquiries for past three years.

(2)   Summary of federal and state EPA, EEO, or other governmental agency inquiries during the past three years.

(3)   Material reports to government agencies for past three years (e.g., OSHA, EPA).

(4)   Copies of all permits and licenses necessary to conduct the Company's business.

(4)   Summary of applicable federal, state and local laws, rules and regulations.

(L)   **Miscellaneous**

(1)   Press releases during the last two years.

(2)   Articles and other pertinent marketing studies or reports relating to the Company or the industry.

(3)   Information regarding competitors.

(4)   Customer satisfaction surveys, if any.

(5)   Current brochures and sales materials describing the Company's services.

Please provide copies of all documents to:

_____

_____

_____

_____

Phone: _____

Fax: _____

A-10

EVALUATION OF A BUSINESS

BIGMOP

B—BALANCE SHEET

I—INCOME STATEMENT

G—GROWTH

M—MANAGEMENT

O—OPERATION

P—PLANNING   Example

Balance Sheet, tangible net worth	$100,000
Opportunity cost, could be earned elsewhere	<u>10%</u>
	$ 10,000
Salary (could earn elsewhere)	25,000
Total	35,000
Average profit (3/5yrs {trend})	50,000
Minus—op cost & salary—	<u>35,000</u>
Total	$ 15,000

Intangible/Goodwill/Marketing Factor multiplier

(0 to 5 depending upon how well established)   <u>5</u>

                                                  $ 75,000

Plus tangible net worth   <u>100,000</u>

Value of business $175,000

GLOSSARY

A

Accounting—process of collecting, recording, reporting, and analyzing a firm's financial activities

Agent—person who agrees to act for the benefit of another

Amortization—the gradual reduction of debts by periodic payments

Antitrust law—legislation intended to prohibit attempts to monopolize markets

Arbitrage—buying at a low price in one market and selling at a higher price in another

Assets—items owned by an entity

B

Balance sheet—financial statement that shows what a business owns and owes at a specific moment in time, a snap-shot of financial status

Bankruptcy—situation when a business cannot meet financial obligations and liabilities exceed assets, and the firm seeks legal protection to repay or restructure debts

Barriers to entry—conditions that create disincentives to enter an industry

Barter—the direct exchange of goods rather than for cash

Board of Directors—group of stockholder elected individuals who oversee governance of an organization

Break-even point—the sales level where revenues equal cost

Budget deficit—government expenditures are greater than tax revenues

Budget surplus—tax revenues are greater than government expenditures

Business—an enterprise that is started and operated for the purpose of its owners

Business ethics—application of moral standards and values to business situations

Business model—a plan that indicates how the aspects of the business work together to generate a profit—how the business makes money

Business plan—written document describing all aspects of the business to determine feasibility, raise money, and provide a plan of operation

Burn rate—rate in which a business is spending its money until it reached profits

C

Capital—produced goods that are used in the production of other goods, wealth in any form that can be used to produce more wealth, the ownership equity in a business

Capital investment—money used to purchase permanent fixed assets for a business

Cash basis accounting—accounting method that recognizes revenues and expenses when cash is actually received or paid out

Cash flow—cash generated after expenses, taxes, and adding back non-cash expenses

Cash management—process of forecasting, collecting, disbursing, investing, and planning for the cash a business needs to operate smoothly

Checkable deposits—deposits in banks or other financial institutions on which checks can be written

Code of ethics—written document that describes the company's general value system, moral principles, and specific ethical rules

Collective bargaining—union bargains with management on behalf of the workers

Common stock—security with voting power representing an ownership right in a corporation

Comparative advantage—when one nation or company can produce a good at a lower opportunity cost than another

Compound interest—interest paid on interest

Conflict of Interest—situation in which one relationship or obligations places you in direct conflict with an existing relationship or obligation

Contraction—the phase of the business cycle when real GDP is decreasing

Contraction fiscal policy—a decrease in government expenditures or an increase in taxation

Contraction monetary policy—a decrease in the money supply

Copyright—government granted monopoly on the production and sale of a creative work granted to the creator

Corporation—an organization owned by stockholders that is considered a separate legal entity apart from its owners

Crowding out—occurs when increases in government spending lead to decreases in private spending

Culture—a particular set of attitudes, beliefs, and practices that characterize a group of individuals

Currency—coins and paper money issued by the federal government

Current assets—assets that can or will be converted to cash within the next 12 months

Current liabilities—obligations that are due within the next 12 months

Current ratio—the ratio of current assets to current liabilities indicating liquidity

D

Debt ratio—the ratio of total liabilities to total assets measuring the percentage of assets financed by debt

Debt-to-equity ratio—ratio of total liabilities to equity indicating how leverage the business is

Deflation—a decrease in the price level

Demand—the willingness and ability of buyers to buy different quantities of goods at different prices

Developed country—has a relatively high per capital real Gross Domestic Product (GDP)

Depreciation—non-cash expense allocating an asset's origina costover the time it is expected to produce revenue

Discount rate—interest rate the Fed charges banks for borrowed reserves

Disposable income—household income after taxes

Dividend—portion of after-tax profits distributed to shareholders

Dumping—the practice of selling exports at a price below that charged in the home country

E

Economic growth—increase in the productive capacity of an economy

Economic system—the way in which a society answers economic questions

Economics—study of how societies use their limited resources to try to satisfy their unlimited wants

Economies of scale—exist when as production is increased and average cost decreases

Elasticity—a measure of the responsiveness of one variable to changes in another variable

Employed—those with paying jobs

Entrepreneurship—the special skills involved in organizing the factors of production, labor, land, and capital, for profit

Equilibrium price—price where quantity demanded equals quantity supplied

Equity—the book value of a business after all debts and other claims, the amount of cash the business owners have invested in the business plus any retained earnings.

Ethics—a set of moral standards and values that help choose between right and wrong

Ethical Dilemma—situation in which there is no obvious right or wrong decision, but rather a right or right answer

Expansion—phase of the business cycle when real GDP is increasing

Expansion fiscal policy—increase in government expenditures or a decrease in taxation

Expansion monetary policy—increase in the money supply

Exports—total foreign purchases of domestic goods

F

Federal funds rate—interest rate one bank charges another bank to borrow reserves (always below the Fed discount rate to avoid bank arbitrage)

Fiat money—money by government decree or fiat

Financial intermediation—process by which banks make depositors' savings available to borrowers

Financial statement—a report summarizing the financial condition of a business

Firm—an entity that employs resources to produce goods and services

Fiscal policy—changes in government expenditures and taxation to achieve economic goals

Fixed cost—cost that do not vary with output

Franchise—the rights to offer specific products or services under explicit guidelines at a certain location for a period of time

Free market—a market in which price is free to adjust up or down in response to demand and supply

G

GAAP—the generally accepted accounting principles that govern the accounting profession

Gross Domestic Product (GDP)—market of all final goods and services produced annually

Gross profit—amount earned after paying to produce or buy products but before deducting operating expense

Gross sales—total dollar amount of sales prior to expenses

I

Imports—total domestic purchases of foreign goods

Incentive—changes the benefit or cost associated with an action

Income elasticity of demand—measures the responsiveness of demand to a change in income

Industry—a group of businesses producing similar products and services

Inflation—an increase in the price level

Internal locus of control—a belief that one's success depends on one's own efforts

Initial public offering (IPO)—the sale of shares of stock to the public for the first time

Interest—the payment for the use of loanable funds

Interest rate effect—when the price level decreases, the demand for money will decrease, causing interest rates to decrease

Intermediate good—a good that has not yet reached its final user, but is an input in the production of another good

Inverse relationship—as the value of one variable increases, the value of the other variable decreases

Investment—the acquisition of new physical capital

J

Joint venture—a business entered into by two or more parties which is intended to terminate upon completion of a specific purpose

L

Labor—the physical and mental effort contributed to production

Labor force—the sum of the number of people employed plus the number unemployed

Laffer curve—indicates that lowering tax rates might actually increase tax revenues

Laissez-faire—policy that the government xhouls not interfere with the economy

Land—naturally occurring resources

Law of demand—price and the quantity demanded of a good are inversely related

Law of diminishing marginal returns—as larger amount of a variable input are combined with fixed inputs, eventually the marginal physical product of the variable input declines

Legal barriers to entry—barriers to entry created by government action

Less developed country (LDC)—country with a relatively low per capital real GDP

License—a permit issued by the government authorizing a person to conduct a certain type of business

Limited liability company (LLC)—a hybrid organization offering the liability protection of a corporation but taxed as a partnership

Liquid asset—an asset that can be converted quickly into cash at a low transaction cost

Loopholes—exclusions and exemption from income, deductible expenses, and tax credits

M

M1—currency in circulation plus checkable deposits

M2—M1 plus small denomination time deposits, saving deposits, and money market accounts

M3—everything in M2 plus some less liquid assets, large time deposits, term repurchase agreements, and term Eurodollars

Macroeconomics—branch of economics that focuses on overall economic behavior

Marginal cost—the change in total cost resulting from producing an additional unit of output

Marginal revenue—change in total revenue from selling one additional unit of output

Marginal utility—additional utility received from consuming an additional unit of a good

Market—all possible customers that might want a product or service at a particular price

Market mix—the combination of product, pricing, promotion, and place (distribution)

Merger—the combining of two separate companies into one

Microeconomics—the branch of economics that focuses on the components of the economy

Monetary base—currency in circulation plus bank reserves

Monetary policy—changes in the money supply to achieve macroeconomic goals

Money—whatever is generally accepted as a medium of exchange

Money creation—increases in checkable deposits made possible by fractional reserve banking

Monopolistic competition—many sellers of similar products

Monopoly—a firm that is a lone seller of a product with no close substitutes

N

National debt—the total amount the federal government owes its creditors

National defense argument—argument for certain trade restrictions based on national defense concerns

Natural monopoly—an industry in which economies of scale are so important only one firm can survive

Natural unemployment rate—the lowest unemployment rate that can be sustained without causing increasing inflation

Net exports—exports minus imports

Net worth—a firm's assets minus its liabilities

O

Oligopoly—an industry dominated by a few mutually interdependent firms

Open market operation—one of the tools of the Fed, buying and selling U.S. government securities in the open market

Opportunity cost—the value of the best alternative surrendered when a choice is made

Organization—an entity that involves people doing work for a purpose

P

Partnership—a firm owned and operated by two or more co-owners

Patent—a government granted monopoly on the production and sale of an invention

Peak—the highest phase of the business cycle

Per capital output—a basic measure of standard of living by dividing total output by the population

Perfect competition—many sellers of identical products

Poverty—a family whose income falls below a minimum established for an adequate standard of living

Preferred stock—stock that gives preference over common stock with respect to dividends or payment in the event of the company's sale or liquidation; may or may not have voting rights

Present value of an asset—the discounted value today of the income stream associated with the asset

Price ceiling—a maximum legal price

Price discrimination—occurs when a seller charges different prices to different buyers for the same good

Price floor—a minimum legal price

Prime rate—interest rate charged by banks to its preferential borrowers

Product differentiation—process of distinguishing a firm's product from similar products

Productivity—measured by the output produced per unit of input

Progressive tax—imposes higher tax rates on higher levels of income

Proportional tax—imposes the same tax rate on all levels of income

Proprietorship—a firm owned and operated by one individual

Prospectus—a complex document issued by a corporation in connection with the offering of securities containing specific information about the business, type of investment, financial data, and other pertinent facts in conformity with security regulations

Q

Quota—a legal limit on the quantity of a good that may be imported

R

Real GDP—GDP adjusted for changes in the price level

Real interest rate—the nominal interest rate minus the rate of inflation

Regressive tax—imposes higher tax rates on lower levels of income

Required reserves—the minimum amount of reserves that a bank is legally required to hold against it deposits

Reserves—vault cash plus bank deposits with the Federal Reserve

Resources—the inputs that makes production possible

Return on assets (ROA)—ratio of net profit to total assets

Return on equity (ROE)—ratio of net profit to equity

S

S corporation—a hybrid entity organized like a corporation but taxed like a partnership

Sarbanes-Oxley Act (SOX)—legislative response to the corporate accounting scandals

Say's law—supply creates its own demand

Scarcity—the problem that human wants exceed the production possible with the limited resources available

Self-sufficiency—a person uses their own resources to produce the goods and services that they want to consume

Shortage—when quantity demanded exceeds quantity supplied

Society—a structured community of people bound together by similar traditions, culture, and customs

Sunk cost—a past cost that cannot be changed by current decisions

Surplus—when quantity supplied exceeds quantity demanded

T

Tariff—a tax on an imported good

Trade deficit—when a nation's imports exceed its exports

Trade restrictions—government imposed limitations on international trade

Transaction cost—the costs of bring buyers and sellers together for exchanges

Trough—the lowest phase of the business cycle

U

Unemployed—those without paying jobs who are actively seeking employment

Unemployment rate—the percentage of the labor force that is unemployed

Uniform commercial code (UCC)—set of business laws that provide a standard way to operate

U.S. government securities—debt instruments issued by the federal government

Utilitarianism—ethical choices that offer the greatest good for the greatest number of people

Utility—a measure of satisfaction received from consumption

V

Value—relative worth and importance

Value system—a set of personal principles formalized into a code of behavior

Variable cost—costs that vary with output

Velocity of money—the average number of times that a dollar is spent annually

Venture capital—early-stage private equity financing; these funds rank behind secured creditors

W

Whistle-Blower—an employee who discovers misconduct and chooses to bring it to the attention of others

Working capital—the excess of current assets over current liabilities

CPSIA information can be obtained at www.ICGtesting.com
Printed in the USA
BVOW08s1450031013

332719BV00001B/14/P